D1251706

Bloody Ground

JOHN F. DAY

Bloody Ground

With a Foreword by
THOMAS D. CLARK
and an Afterword by
HARRY M. CAUDILL

THE UNIVERSITY PRESS OF KENTUCKY

ISBN: 0-8131-1454-3 (cloth); 0148-4 (paper)
Library of Congress Catalog Card Number: 79-57571

Scholarly publisher for the Commonwealth,
serving Berea College, Centre College of Kentucky,
Eastern Kentucky University, The Filson Club,
Georgetown College, Kentucky Historical Society,
Kentucky State University, Morehead State University,
Murray State University, Northern Kentucky University,
Transylvania University, University of Kentucky,
University of Louisville, and Western Kentucky University.

Editorial and Sales Offices: Lexington, Kentucky 40506

Bloody Ground was originally published by Doubleday, Doran and Company, Inc., in 1941.

All of the photographs in this edition are provided by courtesy of the Photographic Archives of the University of Kentucky Libraries. Some have been cropped for reproduction. The photographs by Russell Lee, made for the Coal Mines Administration in 1946, are on deposit in the National Archives, Washington, D.C. Marvin Breckinridge photographs are used by permission of the photographer.

To

Bettie

Thanks

I WISH TO EXPRESS here my thanks to A. B. Guthrie, Jr., city editor of the Lexington *Leader*, who assisted me throughout the writing of this book. I am indebted also to many other persons for their help—to Dr. T. D. Clark, of the University of Kentucky, who aided in collecting material and checking facts; to Julian Wilson, who helped with the photographs; to scores of people in the hills who showed me their hospitality and helped me to gather information; to dozens of writers whose ideas I examined and compared or contrasted with my own. But to my friend "Bud" Guthrie I am most deeply indebted. He read my copy.

JOHN F. DAY

Huntington, W. Va.
July 10, 1941.

Contents

Foreword

Thomas D. Clark

Rereading John F. Day's incisive book *Bloody Ground* almost four decades after its publication brings back nostalgic memories of the author and the post-depression era in Kentucky. In March, 1940, "Sunny" Day wrote a Sunday feature article for the Lexington *Herald-Leader* entitled "Spring Comes to Breathitt County, and with a Lean, Forlorn Hope." Day made some penetrating observations about the stark political, social, and economic realities that faced Breathitt County and other Kentucky mountain communities. Publication of his article was like exploding a bomb. Anger flared out of Breathitt in mushroom-cloud proportions, fed largely by knowledge that Day's charges were true. Day was not a bleeding-heart outsider viewing impoverished mountain society for the first time or through idealistic eyes. He was born and raised on the outer highland fringe and had taught a country mountain school. He had added to these experiences good training as a newspaper reporter.

The *Leader* story quickly gained national attention in the metropolitan press and the weekly news magazines. I recall that in the first burst of local anger a student from Breathitt County came into my office and declared the story was without factual basis. His main contention was that an ancient and decaying log house pictured in the story was not in

Breathitt County. By pure coincidence I knew that the old Hudson Cabin was indeed located just inside Breathitt on the Perry County border, a fact that completely flabbergasted the student. I think other critics of the article were as poorly informed.

Kenneth McCormack, a venturesome young editor in the house of Doubleday, Doran, read comments on the Breathitt article and asked John Day to consider writing a book about Appalachian Kentucky. A. B. Guthrie and I, among others, encouraged Day to sign the contract. We told him it would involve a considerable amount of investigation and research, a thought that must have been sobering to a reporter accustomed to writing brief feature stories and being done with them. Nevertheless he signed the contract with the New York publisher and began to gather notes.

At the time I was also gathering notes preparatory to writing my book *The Kentucky* in the Rivers of America Series. The redheaded young reporter and I set out to gather information about the country along the three forks of the upper Kentucky River. Traveling together we slept in the same mountain beds, ate a lot of greasy food, got a car stuck in bottomless mountain creek mud, and viewed human activities reminiscent of another age in America.

We attended a Hardshell Baptist footwashing, where we committed the egregious blunder of sitting on the woman side of the aisle. A deacons' committee requested us either to leave the church or to take our places among the unwashed. On another occasion, after walking miles up the Carr Fork of the Kentucky, we attended a "funeralizing" or memorial service where we heard a series of preachers from weak nine o'clock beginners to the big-gun eleven and twelve o'clock thunderers preach and pray down hellfire and brimstone on the heads of hardened sinners. On the outskirts of Hazard we attended a "Holy Roller" meeting in which much of the congregation, crammed into a tiny room, became so aroused that they screamed, danced, spoke in unknown tongues, and fell in prostrate heaps of guilt. Among the ragtag communicants was a shapely, young, and scantily dressed woman who floated about the room as gracefully as a maple leaf and gibbered in the unknown tongue until she reached an emotional climax that Sunny observed was as much sexual as spiritual. In a country where many faithful demonstrated the depth of their faith by handling poisonous snakes, we saw practitioners and victims of this literal interpretation of the Scriptures.

I was not along when Day visited the "jenny barn," but I can attest to the truthfulness of his description of these sordid places, which dotted the coal-mining camps and towns under the guise of being recreational centers. William Hogarth in eighteenth-century England never portrayed more sordid gatherings than were seen in Appalachian jenny barns.

In this early era it had hardly dawned on the mountaineers that prohibition had been repealed, for the preachers and bootleggers had voted the counties dry. Try as I might I could never get a moonshiner to let me accompany him to his still. We would start but some mysterious thing always happened to deter us. Day had the same experience. In desperation we appealed to the "revenooers" for assistance. He went with federal men, and I accompanied Kentucky excisemen. Both of us quickly learned that raiding stills was touchy business. We went unarmed, but the raiders carried magnum pistols that could blast the point off a sandstone cliff.

These were among the more dramatic phases of mountain life in the great depression. Day did his homework well and viewed Appalachia through a wide lens of politics, embattled society, and economics. He was able to spot hypocrisy among state and local politicians, economic exploiters, and even charity workers. Local school systems were little short of being bases of political power. Day raised ticklish questions with school superintendents, with Mrs. Mary Breckinridge of the Frontier Nursing Service, and with the administrators of Berea College. He made keen observations about the exploitation of regional resources. His masterful chapter on cutting out the virgin timber is a graphic footnote to Kentucky impoverishment. Mountain loggers slashed timber from the hillsides and floated it away to outside markets from which they received little more than the biblical mess of pottage. He also viewed the blighting of social and economic promises by the coal-mining industry.

Most cogently, Day discussed the breakdown of the judicial process in the local courts and the prostitution of democracy at the polls. He understood that mountain voters were as quick to shoot an opponent in an altercation over the election of a school board member as to shoot a governor. Many an illiterate voter could be aroused over school board elections, though he knew nothing about schools; his interest was in becoming beneficiary of a public job.

Bloody Ground is an eloquent preface to what subsequently became a broader state and national concern about Appalachia. It could not now be written in its post-depression context. Its author, a brilliant young newspaperman, caught a large segment of Kentucky society in a highly revealing still picture. His faithful portrayals of people, time, and place are comparable to those in the Federal Writers Project classic *These are Our Lives. Bloody Ground*'s message is stark and grim. It documents the plight of people caught in the tentacles of social and economic failure in a land that begged for decent leadership and guidance.

In a thoughtful conclusion John Day asked himself what means he would use to solve the region's problems and answered honestly, "I don't know." The people of his book, from the sluttish jenny-barn habitues to the governor of Kentucky, were actors on a tragic stage of Shakespearean proportions, with the difference that here the tragedy never reached a climax.

Bloody Ground

I

Mountain Voodoo

IT WAS AT THE EDGE OF DARK, one late summer day when I drove east along the highway from Hazard. I had left town early because I knew the snake rituals, like other services in the hills, began almost before the sun dropped from sight so that members of the congregations need make only one-way lantern trips.

It had been a parching day, but now the mists were beginning to rise in thin, silvery wisps from the darkening slopes across the gorge the tortuous road followed. Soon the moon would be rising over one of those scraggy hills, and then the mountains would take on something of a primordial beauty the timberman's ax had robbed them of long since.

I turned off the highway into a stony, rutted, twisting little road and parked my car. Walking would be better from here on.

As I trudged along, now climbing sharply as the road clung to the hillside, now leaping from stone to stone as it followed the branch, I fell in with others bound for church, and I wondered whether I looked out of place, whether they would resent my presence. But except for brief, blank stares they paid me no attention

The church was similar to many hundreds in the hills, if a bit cruder. Outside no weatherboarding; just upright boards with the cracks covered by smaller strips. Inside no plastering; just a few printed posters that said: "Trust in the Lord," or "Jesus Is Soon Coming." Benches were rough plank affairs with two boards each for backs. In the center stood a potbellied stove, in the front a table to be used as an altar. Light was furnished by four kerosene lamps like those in farmhouse kitchens, two on the front wall, two on the rear.

I took a seat in one of the rear corners and watched the congregation gather. There were more women than men. Many of the women carried babies. A few were young and not too bad looking, but for the most part they were older, tired-looking, greasy-faced, straight-haired, gingham-clad women.

As the men came in—men of the soil and the mines, men whose very appearances pictured their lack of learning—they hung their hats on nails about the room. I noticed a couple of miners' carbide lights dangling on the wall.

One of the preachers—there usually is one main pastor but anybody preaches who feels the mood—walked over to the table. He was a baldish, knob-nosed, heavy-set man with a scar, probably from a knife brawl, down his left cheek.

He picked up a Bible, thumbed it. "I'm a-goin' t' take my tex' from Acts 19:11."

He might as well have taken his text from the Koran, for he never referred to it again. I looked up that verse later, and it says: "And God wrought special miracles by the hands of Paul." Certainly it had no bearing on what he had to say.

"I'll tell you my people that when you find a man what's tryin' to mock God and the Holy Ghost, you're seein' a man what's headed fer trouble.

Mountain Voodoo

"I heared a story t'other day. Hit war tol' me fer th' truth and hit went like this. The Holy Ghost was a-operatin' on a couple of girls and they got t' talkin' in unknown tongues. A young feller outside the church laughed and went t' town t' paint it red. When he got thar he started to flirt with the ticket seller at the picture show. Th' brother of that girl called th' police and th' police come. When they got thar, that young feller, he pulled his gun. Yes sir, buddy, he pulled his gun right outen his hip pocket. But th' law, they was too fast fer him, an' they shot him down, an' that feller fell flat of his face in th' poolroom door a-shoutin', 'O God, boys, help me.' Yessir, he shouted, 'O God, boys, help me.'

"An' do you think th' boys COULD help him?"

From the audience welled a firm "No."

"An' do you think th' Lord WOULD help him?"

Another "No."

"Nosiree my buddy. When a thirty-eight hits yer heart hit's too late to call on the boys. An' hit's too late to call on God if ye hain't called on him afore."

"Amen!"

"Don' ever speak light of things you don't know nothin' about!" He was beginning to shout. "They's thousands who has paid dear when they did. I'm a-warnin' ye not to sacrifice yer soul for a moment's pleasure."

"Amen! Amen!"

"Let's sing." But the invitation was unnecessary. Somebody already had started softly, "I Will Not Be Denied." Others joined in with voices and tambourines. In a remarkably short time the volume began to swell and the tempo to increase.

Louder and louder grew the chant. Harder and harder coarse shoes patted rough floors. On and on flowed the pounding rhythm of the tambourines, like jungle voodoo drums. The blended sounds rose and fell and rose—monotonous, exciting. The emotional effect was terrific.

Suddenly a woman leaped to her feet, screaming as I have never heard a woman scream before. In that scream somehow was blended pleasure and pain, and on her face was written supreme ecstasy. "Praise be to God," she shouted. "I'm comin' through."

As though her words were a signal, others leaped to their feet. In a moment all hell had broken loose. Men danced, cavorted, shouted. Women quivered, jerked, shrieked. The tambourines pounded on.

The preacher glided to one of the front corners and opened a cheap suitcase. As he did so I heard the ominous rattle that strikes terror to every living creature. A hush more exciting than the pounding rhythm had fallen upon that group of mad people as he opened the suitcase, but then as he lifted a four-foot rattler above his head the shouting and thumping began afresh.

The scarred-faced preacher danced about with the snake around his neck. Chattering in the gibberish of the unknown tongue he passed the reptile to another man.

A big-breasted woman who had been nursing a baby sprang to her feet, sliding the child to the floor and forgetting her bare teat. She snatched the snake and held it in front of her on open-palmed hands. She closed her eyes, opened her mouth, and yelled, "Glory to God, Glory to God." A scrawny girl of ten or eleven, probably a big sister, picked up the baby and tried to hush its squalling.

Two of the overalled men lighted the miners' lights I had seen on the wall; a third snatched one of the lamps from its socket in front of the reflector. The two with the carbides ran the flames over their hands, up and down their bare arms. Not to be outdone, the man with the lamp turned the wick so that the flame ran out the chimney. Then with both hands he held the lamp under his chin. The flames and smoke lapped around his throat and ears as they do around a backlog, yet the popping eyes seen through the smoke evinced not pain but hypnotic rapture.

The smell of searing hair and flesh, the odor of sweating, unwashed bodies, the smoke from the lamps, and the general heat of the night were stifling.

Of a sudden there was a screech that trilled above the general pandemonium. The bare-breasted woman had been bitten. She flung the snake from her, but someone else picked it up and kissed it. No one paid particular attention to the woman, and she, for all she had been struck, did not come to her senses. She seemed, indeed, lost to rationality, self-control, and inhibition. She chanted, "God help me, a sinner! God help me, a sinner!" She began to quiver all over like a muscle dancer, and both big breasts came full into view. She paid no attention. She was in another world.

As the spasms continued she slumped to the floor and rolled in the aisle. Her dress came up almost to her hips, revealing a pair of black cotton bloomers, the likes of which, I believe, are not generally worn in this generation.

Then, as suddenly as she had leaped to her feet a few minutes before, she stopped her hunching on the floor and lay in comparative quiet, breathing heavily and emitting an occasional moan as she rolled her disheveled head slowly from side to side.

Other women were having the type of orgasm I had just seen. Scarface had taken off his shoes and socks and was starting a frantic dance around the bewildered snake he had laid on the floor. Others of the men and two or three of the women joined in the savage gavot. Tambourines had changed hands, but they pounded on.

Not until everyone had reached a temporary state of exhaustion was there quiet, broken only by scattered and fervent, "Praise Gods." The preacher picked up the snake and replaced it in the suitcase.

End of Act I. I knew that Act II and Act III and as many acts as would be performed that night would be the same. Another of the self-ordained ministers would exhort a while. Another song would be started in the same throbbing tempo. Soon there would be bedlam again.

I slipped outside. The fresh air, cool in contrast, was refreshing. My hand trembled a little as I lighted a cigarette. I walked down the road away from the church, stumbling now and then among the larger rocks. I could hear a preacher starting Act II.

I had found the why of the snake services. I had thought perhaps the pay-off came later, after services had fired emotions, but had found the orgies were complete in themselves.

In an effort to put an end to such services the Kentucky legislature passed a law in the spring of 1940. It said: "No person shall display, handle or use any kind of snake or reptile in connection with any religious service or gathering. Any persons violating the provisions of this act shall be guilty of a misdemeanor and punished by a fine of not less than $50 nor more than $100."

It goes without saying that the law didn't stop the services.

Where the snake cult originated it is hard to say. Snakes ever have had a repellent fascination for human beings. In religion they go back to the Garden of Eden. In mythology they are frequently mentioned. The serpent-twined staff of Hermes still is the emblem of the physician.

To the best of my knowledge the sect now active originated in the Ozarks two decades ago, and it gained a following in Tennessee before it did in Kentucky. But wherever the cult had its inception it now has—law or no law—a firm hold in the Kentucky hill country. And although it has no central organization like Jehovah's Witnesses, it is spreading to other states.

In whatever form it may take, the mountaineers' religion is highly emotional and their translation of the Bible is extremely literal. Even so, tests of faith by snake venom are foreign to the beliefs of old-line mountaineers, and most of them look with a mixture of scorn and pity on these latter-day fanatics.

In a literal translation of four verses of St. Mark and one of St. Luke the snake-handlers find excuse for their actions. The first verse of the four in St. Mark 16:15-18 is used by all denominations as a basis for their missionary work: "And he said unto them, Go ye into all the world, and preach the gospel to every creature." The other three in Mark state: "He that believeth and is baptized shall be saved; but he that believeth not shall be damned. And these signs shall follow them that believe; In my name shall they cast out devils; they shall speak with new tongues; They shall take up serpents; and if they drink any deadly thing, it shall not hurt them; they shall lay hands on the sick, and they shall recover."

The passage in St. Luke which the cultists cite is the nineteenth verse of the tenth chapter: "Behold, I give unto you power to tread on serpents and scorpions, and over all the power of the enemy: and nothing shall by any means hurt you."

In 1938 a fellow by the name of Johnny Day visited Preacher George Washington Hensley's church on Greasy Creek in Harlan County. Awed, but not convinced, he swore to warrants at the county seat charging Hensley and two other leaders with disturbing the peace.

That was the case in Kentucky which first brought the snake-handlers to public notice.

Since there was no law at that time forbidding the handling of serpents the three were acquitted on the grounds they were exercising their constitutional right of religious freedom and that those who did not desire to participate were in no manner endangered.

Hensley's followers cheered that victory, but their troubles were only beginning. As the cult grew, so grew the desire of the more reasoning populace to stamp it out. Thus came the passage of the law

On the day after the measure went into effect a newspaper story set forth that: "Kentucky's new law forbidding handling of snakes in religious ceremonies went into effect yesterday, and a violation was reported last night by Deputy Sheriff Floyd Stidham from Vicco."

And continuing: "Warned, the people shouted, 'We can't pay a fine so we'll go to jail and preach.' More services are scheduled for tonight and the remainder of the week. Stidham said services were held last night with two snakes, which appeared to be a rattlesnake and a copperhead about four feet in length. He stated that he saw one man who had his neck and chin badly burned and was told that he had held a lighted oil lamp under his chin while shouting he would be protected. Stidham said he didn't interrupt their services, but as the people came out issued the warning that the services must stop."

But they didn't stop, and a few weeks later Associated Press teletypes rattled out a story which told that Mrs. Clark Napier, 40, wife of a disabled World War veteran and mother of seven children, died at the Hyden hospital soon after she had been bitten four times while handling a rattlesnake at a little country church on Bull Creek in Leslie County.

Less than a week later came another story. This time James Cochran, 39-year-old unemployed mechanic, father of several children, was dead. He had been bitten during services at the Free Pentecostal Church of God in Perry County.

After the first death Lige Bowling, pastor of the church on Bull Creek, was fined $50 for violating the anti-snake law and was held for the grand jury on a murder charge. After the second the victim's brother swore to warrants against twelve members of the Free Pentecostal.

First of the twelve to be tried was the pastor, a healthy

young brute of a coal miner whose appearance made one suspect the real impulse behind the snake services.

As a conglomerate mass of humanity packed the Perry County courthouse his wild-eyed followers gathered at the front of the courtroom, and I saw the tobacco-stained mouth of one man meet the snuff-stained lips of another in the "holy kiss." My stomach turned flips as I pictured myself kissing, smack in the mouth, either of those foul-breathed, stubble-chinned, grimy-necked louts. But to them, apparently, it was the very essence of brotherly love.

Someone in the group started a song, but as the women began to work themselves into a frenzy the county judge pounded the bench for order. "I'll put every last one of you in jail if you don't stop that," he warned.

A witness for the commonwealth took the stand. He told of the orgy that preceded the death of Cochran. He told that the pastor himself "was at the point of death for eight days and eight nights from a snake bite a while back."

"Why," he continued, "they give him up to die and made ready fer t' bury him."

But the heavy-set, low-browed pastor said it wasn't like that at all. He defended himself; he defended his cult; he declared, "I ain't never suffered from a snake bite because I've got th' faith." He told of fasting for a week to "get the power." He asserted that through that power and the laying on of hands a paralyzed child had been cured.

Despite this pretension to the power a jury of six hard-bitten mountaineers found the young buck guilty and fined him $50 and costs. Of course he couldn't pay, so off he went to jail. Trial of the other eleven was set for a later date.

Meanwhile, in other parts of the hills, in Tennessee, in Georgia, in Ohio, in Virginia, snake-handlers and anti-snake-handlers were becoming more active.

In Harlan three were arrested and fined. Our old friend George Washington Hensley instituted a proceeding to test the validity of the new state law. He had been keeping hard at his services on Pine Mountain and had added to his routine a test by poison.

Said he in a statement to the press: "Brother Bradley Shell took a large dose of strychnine powders about 6 o'clock. We stayed with him until 11:30 and there was no bad effect on him because of his faith. The legislature can keep on passin' laws, but it won't keep us from provin' our faith. We are going to appeal to the courts. The Constitution ain't like it used to be when a feller could worship as he pleases."

At Cincinnati, reporters wrote: "The weird emotional outbursts of members of the True Church of God were thrown into a noisier uproar last night when police, under Lieutenant Jacob Schardt, interrupted the ceremonies of the cult to take a copperhead snake away from members who were using the reptile in their strange exercises. . . . Despite this act of police viligance, however, a woman at the meeting was bitten. . . . Schardt threatened to shoot at the snake, he said, as it was being thrown wildly from one to another member as the cultists tried to keep the officers from getting their hands on it."

In Tennessee, "Preacher Jesse Pack, twice bitten while handling poisonous snakes in religious services, was committed to the Eastern State Hospital for the Insane." Pack later died in the asylum—of pneumonia.

In Georgia, "Sheriff's deputies entered the swamps today in search of a young mother hiding her dying five-year-old daughter from medical attention. The mother thought God would take the child if she implied lack of faith in Him by accepting a physician's services. . . . The child had been bitten last Thursday by a deadly copperhead snake, during a religious orgy. A physician who saw but was not permitted to treat the child's swollen arm on Tuesday thought it doubtful that she still lived."

At Richlands, Virginia, "The death of 48-year-old Robert

Cordle, who refused medical aid after being bitten by a rattlesnake during church services, brought 1,500 curious persons today to a funeral home to see his body. While the throngs passed the bier of the Doran resident, the Richlands council passed an ordinance outlawing the use of snakes in religious services and sent officers to the New Light Church to destroy any reptiles there."

I attended the trial of the other eleven who had been arrested after James Cochran's death. Just as they had at the pastor's trial the believers crowded into the front of the courtroom and began to sing. In just a few minutes, even without the aid of tambourines, feet began to pat, bodies began to respond to the rhythm, eyes began to look wild. But the sharp warning of a deputy sheriff cut short the demonstration. "Oh, Lord, I feel so good," shouted one woman despite the admonition. And she looked as though she did. "Glory to God, Glory to God," sang out one of the male leaders of the flock to the jerking of his lower spine.

"I don't believe they can do nothin' with these people fer takin' up serpents. It ain't constitution." The speaker was a watery-eyed, scraggy-bearded fellow of about twenty-five who sat next to me.

"If the Lord could take Daniel through the lions' den and Moses through the fiery furnace He won't pay no 'tention to a few leetle ole snakes," he continued as he saw I was listening. "If a feller goes out in the woods and picks up a snake, is that any business of the law? If a feller brings a snake in an' proves he's got the Lord in him, is that any business of the law?"

"Do you belong to one of the churches where snakes are handled?" I asked.

"I shore do."

"Aren't you afraid to mess with those things? Two people have died around here in the last week or so."

"Well, I was afeared at first, but somethin' stronger than

that got hold o' me. Hit were th' power o' th' Lord, and when that thar gits hold o' ye, buddy, you jest natural got t' act."

"But these people who die and others who lose a finger or an arm as a result of a bite, do they do so because they haven't the proper faith?"

"We tell 'em if they hain't got th' faith to stan' back and not pick up no snakes. You've got to believe in th' Lord and trust in th' Lord and have faith in th' Lord if you're a-goin' to handle them snakes. They'll eat you up if you don't. I've seen a man git bit, an' his finger rotted off, and I've seen others git bit, an' hit didn't even swell 'em. Now onct I seen a man git bit when he was a-puttin' a snake in his shirt an' down in his britches, an' that snake pert nigh et him up. I guess that was good 'nuf fer him, too. The Bible don't say nothin' about puttin' snakes down yer britches. Hit says, 'they shall take up serpents;' take 'em up, like this, in yer hands, an' that's all."

Someone rapped for order. Court was in session. There was a whispered conference among the county judge, the county attorney, and the defense attorney, who incidentally was a candidate for circuit judge and who, it was said, had taken the cases for the votes he might get and not for pay. The defense lawyer beckoned to his eleven defendants and they trailed into an anteroom.

In about ten minutes they returned. There was another conference with the judge. "All right." The judge was speaking. "Then we'll try the cases. I'm not going to grant a continuance." Then addressing himself to the entire courtroom, "I told these people I would dismiss the charges against them if they would promise to quit handling snakes, but they have refused." To the defense attorney, "What is your plea?"

"Guilty. We plead guilty, Your Honor, and ask that you

suspend sentence pending the outcome of an appeal instituted in Harlan County."

"No sir, I'm not going to suspend sentence and have these people headin' right out of here and looking for snakes. The law is the law, and the best I can do for you is give the minimum. Fifty dollars and costs each, and if your clients can't pay they go to jail."

There wasn't $50 in the crowd.

I walked down to the jail a little later to see how things were going along. Three women had taken children to the cells with them. Two of the youngsters were of nursing age. In one case both mother and father were in the lockup. I heard the woman say to another on the outside, "Git some of the Collinses t' take care of th' least 'uns."

They seemed to regard their sentences lightly. They sang and stomped and shouted, "Glory to God; praise be His name; praise Jesus; there'll be stars in my crown tonight."

Some fifty cultists gathered on the outside and heaped condemnation on the legislators who had passed the anti-snake law.

"Why," cried one old crone, "they'll be passin' a law next against speakin' in unknown tongues and against shoutin' and clappin' hands. I'll tell you there can't no law make me quit doin' what th' Lord tells me t' do. I'll tell anybody I'll handle snakes, and if they want to put me in jail, let 'em. That won't stop me nary bit."

"I wouldn't want to be in the shoes of them legislators," ranted another. "I'll tell you them that hurts any one of God's children'll suffer, and hell's walls is a-goin' to be pushed wider fer this business today."

"Amen," shouted one of the brothers as he threw his arm around a second brother and gave him the holy kiss. "We'll git together an' pray tonight till those jail doors swing open. Why, th' Lord kin tear that little ole shambly place down if He sees fit."

One of the sect's disciples was engaging in argument a man who declared proudly that he was a representative of the Cleveland Assembly of the Church of God. The disciple accused the Church of God of fostering the legislation against snake handling. The Church of God man accused the disciple of taking a few verses of St. Mark and excluding the rest of the Bible.

"You sometimes handle snakes too, don't you?" challenged the disciple.

"Only when an enemy brings hit in to test our faith. We don't go 'round temptin' th' Lord."

The disciple criticized the Church of God man for wearing a coat and tie. Turning to me he said: "Now I love this man like a brother. I love ever'body. But look how he's dressed up. I guess if th' Lord came to choose someone he wouldn't choose him—ner you either."

A bystander approached and asked how old the snake-handling cult was.

"As old as God," was the proud reply.

"Then how come I never heard of it until a few months ago?"

"Well, folks has been a-goin' through a dark age, but now they're beginnin' t' see th' light."

II

These Are the People

ALMOST ANY MOUNTAINEER except a mining camp immigrant will tell you his foreparents came from Virginia or from the Carolinas, but beyond that fact he will know little. The exact ancestry of the highlander, indeed, is open to speculation. Many a writer has sounded off about the "pure Anglo-Saxon stock" simply because he has read about it or heard of it and hasn't stopped to investigate. Are the mountain people "pure Anglo-Saxon"? And if they are, what of it? The second question really needn't be answered, because the answer to the first is "No," but I can't pass up that second one without saying that I grow a little weary of hearing "pure Anglo-Saxon" intoned as though it were something akin to being God Almighty.

Most historians agree that many of the early settlers of the hill country were of Scotch-Irish descent, but they disagree about the proportion of the Scotch-Irish to the Germans, Dutch, French Huguenots, Welsh, English, and sundry others. It seems probable, however, that the Scotch-Irish predominated. Who were they? Paradoxically, perhaps, they were very little Scotch and much less Irish. That is they did not belong mainly to the so-called Celtic race but were the most composite of all the people of the British Isles. Called Scots because they lived in Scotia, they were called Irish because they moved to Ireland in 1607 when James I confiscated Irish estates and planted the Scots in Ulster. Geography and not ethnology gave them their name. They were a mixture of the primitive Scot and Pict, the primitive Briton and the primitive Irish, plus the later Norwegian, Dane, Saxon, and Angle.

Whatever the mountain people are, they are not "pure" anything. The popular idea of their Anglo-Saxon origin springs, perhaps, from the fact that their ballads, their singing-games, their dances, their customs, habits, and speech have been until recent years essentially those of Shakespearean England.

A theory that the early mountaineers were largely convicts and indentured servants pushed from the eastern seaboard probably is not correct either, though the fact hardly would be so harsh as it sounds. Many of the "convicts" deported from Europe were charged only with political offenses, and the indentured servants were impoverished Europeans who were looking for a chance in the New World and who had to sell their services to get here. More than likely the theory that the southern mountains were peopled mainly by outcasts or refugees from old settlements in the lowlands has no other basis than imagination.

The evidence points to a conclusion that the ancestors of the present mountain people derived from the middle, or perhaps lower middle, classes of their homelands; that they were good, hardy stock, products of European conflict. They were, moreover, of essentially the same stock as the pioneers in Kentucky's Bluegrass region.

In the decades immediately preceding the Revolutionary War, immigration into the Great Appalachian Valley of Pennsylvania and Virginia was heavy. By 1780 game no longer was plentiful and land prices were high. As a consequence settlers had begun to move westward along the Ohio River or southwestward along the Great Indian Warpath running from Pennsylvania through western Maryland and Virginia and thence along the Wilderness Trail. The first to move, as always, were the hunters and traders, followed, as always, by the seekers of free land.

It is probable that no other route, land or water, played a part so important in the settlement of the United States as the Wilderness Trail. The Blue Ridge, Cumberland, and Allegheny escarpments, forming a well-nigh impenetrable barrier, caused a population reservoir. The Ohio River provided a spillway in the north; the break known as Cumberland Gap and the trail leading through it were destined to provide an even more important spillway in the south. Buffalo and Indian had known the gap where Kentucky, Virginia and Tennessee now meet and had worn trails beyond it to the salt springs. But it remained for Daniel Boone and his contemporaries to make it a white man's passageway.

In 1775 nine men, who had obtained by treaty with the Cherokees some seventeen million acres lying between the Cumberland and Kentucky rivers, employed Boone to lay out a route from the old Virginia settlements through Cumberland Gap to the rolling limestone region of Kentucky. That route was the Wilderness Trail, the trail that moved the frontier westward. Possibly 75,000 pioneers followed it before it became a wagon road in 1795, and countless thousands moved along it in later years to settle the Northwest and the Far West

Once through the mountain barrier the settlers found trails worn by buffalo, Indians, and hunters to lead them into the rich, rolling lands of central Kentucky and the Ohio Valley. But because the Wilderness Road passed for most of its course to the west of the Cumberlands, and because other trails and breaks in the barrier were little known, few settlers moved into the mountains of eastern Kentucky before 1790.

By that time the central Kentucky land had been claimed; thus families turned off the Wilderness Road and followed streams eastward to their sources in the hills. Others came in through Pound Gap or other breaks that had been discovered to the north of the Cumberland River's cut through Pine Mountain. Contrary to a rather common belief these settlers of the mountains weren't homeseekers too lazy to push on, travelers whose "wagon wheel broke." It was easier, really, to go from Cumberland Gap to the Bluegrass than from the gap to the backhill country.

One who looks upon the barren, poverty-stricken, over-populated mountains of Kentucky today may ask, "Why in the world did people ever come here?" There was good reason. Some chose the mountains because they loved them; others because the Bluegrass land immediately to the west had been taken and little was known of the country farther west; others because they had received grants of land in the mountains for Revolutionary War service. Moreover the hills offered suitable homestead sites. There was timber for houses. There were springs of both fresh and salt water. The woods on the slopes and the canebrakes fringing the streams were alive with deer, bear, wild turkeys, pheasants, quail, and squirrels. The Treaty of Greenville in 1795 had ended most of the Indian troubles that had been a deterrent to mountain settlement.

So up the creek beds they pressed, traveling sometimes in parties, sometimes in family groups. The men marched in front, carrying their guns, driving a few head of cattle, hogs, or sheep and leading pack horses. Women walked beside them or rode with children in their laps. There were no Conestoga wagons or Red River carts such as the pioneers of the Far West later were to use, for there were no roads or level fields. All earthly belongings—clothing, axes, kettles, pails, food, seed, and perhaps a spinning wheel or a book or two—were carried on the backs of horses, oxen, and men and women.

Once in the hills the settlers found life to their liking. A man had elbow room there in 1800, with only two persons to a square mile. He still had elbow room in 1850 when there were from six to eighteen. The pioneers felled trees, hewed the logs, and built their one-room homes. They raised a few sheep, carded the wool, spun it into yarn, wove it into cloth, and dyed it with the ooze of native barks for their homespun clothing. They raised hogs for meat and added to the supply with game. They grew patches of corn, gritted it into a coarse meal, and cooked the corn bread with their meat over the embers in great stone fireplaces. They grew sorghum cane for "long sweetnin' " and boiled down the juice from sugar maples for "short sweetnin'." To their diet they added pumpkins, cushaws, and shucky beans. The few necessities they could not make or raise they obtained by bartering skins, ginseng, and yellowroot with traders or at the county seat. The man was farmer, cobbler, blacksmith, and miller. The woman was housewife, mother, cook, and weaver.

In the mountain fastnesses theirs was a full, independent life, and they kept on living it as civilization moved on. Those first arrivals knew how to read, and a few had brought books with them, but there was no need for book learning in the hills. It was better for children to know how to hunt; how to card and spin and weave; how to catch fish; how to churn milk into butter; how to make lights from fat-pine sticks; how to grit corn on a gritter; how to build houses for themselves and their own children.

These things the children and the grandchildren of the pioneers learned, and they forgot the outside world.

That circumstantial detachment from the broader currents of American life was interrupted in 1861 when through the hills was voiced the word that the southern states had seceded from the union and that there was war. Virtually a law unto themselves the mountain people were little concerned with what went on at Frankfort, or at Washington either for that matter, but their fathers or grandfathers had fought to create the union, and they didn't want it destroyed. Furthermore few of them were slaveholders. It was natural, then, that in the vast majority the men joined the Union army, although it was to the astonishment of both southern and northern lowlanders, who knew only vaguely of the strange "mountain whites" who inhabited Appalachia.

It seems that the American mountaineer was "discovered" at the beginning of the Civil War. Confederate leaders, assuming that Mason and Dixon's line was the absolute division between the North and the South, formed a plan to march an army from Wheeling, West Virginia, to some point on the Great Lakes and thus to dissever the North at one blow.

The plan sounded so feasible that it is probable it aided materially the sale of Confederate bonds in England. But when Captain Garnett, a West Point graduate, started to carry it out he got no farther than Harper's Ferry. When he struck the mountains he struck enemies who shot at his men from ambush, cut down bridges before him, carried news of his march to the Federals. Garnett himself, struck by a bullet from a mountaineer's squirrel rifle, fell at Harper's Ferry

Then it was, as John Fox pointed out long ago, that the South began to realize what a long, lean, powerful arm of the Union it was that the southern mountaineer stretched through its very vitals. That arm helped to hold Kentucky in the Union by giving preponderance to the Union sympathizers in the Bluegrass. It kept the East Tennesseeans loyal. It made West Virginia "secede from secession." It drew out a horde of one hundred thousand volunteers when Lincoln called for troops, and it raised a hostile barrier between the armies of the coast and the armies of the Mississippi.

In the mountains the great civil struggle was prosecuted

principally by bushwhacking or guerilla warfare. Marauding bands of both armies lived off the country, killing, burning, looting, and exciting hatreds that led to many feuds of later days. A Union lieutenant and native of Perry County, Abner Eversole, told me of his guerilla days, when it was ride, shoot, burn, and ride again. Other mountain residents have told me of the hell their parents and grandparents suffered.

When the war was over, even the mountaineers who had fought beyond the hills took their squirrel rifles home and resumed their primitive lives. It is natural to suppose that once brought into contact with the America about them the people would have begun to move forward. But the Southern outlanders wanted nothing to do with these enemies in their camp, and the highlanders were content to have it that way; thus the mountaineers' isolation was as complete as ever. The sleepers had been only momentarily awakened, and but few of them were to rub their eyes again until the machine age crashed suddenly upon the hills.

During the 100 years and more between settlement and arrival of the machine age the hills bred a distinctive people. It is an exaggeration to say, "Mountaineers look like this—— Their traits of character are thus and so—— Under certain conditions they will react in this manner——" Even so, similar ancestry, inbreeding, a common fight against poverty, and a century and a half of isolation in an unusual environment have given the Kentucky mountaineers characteristics common to the majority.

Back in 1913 Horace Kephart made a pertinent observation about the mountaineer: "To name him is to conjure up a tall, slouching figure in homespun, who carries a rifle as habitually as he does his hat, and who may tilt its muzzle toward a stranger before addressing him, the form of salutation being:

" 'Stop thar! Whut's you-unses name? Whar's you-uns a-goin' ter?'

"Let us admit that there is just enough truth in this caricature to give it a point that will stick. Our typical mountaineer is lank, he is always unkempt, he is fond of toting a gun on his shoulder and his curiosity about a stranger's name and business is promptly, though politely, outspoken."

The mountaineer no longer dresses in homespun, nor does he carry a rifle to level at strangers. But he is for the most part still lank, and he is apt to have a pistol handy. I don't mean that all mountaineers carry pistols any more than that all central Kentuckians drink Bourbon and go to the races, but the description is reasonably accurate as a generality. At a recent trial at Beattyville thirty men checked guns before entering the courtroom.

An anonymous parody gives an amusing, if exaggerated, picture of certain of the mountaineer's characteristics:

Man born in the wilds of Kentucky is of feud days, and full of virus.

He fisheth, fiddleth, fusseth, and fighteth all the days of his busy life.

He shunneth water as a mad dog, and drinketh much bad whisky.

When he riseth from his cradle, he goeth forth to seek the scalp of his neighbor's wife's cousin's father-in-law, who avengeth the deed.

Yea, verily, his life is uncertain, and he knoweth not the hour when he may be jerked hence.

He goeth forth on a journey half-shot, and cometh back on a shutter, full of shot.

He riseth in the night to let the cat out, and lo! It taketh nine doctors three days to pick the buckshot out of his person.

He goeth forth in joy and gladness, and cometh back in scraps and fragments.

He calleth his fellow man a liar, and he getteth himself filled with scrap iron, even unto the fourth generation.

A cyclone bloweth him into the bosom of a neighbor's wife,

and his neighbor's wife's husband bloweth him into the bosom of Father Abraham before he hath time to explain.

He emptieth a demijohn into himself, and a shotgun into his enemy. And his enemy's son lieth in wait for him on election day, and lo! The coroner ploweth up a forty-acre field to bury the remains of his enemies.

Despite a stoop the mountaineer is of average, perhaps better than average, height. He is sallow and lean of face, sinewy, loose-jointed. His cheekbones are high, his nose straight, his hair a dull brown, his sharp eyes gray or blue. He is rarely fat. His movements indicate latent strength, tenacious rather than robust. He walks with a long, swinging yet uneven stride developed from contact with rough, steep earth. His face is opaque, and his stare is inscrutable. Seldom ill at ease, he can make the outlander feel that way.

The mountain woman is pretty in her youth; pretty in middle age, too, if she is spared the burdens of most. But usually she marries young and fades early. Her lot is indeed a hard one. It is probable that only the peasantry of Europe can show anything to parallel it. In addition to her burdens of incessant child-bearing and child-raising are those of cooking, washing, and housekeeping without modern conveniences, milking the cows, caring for the stock, and helping her man in the corn patch. When she is thirty she may look forty, and when forty, fifty-five. Yet though life defeats her it does not entirely coarsen her. Usually she is simple, natural, shy, and quiet. The man is the lord of the household, and when he yells, "Shet ep!" she generally "shets." There is something striking about an old mountain woman. For all that she may be dirty, wrinkled, and ravaged by time and hardships she has eyes and a smile that go to your heart. She breathes patience and endurance. She has serenity and dignity.

Children and the home are still the centers of existence in the mountains. The mountain man and woman love their children, love them to the point of spoiling the little tow-headed, freckle-faced rascals. Association among parents and children is intimate, and the youngsters start early to follow in the footsteps of their elders. No mortal is more independent and self-satisfied than the mountain child. Circumstances have wrung much of the self-importance from the mountain man, but it is yet instilled in his children. The mountain boy has few "brought-on" toys, no footballs, bicycles, or ponies. By the time he is six or eight he may be wielding a hoe alongside his mother in the corn or garden patch. When he is twelve he may be doing a man's work. The fact that he works doesn't mean, however, that he has no freedom. For all their raucous shouts of "I'll whup you" his parents are lax in discipline, and by the time he is twelve he may smoke, drink, chew, and swear. When the work is up he does as he pleases—hunting, fishing, going to school only when he feels the urge or when the truant officer gets unusually diligent. The mountain girl's future is marriage, and since she's on the cull list by twenty she starts early to prepare for married life. She, like other girls, nurses dolls until she is six, but then she nurses the "least 'uns" until she is sixteen, her own after that.

Probably the most widely recognized characteristic of the mountaineer is his individualism—that independence that expresses itself in a determination to do as he damned well pleases. The trait is too deeply implanted to be uprooted in a few decades; yet uprooted it will be. The reason: poverty. As population pressure has increased, as resources have been depleted, as the task of eking an existence has become more and more difficult, independence has been choked. It's still there, to be sure, but under a restraint an earlier mountaineer would have found intolerable. It is fighting a rear-guard action. A man, however bred, can't maintain much independence on relief, and a large proportion of the mountain population has depended upon the WPA for existence during the last eight years.

In the past, independence has been carried to an extreme.

The mountain man made the worst possible workman, for at an order he didn't like he'd balk like a mule. But it is tragic nonetheless that this trait should vanish. "The independence of the mountain farm must be preserved, or the fine spirit of the race will vanish and all that is manly in the highlander will wither to the core," Horace Kephart said. If that is true, and I'm afraid it is, the highlanders are doomed to a status no better than that of the Georgia crackers.

Hospitality is another well-known trait. Unhappily suspicion and mistrust, always present in the mountaineer's nature, have suppressed it among those whom civilization has reached via the highways, but it still flourishes in the back country and it is evident along the roadways when suspicion has been allayed. Many times I have been asked to "get down and eat a bite" or to "take the night" in a section where I was a total stranger. I recall eating one day with a family who had only corn bread, water-and-grease gravy, and cooked onions. They shared the food gladly and offered no apologies other than, "We'll eat better when our garden comes on." One is bound to have a tender spot in his heart for such people.

Much has been said and written about the universal honesty of the mountaineer. It is a virtue that is passing because of the encroachments of "civilization" and the press of poverty. Especially in the mining camps and other towns is the charge of larceny being added to the criminal court dockets. An old storekeeper told me that thirty or forty years ago he had no qualms about leaving his store, and even his cash drawer, unlocked but that now he has difficulty in keeping either sufficiently secure.

Several decades ago larceny was almost unknown in the hill country. A mountaineer who would think nothing of shooting his neighbor for damage done by a roving shoat would consider it a heinous crime under any circumstances to steal that shoat. The extent of change from such a high regard of honesty is shown not only in minor thefts but in major frauds. In the early 1930's, for example, residents of Clay, Breathitt, Magoffin, Knox, Bell, Perry, and Knott counties perpetrated one of the biggest mail-order frauds of all time. Since about the time of the first World War the tempting catalogues of Montgomery Ward and Sears, Roebuck had replaced the Bible in order of importance in mountain homes. Unable to visit cities and their big department stores the hillsmen looked hungrily at the thousands of fascinating pictures in these wonder books, and often such hard-earned cash as they were able to obtain went for some especially attractive article in the catalogue.

Then someone found that a check, even though against a nonexistent fund, would bring that longed-for rifle, gay new dress, or pair of shoes. In three years eastern Kentucky "customers" swindled Montgomery Ward and Sears, Roebuck out of $1,000,000 worth of merchandise. As the companies took steps to plug the leaks the purchasers grew more crafty. Seldom was the same name used twice, and forged cashiers' checks began to appear. So clever were many of the forgeries that company officials became convinced a big-city ring was using the mountaineers as "fronts." Thirteen detectives were sent into the hills and thirteen detectives came out on the run.

Later, in 1933, Mrs. Katherine Keeler and Mrs. Jane Wilson, of the Northwestern University Crime Detection Laboratory, went into the hills to investigate after a careful study had convinced them that more than 200 persons had written the forged checks. They posed as university graduate students writing theses on the racial stock of Kentucky highlanders. Always proud to be the objects of such attention the mountaineers signed questionnaires after the young women had filled them out. Comparisons of several thousand signatures thus obtained with signatures on the checks led to the arrest by federal officers of 137 persons, about half of them women.

One of these women while free on bond wrote still another check to "git me a fitten dress t' come t' court in." At London in May 1934 all 137 pleaded guilty. Ninety-three were probated five years, and forty-four were given sentences ranging from three months to three years.

I have read many treatises holding that the mountain people are not lazy, but boiled down they all say, "Honest, they ain't lazy; they just don't like to work." Personally I know of only two types of people who are lazier or less ambitious than the mountaineers–Negroes and Southern white trash. To be sure, the mountaineers have physical energy. They'll walk ten miles to a social meet and hike all night on the trail of a 'possum, but in too many cases they just don't give a damn if the porch falls in and Susie Belle cooks on a three-legged stove. I don't know; maybe it's contentment; maybe it's a fatalistic feeling of "what's the use"; maybe I wouldn't do any better under their circumstances. But, infrequently, I've seen a man making a decent living for his family off fifty acres of hill land, and hundreds of times I've seen the weeds taking the crop, rot taking the house, and rickets taking the kids while the old man spat tobacco juice and looked speculatively over the 100 acres his grandpappy left him.

A characteristic the mountaineer has in full measure is loyalty. No friend will spring more quickly to your aid and cling more steadfastly and courageously. While his friend is in trouble the mountaineer's trouble does not end. He is loyal also to his clan, his hills, and his country. The love of the highlander for his home, his children, and his mountains has been mentioned. That love is inextricably bound with a dogged, unreckoning loyalty.

But if a mountaineer is loyal to his friends he is fully as implacable toward his enemies. Never will he forgive or forget a real or imagined insult, and his desire for revenge never lessens until the score is settled. His is a simple, sensitive spirit, and the emotions of love, anger, hate, and revenge are fierce and primitive within him.

Primitive, too, is his Indian-like dignity and reserve, inherited from those who were born to isolation and loneliness, though on proper occasion he can be friendly, talkative, and even garrulous.

In the matter of neighborliness the mountaineer is a paradox. He is courteous to his neighbor. He will lend him anything he has. He will invite him to eat or stay with him. He will help him with his crops. If the need is great he will share his food and clothing with him. But let that neighbor decide the boundary line should be moved ten feet in the south hollow and he'll blow the livin' hell out of him. Under all the neighborliness is suspicion and mistrust, an ever-present fear that some advantage will be taken. Such a spirit makes community endeavor well-nigh impossible.

Although the mountaineer's actions may seem gross and his speech coarse when compared to the actions and chatter of the socially elite around the tea table, he is singularly able to acquit himself well under any circumstances. Perhaps it is his innate dignity, perhaps it is his firm belief that he's as good as anybody else, perhaps it's sheer nerve that makes him free of the manifestations of self-consciousness. Whatever it is, he has it in abundance.

And the hillsman has his code of manners, however crude they may appear. When a mountaineer approaches the house of a friend or stranger he stands in the yard and shouts, "Hello." It would be as unmannerly for him to pound on the door as for you to walk in without knocking. His manners, too, command that he visit the home of the sick, and this he will do though the patient grows sicker as a result. While making rounds with a county physician I have seen as many as ten people in an airtight room with a person seriously ill. They smoke, they chew, they talk in loud voices while the patient suffers in silence. He knows they consider it their duty and privilege to "come and set up."

Many of the highlander's manners are manifestations of a belief in male dominance. A backcountry mountaineer does not tip his hat to a woman, but he offers his chair to a visiting male neighbor. When he and his gal are trudging to a big meetin' they walk hand in hand, but he doesn't take her arm to help her across the rough places, and when the gal has become his woman he walks in front and she heels, carrying the least 'un and leading a couple of others. Women generally do not eat with the men, and if they do the food is not passed to them first. Usually the women stand and serve. The hillsman doesn't consider it his part to aid the housewife. He doesn't bother to close the door or to clean his shoes before entering. He'd no more think of wiping the dishes than of refusing shelter to a friend.

I have never been able to determine in my own mind whether the highlander's thoughts flow deeply. At times I have been startled by the depth of an observation. At others I have been disgusted by sheer tommyrot. Many persons hold to a theory that the American mountaineers represent an accumulation of fertility that is potentially the finest the human race affords. That possibly was true a hundred years ago. It is not true today. Certainly there are many persons of superior intelligence and physique in the mountains today, but the average mental and physical strength is below the average for the nation. The three basic reasons are excessive inbreeding, selective migration, and unfavorable environment.

Intelligence quotient tests are far from infallible, but they furnish the only known scientific method of arriving at conclusions regarding intelligence. After carefully testing 2,000 subjects in three counties of eastern Kentucky, Dr. Nathaniel D. M. Hirsch, of Duke University, observed that the most important single discovery was the low I.Q. rating of the subjects; that lowest I.Q.'s were found in the districts where close intermarriage occurred; that environmental factors were responsible for 25 per cent and hereditary factors for the other 75 per cent of the subaverage mentality of the people tested.

For one hundred years migrations have played an important part in lowering the intelligence level. The first migration took place around 1840, when game and fish resources were depleted and an arduous type of agriculture became the basis of existence. The Civil War took a heavy toll of the best mountain men, and for several years after the war many intelligent and venturesome youths went west. About 1880 another general migration took place, and between 1910 and 1930 many workers moved from the hills to the industrial centers. The majority of those who left were the most energetic, ambitious, and intelligent.

Between 1930 and 1935 possibly 100,000 persons returned to the Kentucky hills, spreading poverty even thinner, but this reverse migration did little to help the stock. Many who returned were those who couldn't succeed outside.

Hill dwellers have, as someone said, "married back and forth and crossways and upside down until every man is his own grandmother if he only knew how to figure it out." On this point Hirsch said, "Close inbreeding of people that are generation after generation losing their most energetic and most variable types through migration can only result in the production of a stolid but stable stock at the best, and at the worst in subrepresentative types of humanity."

Others who have made tests in the mountains have brought forth similar reports. In one survey a question asked was, "What is the thing for you to do if it is raining when you come to school?" and the universal reply was, "I wouldn't come." When several of the children were asked, "What would you do if it was not raining?" they replied, "I wouldn't come anyway."

One sees many mental defectives in the hills of eastern Kentucky. It does not follow, however, that an undue proportion of the people are imbeciles or idiots. The mentally afflicted are kept at home because ties are strong, because the mountaineer has a horror of institutions, and because the state, having insufficient space, pays families to keep them there. In many cases the $75 a year the state pays the parents of a moron, imbecile, or idiot is an important part of the family's cash income, and the parents would far rather receive this bounty than to have their offspring in the Feeble Minded Institute at Frankfort. That practice is tragic socially, for many of the moronic class reproduce their kind.

The highlander knows little of intricate conventions, and thus in the light of the country's generally accepted code he is immoral. During the last few decades he has aped the vices but not the virtues of the outlander. Not all his transgressions, however, can be laid to "civilization," for always his morals have been lax. In 1901 Ellen C. Semple wrote: "There seems to be no higher standard of morality for the woman than for the man, and for both it is low. The women are modest, gentle and refined in their manners, but their virtue is frail." Combined in the mountaineer are a primitive amorality, a gross materialism, frankness, and the acquired vices.

In the idleness of the hill country sex assumes tremendous proportions. Sexual intercourse is the "poor man's only recreation," and to the mountaineer it is, moreover, an experience that is vital, taken for granted, and indulged in at an early age. When Miss Semple said the virtue of the women was "frail" she didn't exaggerate. Having fewer inhibitions than the outland girl and less to lose they yield more readily. If a girl is so unfortunate as to turn up pregnant, the cause of her trouble probably will marry her—either out of regard for duty or the trigger finger of an aggrieved parent. But even if he doesn't she is by no means so disgraced as her sister of the lowlands. The child may be given the father's name and still be a member of the mother's household. Very little stigma is attached either to the girl or to her illegitimate offspring, and her misstep is not likely to stand in the way of a future marriage.

The virtue of the married man and woman is no more unsullied than that of the unmarried. The woman is apt to welcome a little change in her burdensome life, and the man is prone to stray to other pastures. In fact he may stray so far he forgets to come back. In such a case he probably will find himself a "widder woman" somewhere, and his own "widder woman" may find herself a stray.

Doubtless there are many cases of incest in the hills. A low living level and one-room cabins that house males and females of all ages are conducive. But doubtless, also, incest is by no means as common as this Rabelaisian tale on the mountaineers would suggest:

A young hillbilly culminated a pie-supper courtship by marrying a pretty sixteen-year-old from across the ridge. After the ceremony, the big dinner, and the shivaree, the bridegroom hied his bride to the privacy of her parents' loft. Presently he jumped out of bed, pulled on his overalls and shoes, and headed for home.

As he crawled in the bed among his brothers and sisters, his pappy raised up on one arm and queried, "What air you a-doin' back hyar, son?"

"I guess I got good reason, pappy," the son replied. "That thar gal I hitched up to war a virgin."

"You done right in leavin', son," the old man agreed as he settled back down on his corn-husk tick. "Iffen she hain't good 'nuf fer her fambly, she hain't good 'nuf fer ourn."

Courting in the hill towns is much the same as courting any place else, but courting in the hill country is talkin' to a girl, and when a fellow is talkin' to a girl in earnest, marriage is supposed to result in a few months, especially if the "layin' acrost the bed" stage has been reached. "Me and my man didn't talk long," a woman told me once. "We talked about three months, I guess; then I got used to him and we married." When a girl is being courted steadily she'd best not smile upon another, else the two swains are apt to shoot it out. One of the most derisive statements that can be made about a young lady of the hills is, "That gal, why she's talked to pert nigh ever'body 'round hyar."

The phrase, "talkin' to a girl" is descriptive. There are mighty few places a mountain beau can take his love, so he talks to her. In time, of course, talking leads to acting, and so comes "layin' acrost the bed," another custom born of necessity. Mountain homes are short on chairs, and such a thing as a divan or davenport is almost unknown. Hence, they "lay acrost the bed," and it is probable the girl finds the practice more efficacious in determining the identity of her future husband than little whims in which she likes to indulge. She may, for instance, swallow a thimbleful of salt before retiring so that in her dreams she will see the face of her future husband as he brings her a glass of water. She may get up before dawn to find a cardinal and recite, "See a redbird before it's light, see your man before tonight." Or she may find a snail whose trail will spell out his name in a plate of corn meal.

When the day of the wedding comes the two are joined by a justice of the peace at the county seat or by a preacher at the home of the bride. Church weddings are rare. The ceremony often takes place before noon, but the time isn't important so long as it isn't raining, for if it is, "the bride will shed as many tears as the rain drops that fall." And if she takes a bath that day, "she musn't get her belly wet, else her man'll be a drunkard."

When the maiden has been made a bride her father perhaps will tap her on the left cheek with an old shoe for good luck and her mother may hand her a little "poke o' wheat" for fertility. After the ceremony friends and neighbors join the bride and groom in a big dinner. During the meal the groom is the butt of many jests. Later he is ridden on a rail or subjected to even rougher treatment during the shivaree.

On the wedding night, unless the bride's parents happen to be "religious," the liquor flows freely and the furniture is cleared away for a square dance. Until late at night they pound the boards; then some go home and others sleep where they can find the room. Next day, called by some the "Infare Day," the celebrants move to the home of the groom's parents, and after another big dinner there they at last leave the young couple to themselves. There usually is no honeymoon trip. The two make their abode with parents or begin to build themselves a shelter a "little ways up the hollow."

Birth, marriage, death—every phase of the life of the Kentucky mountaineer has been shaded by poverty and isolation. He came into the hill country with an eighteenth century civilization, and through the combination of isolation and poverty he retrogressed, even reverting to customs and usages already abandoned when he left Virginia and the Carolinas. Today the machine age has him in its mad whirl, and his isolation is nearly gone. But poverty has grown more stark, more real, more pressing. Up and up the hollow he has gone until there's no more room at the head. Charity he has always scorned, but charity today he is forced to accept. "Servility," said Kephart, "is literal hell to a mountaineer, and when it is forced upon him he turns into a mean, underhand, slinking fellow, easily tempted into crime." Servility is upon the mountaineer.

III

In a Manner of Speaking

PREACHIN' CHARLIE he'd ben funeralizin' for three days runnin', but his Scriptur' juice warn't sca'cely tapped yit. He'd trickle a bushel o' Bible ary rod o' the trail. Sometime hit u'd sample pure Charlie; which hit was purely nacheral, seein' Charlie hisself had been samplin' more strongerer waters than Moses's for to season his sarmons with.

That paragraph is from Percy Mackaye's *Tall Tales of the Kentucky Mountains*. It is just one chosen at random from page upon page of the same dialect. It's very pretty dialect too. The only trouble with it is that Kentucky mountain people don't talk like that–and never did. Mr. Mackaye has written interesting stories and plays, but he got off base when he tried to make the mountain dialect conform to rules and every character speak according to the resulting pattern.

The only consistent thing about the Kentucky mountain dialect is its inconsistency. Not only do people in various parts of the mountains speak differently, but families in the same neighborhood speak dissimilarly, members of families speak unalike, and even an individual will use a word one way one time and another way another, sometimes in succeeding sentences. No one person uses a large number of quaint or obsolete words. They still may be heard from the lips of older persons in the remote areas, but in and around towns they have passed on with the coming of consolidated schools, daily newspapers, and the radio. The mountain speech has changed as much during the last twenty or thirty years as have modes of living. Lucy Furman and Louise Murdoch wrote the best dialect of the era prior to 1920; James Still writes the best dialect of today. It is impossible to give in a paragraph or so a complete picture of an author's dialect, but perhaps these two excerpts will indicate the change:

From Miss Furman's *Glass Window*:

My sympathies allus was with the women-folks anyhow; 'pears like the universe is ag'in 'em, and God and man confederates to keep 'em downtrod. In all my travels I have seed hit, and hit's been the same old story ever sence Eve et the apple. I gonnies! Ef I'd 'a had the ordering of things then, I'd a predestyned the female sect to better things. If replenishing the earth was to be their job, I wouldn't have laid on 'em the extry burden of being everly subject to some misbegotten, hell-borned man-brute! Yes, dad burn my looks, when I see a puny creetur like Cory there, not only childbearin' ever year reg'lar, but likewise yearning the family bread by the sweat of her brow, hit fairly make my blood bile, and eends my patience with the ways of the Lord. Yes, taking Him up one side and down t'other, God Almighty sartain does as much harm as He does good, if not a leetle more. His doings is allus a myxtery, and sometimes a scandal!

And from Still's *River of Earth*:

The man with the rooster scoffed. "Hell shot a buck rabbit!" he said. "You can't git above your raising. Born in a camp and cut teeth on a tipple. Hit's like metal agin loadstone. Can't tear loose. Whate'er you're aiming to be, you'll end snagging jack-rock.

The only criticism I have of either of these paragraphs is that the mountaineer seldom sounds an "ing." He doesn't say "raising"; he says "raisin'." He doesn't say "snagging"; he says "snaggin'." It's true, however, that too-frequent use of the apostrophe, even though it must be used to give a faithful portrayal of the dialect, detracts from the appearance and readability of the dialogue. Elizabeth Maddox Roberts eliminates many apostrophes by writing the suffix "en" instead of "in'."

Passing from use are many old words, some of which trace directly back to the days of Shakespeare and even of Chaucer and some of which are corruptions of good English words. Seldom heard today are:

Swounded (fainted). Mischievous and onbiddable. Whilst. Titlement (title). Troublous. Blasphemious. Mought (might). Holp or holpen (help). Beasties (horses). Cow-brute. Beholden (indebted). Buss (kiss). Gorm (muss). Begone. Wropt (wrapped). Asshorance (assurance). Beyand (beyond). Fittified (subject to fits). Level-lander (one who lives outside the hills). Unbeknownst. Traipsing. Quile (coil). Poppet (doll). Pindling (puny). Passel. Peacified. Tale-idle (gossip). Tooth-dentist.

And such sentences or clauses as these are rare:

When I war jest a leetle set-along child. He's got sech a lavish of it. That's an antic (playful) dog. I'll tell ye if he worsens. She knows naught. Hit's jest a frolic (It's easy). Hit would pleasure me to stay a spell. They's al'ays a-faultin' me (finding fault). I'd say hit's 'bout a smidgin (mile). I'm fexatially whupped down (amazed). He's eleven year old, a-risin' twelve. If I had my druthers (my way). Hit's lasty water.

There are other old words that are heard more often than those just listed, but which themselves are becoming increasingly rare. They are heard fairly frequently in the back country today, but in a few years they will have disappeared. They include:

Main-chiefest. Misfortunate. Main-oldest. Yearnt (earned). Destructious. Contrarious. Cyored (cured). Franzy (frenzy). Layway (waylay). Fotched (carried). Cotched (caught). Riz (rise). Sot (set). Sont (sent). Glimp (glimpse). Amongst.

In the same class are these sentences:

I'm bounden to go. Hit's sightly (pretty). Hit'll bring easement. I neglect what you said (I didn't understand). He was here a month ago, er sich a matter. I shore do disgust turnips. She's a fine-haired gal (blond). His name is Jonse er Anse, one. Come spring, I aim t' plow that land. What d' you foller? (What's your occupation?) He named it to me yesterday (suggested or told). I'll tell ye fer why he done that. He's a knowin' man. I don't fancy him none. Is Skid 'bout through layin' by? (Has he harvested his crop?) The preacher give it out (said or told) there'd be a meetin' next week. I shore sot a heap o' store by that boy. His woman's been called to straw (She's about to give birth). Set down an' make yerself pleasant (comfortable). Over thar in th' woods they was a-treadin' so you could see th' trees a-shakin' (They were having sexual intercourse). He thumped him right cot dob in th' belly. What do you mean shy-keenerin' around my farm like that? She's kindly fancy like; she likes fill-dalls on her clothes.

Some word usages are heard constantly in town and country. They are so much a part of the mountaineers' speech that even those who have college educations and those who have lived away from the hills for years revert to them occasionally. First of all, there's the pronoun "hit." Hit comes right down from Chaucer, and hit's an integral part of the language today. Hit is not always substituted for it, and there seems to be no reason, except possibly a sense of euphony, for using one instead of the other. "Shore" nearly always is substituted for sure, "pine blank" or "pint blank" for point blank, "right smart" for much or many, "agin" for against, "shet" for shut, "pack" for carry, "kindly" for kind of, "poke" for sack, "pieded" for pied, "axed" for asked, and the prefix "on" for "un" in words such as unbearable, unknown, and the like. Many of the words heard most commonly simply are examples of bad grammar, and they are by no means peculiar to the hills. Yet they are so much a part of the mountaineers' speech they cannot be omitted. They include "he come," "I seen," "he's growed," "I knowed," "I heared," and "feller" for fellow.

For some reason the idea seems to have gotten around that the mountaineer speaks with a pronounced drawl. Nothing could be farther from the truth, for in fact his speech is clipped. Occasionally, of course, he inserts sounds where they don't belong, as in "cyards" for cards and "gyarden" for garden and "bornded" for born, yet generally he elides to such an extent there are almost as many apostrophes in a sentence as there are letters, and his delivery isn't as slow as that of the southern lowlander.

The mountaineer usually adapts his speech to the company he's in, and if he has the least suspicion he'll be laughed at he'll be careful of the words he uses. The stranger generally can hear the so-called quaint usages only if he listens unnoticed to conversations.

The interchangeableness of hit and it has been mentioned. There are other words that are interchanged, sometimes in the same sentence. They include took and "tuk," can and "kin," you and "ye," can't and "kain't," such and "sich," always and "al'ays," after and "atter," to and "t'," the and "th'," there and "thar," was and "war," set and "sot," just and "jest," here and "hyar," heard and "heared" or "heern," aren't and "ain't" or "hain't."

Words such as "clever," "common," "queer" or "quare," and "pert" or "peart" have several meanings. If a mountaineer says, "He's clever turned," he doesn't necessarily mean the subject is talented or skillful. He may mean he's generous.

In the same manner, common may mean pretty, healthy, friendly, or ordinary; quare may mean unusual, unbalanced, large, strong, or good, and peart may mean expert, skillful, keen, clever, or active. Other words with double meanings include "sight," which may mean a short distance or a great deal; "proud," which may mean well (physically), glad, or self-esteeming, and "pretty," which may mean nice, obedient, or good-looking.

One who listens casually to the conversation of a couple of hillbillies meeting on the street or to the laconic exchange of words that takes place when one mountaineer passes another's house may arrive at the conclusion that their vocabulary is limited to a hundred words or so. Here, for example, is a typical conversation that ensues when a hill dweller astride a mule rides up the creek bed and halts in front of a neighbor's door, the man on the porch speaking first:

"H'lo, Josh."
"Howdy, Mose."
"Come in an' set a spell."
"Nope, guess I'd better not."
"Looks like rain, don't it?"
"Kindly. Guess we could use a little."
"Your crap hurtin' any?"
"Not bad. Jest outen th' first weeds though."
"Supper's pert nigh ready, I reckon, better come in an' eat a bite."
"Guess I kain't."
"Won't you take a night with us?"
"Better git 'long I guess. Come an' go round."
"Can't go now, I reckon."
"Wal, come when you can. Giddap!"
"I will, you come back."

The number of words hillsmen employ in usual conversation is limited, but when they really get strung out in a tale-telling or the like their descriptions are colorful and they may use correctly such words as dilatory, mustered, countenanced, and replenished—words that one seldom hears other than in speeches or formal conversation. Occasionally when they can't think of a word that fits they coin one, although unhappily for the picturesqueness of the language that practice is passing. The coining of words from English roots has resulted in the use of nouns as verbs and verbs as nouns. Such usages, however, are seldom heard today except in the remote sections. As examples of the use of verbs as nouns consider these:

There's about one more gittin' of blackberries left. Ever'body got drunk at the big to-do at town las' night. I didn't hear no give-out about it at church.

And of nouns as verbs:

I don't think my gal confidences me none. It shore is a-breezin' out thar. That man, he's al'ays prankin' with th' children. This ham ought t' meat us a month.

An amusing instance of this use of words occurred not long ago when a U.S. commissioner was holding a preliminary hearing on a moonshining charge. Among the defendants was a girl of about sixteen.

"What were you doing at the still?" he asked.

"I was cowing," the girl replied.

"What do you mean, 'cowing'?"

"Why, lookin' fer my cow."

"Well I'll be—— I've heard of a cow bulling, but never before of a girl cowing.

Occasionally one hears an adjective used as a verb. "He slipped in th' lot and nastied himself." The past participle is used without the auxiliary. "He drug me along."

Pleonasms are heard frequently, even around the towns. A mountaineer may speak of "a job of work" or "a chuffylike, big, large, fleshy woman." And I have heard: "There's a spring close nearby." "It were a little, bitty tiny knoll, hardly much bigger than a ant hill." "This here's a strong, stout horse." "We shorely undoubtedly will be thar 'fore long." "He's done done it."

Redundant nounal compounds give added color to the dialect. There are:

Beetle-bug. Spruce-pines. Play-parties. Rifle-gun. Pot-vessel. Biscuit-bread. Women-folks. Church-house. Men-folks. Granny-woman. Ham-meat. Speller-book. Song-ballad. Nurse-woman.

There are other compounds, too, which are not necessarily redundant:

Wrong-doer. Marriage-bed. Ambitious-minded. Rock-cliff. Back-track. Corn-liquor. Court-time. Fotched-on or brought-on (brought in from outside the hills). Friendly-like. Fur-off. Head-piece. House-seat.

Some of the most amusing bits result from the incorrect use of comparatives and superlatives. One may hear:

More sweeter. Ignoranter. More happier. Worser. Welcomer. Civiler. Skeerier

Particularly with superlatives do the mountaineers have fun:

He's the keen-tonguedest man I ever heared speak. He's th' up-and-comingest youngster of 'em all. She's the most contrivingest woman I ever seen.

Others include:

Most nighest. Almightyest. Amazingest. Smilingest. Sewingest. Outlandishest. Friendliest. Deceivingest.

Most any word, be it noun, adjective, or what have you, may be made by the mountaineer into a comparative or superlative by adding an "er" or an "est."

Double negatives are common: "I ain't got no money." Triple negatives sometimes are heard: "I ain't got nary none." At times, even, a quadruple negative may pop up. I heard one fellow say to another, "Jim, Tom's done broke his arm an' can't work." The reply was, "He ain't never done no work nohow."

"Ary" is used frequently, but not as Mr. Mackaye used it in the quotation at the beginning of this chapter: "He'd trickle a bushel o' Bible ary rod o' the trail." It does not mean every. It is a contraction of a contraction: e'er a. "I ain't seen ary hog." In the same manner "nary" is a contraction of ne'er a.

Little regard is shown for tense and number:

The men does a heap o' fightin'. I come up the hill by myself. Pass me them cabbage. He give me a nickel fer it. He's six year old.

"You-all" is one of the few southern expressions used by the hillsmen. Unlike the southern lowlanders they pronounce their *r's*. They don't say no'th or niggah.

Everyone who hears a mountain dweller talk notices the pronunciation he gives night, bright, light, and tonight. He sounds an extra-long *i*.

Mountain speech today is a mixture of good English, bad English, Old English, and slang. Unfortunately the Old English is going out and slang is coming in.

IV

They Read No Greek

IT WAS A STUFFY JULY MORNING in 1932, and the mud road in Kentucky's foothills was gooey from the night's heavy rain. As the mail carrier's buggy topped a steep rise from the creek bed I saw the school building—the school building in which I was to teach.

There it sat, an ugly gray frame structure on a grassless red-clay knoll. Half the weatherboarding was missing from the side nearest me. One remaining window shutter dangled from its upper hinge. At the foot of the knoll, about 100 feet apart, were two outhouses. One had no door. The other lay on its side like an uprooted tree.

A bareheaded, overalled youngster appeared around the side of the building, abruptly disappeared, then reappeared with eight or ten others.

"Hello," I called. Two or three answered thinly.

They slid down the bank in front of the school as the buggy approached and watched as I rolled up my pants, climbed out over the wheel, and pulled my suitcase after me.

The front door was nailed shut—useless precaution, for there wasn't a whole window light in the building. One of the older boys handed me a key. "The trustee said give you this. Hit's to th' back door. We ginerally never use th' front one. Th' floorin' in the coatroom hain't much good."

The inside was a mess. Glass, leaves, dust, and nutshells covered the floor. The initial-scarred, two-seater desks sat every way but in rows. The blackboard and the pipe that connected the little wood stove to the chimney were riddled with bullet holes.

I picked my way to the teacher's desk, gave one leg of it a kick so it would stand up straight, and opened the drawer. A mouse scampered up my arm. I jumped and clawed frantically. The children laughed.

"Nice shape your building's in."

No answer.

"Do you know where I can get a broom?" I asked one of the girls.

"I guess you can borry one from Miz Hall. She lives close."

"Would you mind getting it?"

She scampered off.

Seven or eight others joined the group that watched my inspection. They peered in at the windows and the door. Some ventured inside and kicked the dirt around with their bare feet.

"Boys, help me straighten up the desks, will you? You girls see if you can get some of the trash on the outside when the broom gets here." They aided willingly, fussing over turns for the broom, and in fifteen minutes or so the place looked considerably better.

"Now, boys, the next thing we've got to do is set that toilet up—I know, you probably shoved it over, but now comes the settin'-up time."

We righted it and propped it with a pole.

"Is this the boys' or girls'?"

"Boys'."

"What in the world do the girls do for a door?"

"Dunno," they snickered.

I learned later they went in threes and fours. Two stood guard to keep the boys from peeking.

I found a battered water bucket and a dipper in the cloakroom and started for the well I had noticed near the building.

"That water ain't no good," said the boy who had handed me the key

"What's the matter with it?"

"Dunno. Teacher had it tested 'bout three year ago. Said it had germs-like."

"Where do you get your water?"

"They's a spring up the road a piece. We carry hit from there."

"How far is it?"

"Oh–quarter of a mile I reckon."

"That's a mighty long piece to carry water for the school. Why hasn't the superintendent done something about the well?"

"Dunno. But us boys don't mind packin' it," he grinned. "Teacher always let us biggest 'uns go git th' water."

"I know. That's a good way to get out of school for a while. But what I want to know is why something hasn't been done about the well. How do you know the spring water is all right? Did the superintendent say anything about it when he visited the school the last time?"

He looked at me blankly. "I hain't never seen th' superintendent."

"You've never seen him! How long have you been going to school here?"

"Well, I commenced when I was six, an' I'm fourteen a-goin' on fifteen now."

"Great day in the morning! No wonder this school's in such a shape—— What grade are you in?"

"Fifth reader."

"You should be farther along than that. What's the matter, don't you study?"

"Yeah-h-h, I study when I come, but I don't git to come reg'lar. I have t' help out at home a lot. Then th' teacher that was here, he was an old-like feller, an' he didn't keer whether we learned nothin' er not—just so we kept quiet."

"How many children come to school here?"

" 'Pends on th' time of year and whether hit's cold er not. Most th' big ones has to work in th' crops in the summer and the little ones can't come when hit's real cold. I guess they's twenty comes reg'lar, but then some days I've seed as low as five er six."

"How many children are there in the district, you reckon?"

"Must be forty. There's old Mose Jenks. He's got about ten and he don't send none o' his'n. Then there's lots of others that don't never come—'cept maybe on th' last day fer th' treat."

"Well—I guess I'd better ring the bell. It's about time to begin."

"Teacher . . ."

"Yes?"

"There ain't no rope on th' bell."

"Well for! . . . How do I get the kids in?"

"Just holler 'Books' and they'll come."

"O.K. Books! ! !"

I taught that school two terms and a similar one a third. In the thirty-four mountain counties of Kentucky there are still 1,840 like it, as compared to about 330 of all other types. Some of the one-roomers are better, some are worse—depending upon the degree of poverty of the county, the ability of the county superintendent, and the education and perseverance of the teacher.

It may be very well for the older generation to romanticize

the "little red schoolhouse," but there's nothing romantic about the one-room schools of eastern Kentucky. They're not even red—or generally any other color for that matter. Indeed they are little houses on a little ground where little teachers at little salaries for a little while teach little children little things. Many of them are inaccessible by automobile except during the summer months. About a fourth have no water supply other than a neighbor's spring or well. The toilets all are filthy. In one county the health officer advised the superintendent not to build toilets. His idea was that it was better to place a hoe in the corner and let the children take it with them to a nearby cornfield. Very few boast a water cooler. In most, a bucket and a common dipper are still in use. If there's any place on earth hotter in the summer or colder in the winter than one of those squat buildings I haven't found it. Many are roofed with tin, which makes them ovens in July, August, and September. Many have loose window sills, cracks in walls and floors, and missing weatherboarding. They are iceboxes in November, December, and January. Jacketless stoves may glow by dint of constant fueling, but teachers and children alike freeze on one side and scorch on the other. Possibly 2 per cent of the schools have electric lights. During dark, winter afternoons in the 98 per cent it is almost impossible to read. There is no playground equipment. At some, as at the one I first taught, there isn't even a playground. The children play fox and dog until they tire of that, then they pick fights or throw rocks. They seem to get a savage thrill out of the tinkling crash of breaking glass. Thus the scarcity of whole windowpanes. If there are any teaching aids—maps, globes, books, magazines, phonographs, modeling tables, and the like—the teacher buys them from a pitifully small salary of $50 to $75 a month or from money earned through a school project.

Ninety per cent of the children in such schools never go to high school. Few, in fact, finish the eighth grade. While discussing a particularly isolated school with a county superintendent I asked, "How many of the children who finish the eighth grade here go on to high school?"

"Every one," he replied.

"I can't believe it!"

"None ever finishes the eighth grade," he smiled.

Most mountain counties have seven-month schools—an improvement, at that, over the four-, five-, or six-month terms of yesteryear. Carter, Lawrence, and Letcher counties are the only three that have eight-month terms, and Boyd, where the capital of eastern Kentucky, Ashland, is located, is the only one with a nine-month term.

School attendance in most mountain counties is extremely poor. Percentages of school-age children actually in school range from 60 to 85, with 70 about the average. Terms start early, in order that bad weather may be avoided, but children don't go to school if there's anything else to do.

Accessibility of schools is closely related to attendance. Rural educators have fixed one and one-half to two miles as the maximum distances children reasonably should be expected to walk, but there are school districts in all sections of the hill country in which children must walk twice that far. Facing a six or eight mile round trip, children simply stay at home when the creeks are up or snow is on the ground. I had a boy who made an eight-mile trip every day, and his clothes on the coldest, snowy days consisted of shoes (no socks), overalls, a shirt, a sweater, a worn suit coat, and a cap. His clothing was no different from the average, but his attendance certainly was.

High percentages of retardation result from inadequate facilities and poor attendance plus a low intelligence quotient found among many mountain children. In only three of the thirty-four mountain counties of Kentucky is there less than 30 per cent retardation. In others, as high as 55 per cent of the children are older than the normal for their grades. The average is about 45. When children get behind they tend to drop out of school. Thus a large percentage of the mountain children get no farther than the fifth or sixth grade.

If illiteracy means the inability of a person to write his name or read it when it's written, about 12 per cent of the people of eastern Kentucky are illiterate. However, so many more are able to do no more than write their names the percentage does not give a full picture of the lack of education.

The education level of teachers, however, has been raised. Ten years ago 70 per cent of the teachers in the public schools of eastern Kentucky had only high-school educations or less. Today, although there is wide variation among counties, perhaps 90 per cent have at least two years of college, and those who obtained life certificates with only eighth-grade or high-school educations are rapidly being replaced.

Progress is being made also in consolidating schools, largely as a result of the expenditure of WPA funds for roads and native-stone buildings. Even so, the old one-room schools still are the rule.

There is, however, something to be said in behalf of one-room schools. Molly Clowes, in one of a series of articles in the Louisville *Courier-Journal*, quoted a county superintendent:

> In the interest of education, I'd be inclined to say we'd be better off if we could do away with the one-room school—if we could pick up our children and educate them in modern surroundings, with paint on the walls and a good roof over their heads. But in the interest of our people, as we're living today, I'd say let's leave the one-room school as long as we can. Bare and uncomfortable as it is, it's about the only meeting place left us. We listen to speakings there; we meet neighbors and hold gatherings, and any preacher that has a mind to is free to talk there if the people want to listen.
>
> Our people don't come down much to the new high school. It's

too far from the hollows. Then it's so fine, they begin to notice their clothes and feel out of place. And anyway, most of the children in our county never get past the grades.

Eastern Kentucky counties are handicapped in their school programs, as in all other programs, by a lack of money. To the $12.33 per capita they receive from the state they add returns from the maximum tax rate of seventy-five cents. That latter fund, however, doesn't amount to much in a county like Leslie, where land is assessed at an average of $10 an acre. The amount of taxable wealth to each teacher ranges from less than $50,000 in Laurel, Rockcastle, Jackson, Wolfe, Rowan, and Elliott to $250,000 in one county, Boyd. Lee has between $200,000 and $250,000; Harlan, Perry and Pike have between $150,000 and $200,000. The others range from $50,000 to $150,000. Most of them are in the lower bracket.

A close correlation exists between the amount of taxable wealth and the school expenditure for each teacher. In Jackson, Owsley, and Elliott the amount spent each year for each teacher, including salary and school upkeep, is less than $500; in Leslie, Clay, Morgan, and Clinton it is between $500 and $600; in Knott, Breathitt, Magoffin, Rowan, Wolfe, Menifee, Knox, and Wayne it is between $600 and $700; in Floyd, Martin, Laurel, Rockcastle, and Powell it is between $700 and $800; in Perry, McCreary, Whitley, Pulaski, Estill, Carter, Lawrence, Pike, and Johnson it is between $800 and $1,000; in Letcher, Harlan, and Bell it is between $1,000 and $1,250; in Lee and Boyd it is more than $1,250.

In the richer counties salaries and expenditures for school maintenance and construction are inadequate. In the poorer counties they are disgraceful. The situation can be corrected if state school funds are distributed to the mountain counties and central and western Kentucky take care of themselves.

Legislators from the Bluegrass counties, where one-room schools are rarities, always have fought redistribution proposals, but despite such opposition the 1940 General Assembly took a step in the right direction. It approved a suggestion of the governor and leaders of the Kentucky Education Association that a constitutional amendment be submitted to the people for a vote at the November 1941 general election. Should the amendment be adopted, 10 per cent of the school funds, in addition to the per-capita allotment, will be distributed to the poorer counties. Should it be rejected—and it probably will be—the mountain counties will remain Kentucky's back yard.

Problems of mountain educators are aggravated by the large percentages of school-age children. At least 42 per cent of the population in every county in eastern Kentucky is under fourteen years of age. In Knott and Leslie counties, where birth rates are extraordinarily high, more than 50 per cent of the people are of school age. Seventy per cent of Knott's people and 72 per cent of Leslie's are less than twenty-five years old.

A county's school system depends to a great extent upon the superintendent. If he is just a politician, as too many of eastern Kentucky's superintendents are, his teachers are political friends who may or may not be educated, his buildings are dilapidated, his attendance is poor, and his system is not worth its cost. If he is a capable, energetic person he achieves much despite meager resources. He gets the best and highest trained teachers available. He fosters modern teaching methods. He keeps his buildings in repair and establishes consolidated schools as road and financial conditions permit.

In Wolfe County the superintendent's office was held for many years by virtue of political strength rather than ability. An educator's 1940 report on Wolfe County stated that the average school building was unpainted and had some weatherboarding torn off; that steps were broken, the interior dark, and some of the window glasses broken out; and that desks were hand made of rough oak lumber thirty years ago. The superintendent has not visited the average school in three or more years. There is a large primary class, small second and third grades, and a continuing diminution through the eighth grade. In most of the one-room schools there are two teachers who hear recitations independently of each other and usually in tones that cause confusion. The teachers permit sing-song word-calling to pass for oral reading, and they keep a switch in evidence for disciplinary effect. In the county are eight teachers who have not had college work, and they are not the worst on the staff. Since 1936 twenty-seven teachers have been added to the staff despite the fact that enrollment has increased little. Twenty of the fifty-five schools are not located on hard-surfaced roads, and thus the children who finish there could not get to a high school even if the county provided transportation—which it does not.

On the other hand the same educator reported that McCreary County made phenomenal progress between 1935 and 1940 under the leadership of its superintendent. The school board's debt was increased $20,000, but the value of buildings was increased $350,000. The superintendent not only made use of WPA grants and labor but also of NYA centers, where girls were taught sewing, weaving, and canning and boys were taught trades. The county provides transportation for high-school students and for pupils who attend consolidated schools.

In the same manner a young and capable graduate of the University of Kentucky law college, Town Hall (and that's his name), has made progress in Floyd County. In three years he has spent $425,000 on new buildings and equipment. Nearly all his teachers have college training; many are graduates. He has increased attendance 10 per cent and believes he has 85 per cent of the school population actually attending school regularly. He has built consolidated schools and added busses. He has fostered such activities as building trades classes, bands, science clubs, Girl Reserve clubs, glee clubs, and literary clubs and has encouraged 4-H and Future Farmer groups. In short he has built a modern school system in a county that is not among the richest.

Breathitt is a county in which the superintendent, Mrs. Marie Turner, is striving to improve school conditions. She faces the same problems as the other superintendents—small school revenue (Breathitt's total assessed valuation of about $5,000,000 has been decreasing annually since 1931), low salaries (average $72 a month), rapid teacher turnover, scarcity of good roads, inaccessibility of schools, and attendance difficulties. Since 1935, however, she has operated, with the help of state and national educators, a child-guidance program that is showing results despite the fact some of the teachers have only a vague idea of what it's all about.

The program operates through a case-history procedure. Before a school term starts, the year's work is outlined at a conference at Jackson. For the next three or four days each teacher visits the homes in her district to gather data on the children's families and environment as well as upon children themselves. An open record is kept for each child, indicating, in addition to other data, his ability, his interests, and his progress. The case histories are valuable to the teacher, for she gains a better understanding of the child's difficulties, and through encouraging his interests may keep him in school when otherwise he would drop out. They are valuable to the new teacher, for she has a record on each of her pupils. They are valuable to the high-school staff, for they furnish a ground for orienting pupils who go beyond the eighth grade. They are valuable to the superintendent in dealing with problem children, for periodically she and trained psychologists discuss cases with the teachers.

Mrs. Turner told of a girl who presented an unusual

problem. A pretty girl of seventeen, she was in only the fifth grade, yet her intelligence was normal. She had gone to school irregularly because her mother died when she was a small child and she had to help raise four younger children. This girl kept both the school children and the parents in turmoil by spreading invented or exaggerated stories. Friendly talks were of no avail. She denied having started the rumors, then started more. Punishments of various sorts were meted out, without result. Since the girl seemed interested in her school work and had professed a desire to become a home-economics teacher her instructor started her on a sewing project, confiding that a teacher must not gossip maliciously as she had done. This also failed. Finally one of the teachers suggested that since the girl had such a vivid imagination she be put to writing a book. The manuscript is developing, and it has kept her occupied.

In addition to being of immediate use the guidance program should be valuable in the future in reorganizing the school program to meet community needs, in placing individuals in occupations for which they are fitted, in developing, possibly, occupations new to the area. "New occupations" might include management of producers' or consumers' co-operatives, raising game birds, work in rural electrification and resulting industries, and management of summer resorts.

Guidance advocates set forth that there are at least two important reasons why a vigorous and socially purposeful program should be developed and maintained in Breathitt and other similar counties of the southern Appalachians.

In the first place, they say, large numbers of people do live there, and they are likely to continue to live there for some time to come, if not permanently. The educational and other individual and social opportunities they enjoy will affect greatly the region and the nation. It is important, therefore, that they should be aided and encouraged to develop all possible resources and potentialities of the area, that they be afforded every opportunity to make the most of the circumstances that surround and condition their lives.

In the second place, they continue, if the great social experiment looking to the territorial redistribution of the population as a means of ameliorating underprivilege is ever realized it is likely that in large part such redistribution will come through a more complete understanding of its purposes by the average man. In short, in a democratic nation some reliance must be placed upon the enlightened will of the people, particularly those most affected. One of the major purposes of the present guidance experiment in Breathitt County is to help the people, especially the younger, to analyze their community and its conditions, its advantages and assets, and also its disadvantages and liabilities. And thus, in the light of a more comprehensive knowledge, individually there may be decided the question of population redistribution. It is likely, the program's supporters contend, that through education and guidance people will tend to seek those areas which for them provide greatest privilege and opportunity. This really is the philosophy of redistribution through effective education and guidance.

Whether or not such a goal is obtained the school system has been improved through the program and through the efforts of trained teachers. Beside a dirt road that runs along the Middle Fork of the Kentucky stands one of the best one-room schools in Breathitt. The teacher knows the background of every pupil. She keeps them interested, and she keeps them in school. Boys who can't be kept at books long don't idle. They make desks and chairs, sand-modeling tables, and wood carvings. Girls make posters, clothing, maps, and school-room decorations. The instructor uses manuals in teaching writing and reading. She strives to prevent the sing-song calling of words that passes for reading in most one-room schools. (I found at my schools that the students not only sang the words but had memorized them through association with pictures on the page. When the pictures were covered the pupils couldn't recite the words.) She organized a P.T.A. No one came on the first call, but she found the mothers were delighted with a little entertainment. Now they come regularly and are interested in the school. Though there is hardly such a thing as surplus food in Breathitt, she realized $15 by marketing vegetables the children brought to school during the garden season. She bought a weanling pig. Families in the district took turns caring for it. When it was a hog she sold it and used the profit to buy school supplies.

At the time the guidance program was inaugurated the Breathitt County high school obtained permission from the state Department of Education to depart from standard requirements for part of its students. Freshmen are given placement tests. On the basis of these and the guidance records they are divided into three groups. Those in the upper group take a course similar to that in other high schools, leading to college work. Those in the lower group, according to the high-school superintendent, "get about what they can out of high school—art, manual training, agriculture, home economics, or perhaps some of the English, mathematics, or other courses offered the upper group." He said one boy was interested only in gymnasium work, "so we let him do gym work and he stayed around until gradually he got interested in a few other classes." Those in the middle group are the "in betweens" who are gradually absorbed into either the higher or lower brackets.

Superintendent R. M. Vanhorn, nevertheless, is somewhat doubtful of the practicality of the guidance program. "You can tell a boy he should do thus and so on a farm," he said, "but if he has no money and no way to get a start, what good does it do? The same applies to 'new' occupations. Nearly all take some financial outlay for a beginning."

Of an individual's future in the mountains he said: "If a

boy or girl has enough brains to get through high school and into college he or she must, in nearly all cases, get out of the mountains to attain anything. For those who stay the best that can be hoped for them is that they will be able to support themselves."

V

For Sweet Charity

IN A KNOTT COUNTY valley so narrow you can spit from slope to slope huddles the Caney Creek Community Center and Junior College.

Caney is one of the hill country's many charitable institutions known as mission or settlement schools, but it resembles its kin about as much as a dinosaur resembles a chameleon. The reason is that Mrs. Alice Spencer Geddes Lloyd is the Caney school, and Mrs. Alice Spencer Geddes Lloyd is an unusual woman.

It was back in 1916 that Mrs. Lloyd, a Radcliffe College alumna, came down from Boston to Knott County for her health. She's been there ever since, for a native named Abisha Johnson persuaded her to start a school in his isolated section.

In those days when one said "isolated" he meant it. There was a railroad at Wayland on the Floyd County line, twelve miles down the creek from Caney, but there wasn't a road within miles of the school until 1931, when a traffic-bound highway was completed between Hindman, the Knott County seat, and the Hazard-Jackson road. In the fall of 1940 a WPA road was finished from the Hindman–Prestonsburg highway to the school, and the students rode to classes for the first time.

Abisha donated a piece of perpendicular slope and a tiny square of his precious bottom land, and in 1917 Mrs. Lloyd started her school in a one-room shack. As attendance grew and donations came in from the great outside she purchased land and added buildings until she had acquired 153 acres and a plant worth about $200,000.

Mrs. Lloyd is a tiny, gray-haired woman in her sixties. Her thin lips only partly cover teeth that tend to protrude, and her sharp blue eyes peer from behind heavy shell-rimmed glasses. Partly paralyzed for years, she works daily from 9 A.M. to 9:30 P.M. behind an old Oliver typewriter in a stuffy, crowded little office in her board-and-batten Administration Building.

To all who have worked with her or under her Mrs. Lloyd is an enigma. She will not talk about herself, hence little is known about her life before Caney. She has not left the school more than half a dozen times. She is both kindly and stern, but at all times strong-willed. She has the most advanced ideas on some subjects, the most reactionary on others. She works almost frantically at her task, yet feels its hopelessness. She must know that the school, as she has built it, cannot exist when she is gone; still she toils to make it conform to her ideas —and hers alone.

Her mother and chief helper, Mrs. Ella Geddes, must be eighty-five, but looks little older than Mrs. Lloyd. Mrs. Geddes keeps the records and is so accurate that when a discrepancy occurs between her figures and the bank's, the bank checks its figures. She fell a year ago and broke her right arm. She learned to write with her left, and carried on.

"In humble cottages live the college men," Mrs. Lloyd says in her handbook, and when she says "humble," she doesn't exaggerate. I stayed three days and nights in one called Summerfield, located as far up the hill as one can get without a ladder. Made like a summer camp cottage of upright boards, it has three small rooms. The floors are bare, the walls are covered with cardboard boxes. Drooping pieces of chintz are the curtains. In the largest of the three rooms are a potbellied stove, a rickety table, bookshelves, two cane-bottomed chairs, and a sway-backed cot. In the second room is a bed and some wall hooks for hanging clothes. The third room contains a small cookstove, a wash pan, a water bucket, and a dipper. The boys get their water 100 yards down the hill. I don't blame them for not bathing more often.

It was summer when I was there, and the screens had rusted away. I stomped spiders and roaches; swatted at mosquitoes, moths, and flies. The boys told me I was lucky. There were no bedbugs at Summerfield.

The girls' cottages are similar except that a feminine touch has been added.

In naming the cottages the mountain youths, like their grandfathers who named the creeks, hollows, and hamlets, have shown a propensity for using odd titles. The registrar's office is named "If," from Kipling's poem. Then there are "Galahad," "Firing Line" (the students say "Firing Line" is the last stop before they "cross the hill" if scholastic standings get too low), "Opportunity," "Pilot," "Atlas," "Gloria," "Plank Side," "Syracuse," "Sycamore" (because of a large tree beside it), and "Up Yonder." The last had no name for some time; thus when a student was asked where he was staying he replied, "Up yonder." The name stuck.

Caney is a settlement, but you won't find it on the map. However if you look hard you may find Pippapass. That's the post office, and until the WPA road was completed Pippapass got its mail once a day from a carrier who made a wagon trip down the creek to Wayland and back.

Six of Caney's buildings are of stone. They are the library, the science building, auditorium, liberal arts building, one of the "dormitories," and the high school building, erected in

1940 by the county, the WPA, and Mrs. Lloyd. These six and the frame graded-school building are located on comparatively level land along the creek. All others are log or rough-lumber structures whose unbarked pole foundations anchor them to the hillside.

The grammar and high schools are joint efforts of the county and Mrs. Lloyd. The junior college, which has an average enrollment of 187, is her own. Unlike other settlement schools Caney is a liberal arts and normal school and does not emphasize trades or vocational training. It is not an end in itself but a step for those who wish to be teachers, doctors, lawyers, engineers, ministers, nurses, and business men and women. It is an accepted two-year college, and its graduates enroll as juniors in the best universities of the country.

Those who are able pay a little tuition, but most of the boys and girls "work their way"—in the kitchen, in the dining room, on the campus, in the buildings, in the laboratories, in the offices.

Mrs. Lloyd sets forth in her catalogue this objective: "The training of selected mountaineers as professional men and women for efficient and consecrated leadership in the Southern Highlands."

And while we are speaking of catalogues, Mrs. Lloyd's publications, all of which she prepares herself and has printed in her own print shop, are masterpieces. Here is an excerpt from a newsletter she entitles "Civilization?":

Lou-Rainey . . .

She was always thoroughly clad in her hand-woven crimson skirt, pleated to her ankles.

Her sinewy, browned throat (only) was revealed from her yellow blouse.

Around her classical head was wrapped her plaited hair.

Her calloused feet, firm and muscular, were bare.

Along around dusky-dark of an afternoon, she would leave

her steaming sorghum pans stretched under the willows and, shuffling through the leaves and munching an apple, would casually splash through the flowing creek to her split-rail fence, and in her shrilly-musical voice, holler to her next-cabin neighbor,

"Hain't th' mail-mule came?'

Lou-Rainey's daughter . . .

Her clothes, bought by mail-order, are form-fitting, sleazy, scarlet silk with purple zippers.

Her arms and neck are smooth-shaven, revealed from the halter that is her blouse.

Emerging from her head is a frizzled permanent.

Her feet are clad in high-heel spikes and striped anklets.

When the mining whistle blows, Lou-Rainey's daughter, chewing her gum between her rouged lips, clatters over the cement walk of the sooty mining town toward the freight car that is the railroad terminal and, in a real lady-like voice, screams to the boy at the pop and peanut stand,

"Hain't you saw th' mail-train comin' yit?"

As at boarding schools of a past era Caney's girls wear low-heeled shoes, white middies, and long white skirts reaching nearly to the ankles. Cosmetics, jewelry, silk stockings, and fancy coiffures are forbidden.

The boys must wear coats and ties to classes except in hottest weather and to the dining tables the year around.

"There are but four arbitrary rules of moral conduct that must be subscribed to by the student who is applying for admission to the Caney Junior College," Mrs. Lloyd sets forth. "It is understood, when accepting the hospitality of the Caney campus, that these four rules must be observed at all times, and under every circumstance: (1) No tobacco or playing cards; (2) no liquor; (3) no fire-arms; (4) no unauthorized meetings with the opposite sex."

No "unauthorized meetings with the opposite sex" means no meetings at all, for the girls and boys are not allowed to mix. Their dormitories are as widely separated as possible. They sit on opposite sides of the classrooms. They use the library at different hours. They sit at opposite ends of the long dining hall. There are no "date nights" or social hours for mixed company.

But despite the rules many of the boys smoke—some simply because smoking is forbidden—and occasionally indulge in a little card-playing, a little liquor-drinking and a little gun-shooting. They have, moreover, devised a pastime they call "Wahooing." Wahoo is the name they give to a kind of magnolia tree; so when, in the late night hours, they climb one of the trees to a girl's window—and sometimes even through a girl's window—it's "Wahooing."

A campus guard patrols the hillside, however, and when a boy, or girl, is caught breaking a rule Caney days are over.

Mrs. Lloyd helps her more promising graduates to complete their educations, and at the University of Kentucky she has a house called Caney Cottage. Her rules there, as at the junior college, are severe: "No cook, no valet, no janitor, no guns, no cards, no liquor, no tobacco, no gambling, no joy riding, no fraternities, no automobile, obedience to the matron. Do your own cooking and dish-washing; make your own beds; press your own clothes; $2.50 a week for food."

Though some observers have termed the Puritanic rules "vicious" and the rough living conditions "outrageous," one thing cannot be denied. Mrs. Lloyd gives more young men and women better educations for less money than any other school in the mountains. On a budget of $50,000 a year she runs her school and helps her graduates through such universities as Yale, Harvard, Tulane, Vanderbilt, and Kentucky.

"I have about fifty-five graduates a year, and 92 per cent of them go on for higher work," said Mrs. Lloyd as she leaned over her typewriter and looked at me intently. "The school is open to mountain boys and girls of this and other counties, and it costs them practically nothing. But I pick my students. I pick them for academic ability, character, and consecration to mountain work. There is an unwritten pledge that every student I educate must return to the mountains. Those who do not are traitors. My purpose and my hope is that I can train mountain leaders.

"Not more than 25 per cent of the local people have the mental capacity for more than the most elementary education," she continued. "Intermarriage—oh, terrible intermarriage!—has resulted in the development of racial weaknesses—low intelligence, bad eyes, epilepsy, and so on. This together with economic poverty and isolation have brought about a sad decadence of the proud mountain stock. Those who stay in the hills are barely able to exist and those who migrate cannot cope with the competition of the outside world. Thousands came back during the depression and have made no effort since to leave.

"It is extremely difficult even to keep those in school who have the capabilities. I would say there are 2,200 children of school age in Knott County who are not even enrolled. If all the children attended who should attend there wouldn't be building space enough for them. The average pupil goes to school from one to twelve weeks a year, then quits at the fourth or fifth grade. The only way to get them in school and keep them there is to have truant officers who go out and beat the bushes and bring them in. Some stay away because they haven't enough clothes to wear; some because they are so far from schools, some because of physical defects, and some because of ignorant parents. I remember asking a father to send to high school a child I considered particularly bright. He snorted, 'The only high school is in heaven.'

"I tried moonlight schools for the older people for a while but gave it up. What's the use teaching old men to sign their names to checks when there are so many children to be taught? I tried an industrial school but found there was no cooperation on the part of the people. The mountaineer is suspicious, independent, and uncooperative. If any new ideas are to be instilled they've got to be instilled from the bottom up, not from the top down. I know of a man who started a goat farm in the county—a good idea except that it didn't work. The people never had drunk goat's milk and they had no intention of starting something new.

"The mountain people are not good workmen to hire. They have to be circumvented like children. For instance I had a man fixing one of the porches. I looked it over and said, 'That board there isn't straight. Don't you think you'd better take it up and straighten it?' He glared at me, dropped his hammer, and said, 'Do it yourself if you don't like it.'

"I get along with them very well though. I don't interfere with their religion, politics, or moonshine. Eighty-eight per cent of the people in the vicinity are Calvinistic Baptists, but I don't hire Baptist preachers or any other kind of preachers for teachers. They're forever proselyting despite your best efforts to keep them from it.

"The honesty of the mountaineer, so far as not stealing is concerned, is high, but his ethical standard is low. For example I always put this question to my students: 'A man had a mule that had a bad habit of running off and throwing its riders. He sold the mule without guaranteeing it but without making any mention of its bad habit. The mule ran off and killed a little girl. Was the original owner morally responsible for the death of the child?' I have never yet found a student who considered the man in any way responsible. I can excuse this only on the ground that they have been exploited until their feeling is a self-defense mechanism.

"Perhaps you wonder why I try so hard to keep the boys and girls of the school separate. That goes back to the awful intermarriage problem. Nearly everyone in the school is in some way kin to everyone else. When a student enters here I can almost tell by his family name what his defects and his abilities are. Honestly, I can do better with an illegitimate child, for generally he has a new strain of blood in him. I try to keep the boys and girls here from forming relationships that will lead to marriage. I want them to get out and marry people on the outside of their little purlieus. Often I have considered running a school for boys only. I educate girls and then they get married and do not carry on the work I designed for them. Still I considered it would not be fair to bar girls, so I have tried to carry on a co-educational school.

"At Caney we do not teach manual arts as they do at other mountain schools, because I feel it is useless. Now just suppose I teach the girls to weave. All right, they know how to weave, but they don't have the materials to weave with, and they haven't the business ability to market the finished goods. No, my only hope is to train chemists, engineers, doctors, lawyers, teachers—men and women from the mountains to become mountain leaders. A statement of Horace Kephart's has been my guide: 'The great need of our mountains today is trained leaders of their own. The future of Appalachia lies mostly in the hands of these resolute boys and girls who win the education fitting them for such leadership.' "

In other valleys of Kentucky's hill country are many mission schools quite unlike Caney. I do not know the exact number. "Home missionaries"—some self-appointed, some supported by churches—produced them wholesale twenty to fifty years ago. A number flourished; many perished. New ones still are being started, and old ones are dying or being absorbed into the public school system. Dr. E. O. Guerrant, a Presbyterian preacher-physician and one of the best known of the mountain missionaries, established more than fifty schools at about the turn of the century. Only two remain: the Highland Institution, at Guerrant, Breathitt County, and Stuart Robinson, at Blackey, Letcher County.

A few of the mission schools are nonsectarian, but most are denominational, and practically all were started as religious efforts. Stuart Robinson, by way of example, had its inception in a Sunday school. The extent to which it still emphasizes religion may be seen in a statement by Superintendent W. L. Cooper. "The ultimate objective," he said, "of all the school's service is to bring about in those whom it touches a deeper sense of responsibility to God. . . . Our subject matter is prayerfully selected, and so organized and taught that boys and girls are daily brought under the influence of the principles that our Master Himself taught. For instance, our mathematics teacher is more vitally interested in bringing the boys and girls of her class into contact with Christ than she is in getting across to them a few mathematical formulas."

It seems that many of the mission schools have done a little too much "prayerful selecting" of subject matter, but this does not apply to Stuart Robinson for all its emphasis on religion. It has good balance between its academic and its vocational subjects, and it has been a progressive, successful school.

Here are a few pertinent facts:

It had 432 students, seventy of them boarders, enrolled last year in the grammar and high schools, but the average daily attendance was about a hundred less. Because it is in a mining community it has a tremendous student turnover. Regarding this floating mine population Mr. Cooper said, "One year our school opened with the second grade numbering thirty-three. We closed the year with about the same number but with only three of the original pupils." In an effort to cope with the rapid shift of students the high school offers two subjects a semester instead of the usual four and gives two full credits instead of four half-credits. The school has a 150-acre farm and a 35-cow dairy, which aid financially. The county furnishes the graded-school teachers and Stuart Robinson the high-school teachers.

The institution's sources of income indicate how a mission school is financed. During a seven-year period it realized

$32,106 from a clothing business (sale of clothing sent in as gifts); $97,539 from the Assembly's Home Mission Committee (of the Presbyterian Church, South); $14,720 from tuition; and $35,178 from individual donors. To these assets were added the income from the farm, run by the students, and the payment of grammar-school teachers by the county.

Stuart Robinson, the Pine Mountain Settlement School in Harlan County, and the Hindman Settlement School in the Knott County seat might be termed "typical" of the best mountain mission schools. Started as independent institutions they now are associated with public-school endeavor. They offer courses through a high-school level, and they emphasize vocational training and "moral living." Miss Katherine Pettit and Miss May Stone founded Hindman in 1902, when the trip from Jackson was a two-day, jolt-wagon journey, and Miss Pettit and Mrs. Ethel deLong Zande started Pine Mountain in 1913.

The nineteen buildings of the Pine Mountain School lie in a valley much wider than Caney's, and most of them are handsomer and sturdier. For many years after the school was founded it could be reached only on horseback or afoot, but now a gravel CCC road winding eight miles over Pine Mountain connects it with the Harlan-Whitesburg highway.

Pine Mountain's entire atmosphere differs from Caney's. An easy relationship exists between boys and girls. Regulations are less severe. Living quarters are more comfortable and attractive. Pine Mountain has a swimming pool and other facilities that would be considered luxuries at Caney.

The school places its emphasis on vocational training, and only 15 to 20 per cent of its graduates go beyond the high-school level it offers. It has courses in printing, woodworking, auto mechanics, agriculture, home economics, nursing, and weaving. For good or bad it sets great store in "perpetuating the culture of the mountain people"–ballad-singing, folk-dancing, and the like.

In comparison to Caney, Pine Mountain is a "rich" school. It has an endowment of about $300,000. It has 336 acres of land, thirty-six of which are under cultivation as the school farm. It has a staff of twenty-five, fifteen of whom are classed as teachers, although there are only about ninety boarding and thirty day students. It charges an entrance fee of $10 and tuition of $7.50 a month, paid by about 50 per cent of the students through work at the school. It operates a medical insurance plan for the community and has a ten-bed hospital.

Important because of its success among an inherently uncooperative people is a co-op store managed by tenth-grade pupils. Started in 1937 it sells school supplies, canned goods, staples, and confections. Shares sell for twenty-five cents apiece, and the shareholders elect officers, who do the purchasing and sales planning. The shares earn a small interest, but most of the cooperative's earnings are returned to the purchasers through lowered prices.

Staff members keep records on all students but give neither grades nor credits, because "working for them brings hypocrisy and superficiality."

An effort is made to teach good citizenship, and nearly every older student has some trust for which he is responsible to a citizenship committee.

Operated in conjunction with the school and located about four miles from it in different directions are two outposts or community centers. Their programs call for medical clinic days, singing, sewing and canning classes, mothers' "get-togethers," lending library services, boys' playground activities, and periodic "socials" or parties. It seems, however, that their programs are not always carried out. The outpost called the Medical Settlement was run in 1940 by a woman who had no more understanding of the mountain people than she had of Einstein's theory of relativity. A "northern outlander," she hadn't even visited most of the homes in her district. She said she tried to have parties once a week, "but the boys got drunk, so to punish them I quit having parties." She said she tried having square dances, "but some of the people got converted and objected, so I quit having square dances." She planned sewing classes, but the women said they were too busy to come—so, what did she do?

Many, perhaps a majority, of the staff members of settlement schools are well trained, capable, and sincere, but all too large a number are men and women who simply couldn't make the grade elsewhere.

At the Medical Settlement was one of the University of Kentucky's so-called radio listening centers. Brain children of Publicity Director Elmer G. Sulzer, the listening centers have been successful in gaining national publicity for the university, but they have been pretty much of a failure in "bringing the best in educational programs to the isolated districts of eastern Kentucky." (The latter fact, however, is not generally acknowledged yet.)

The idea was something like this:

The university broadcasts educational programs daily, and Sulzer figures, "Maybe the mountain people don't profit from the programs because they don't get them, and maybe they don't get them because they haven't any radios." So he gets himself an old battery set and, with a sendoff in the newspapers (from publicity handouts), hies himself up to Cow Creek and sets 'er up in the general store. Then he tells the storekeeper-postmaster, "Now here's a radio and here's a program of the university broadcasts. You invite everybody in the neighborhood to come in at the hours these programs are scheduled, and then you turn on the radio. Presto! The great outside world is brought right to them and they will become educated." Then national magazines carry stories called "Radio Comes to Cow Creek"—all about how the quaint and folksy folks leave their corn patches and their stills, swing the young 'uns up on their hips, mount their mules, and in great excitement ride to the general store to hear Professor

I. M. Manure tell in his inimitably witty fashion how to grow more lespedeza by spreading triple superphosphate.

Bunko! I've seen perhaps half of the thirty-odd centers from time to time, and I've never yet seen one operating as it's supposed to. In most cases the radios aren't even working, and if they are, two or three loafers are sitting around listening to the ball game or to Uncle Ezra and his Coon Hunters.

The radio at the Medical Settlement whined and popped and cracked like a machine gun, but it didn't matter much. Many of the families in the neighborhood had radios anyway.

That the mission schools have aided the causes of education and "social enlightenment" cannot be denied, but it is highly possible that the millions poured into them could have been spent better than in taking over a state function. Moreover the mountain people are resentful of many of the schools' practices. Admittedly it doesn't take much to make the mountain people resentful, but perhaps they have cause enough in being made to feel daily that they are dependent upon charity for their educations and in being made the subjects of fund-seeking literature. At any rate the day of the charity schools is passing. The trend is toward state maintenance and control, and it is probable that in a few years only those with large endowments will remain private.

To Berea College on the eastern tip of Madison County go many of the mountain youths who seek educations higher than the mission and public high schools offer. It is not the only eastern Kentucky school offering low-cost education to mountain students, but it is the principal one.

Berea is an old school as American institutions go. John G. Fee founded it in 1855. From a one-building district school it has grown to an institution with an enrollment of 1,850, including 542 in the foundation school, 473 in the secondary school, and 835 in the college. In addition to the many buildings on its central campus it owns 6,284 acres of land, a hotel, a dairy, a cannery, and weaving, baking, clothing, furniture-making, printing, broom-making, and pottery-making industries.

The school's work program makes it in a sense a small communistic society. Seven hundred of its present enrollment started to school with no more than $25 each. These 700 are half-day students; that is, they work half a day and go to school half a day. Every other student pays an annual tuition of just $150, but he works two hours a day no matter whether he has money or whether he doesn't—and there are few who do. The students are responsible for the upkeep of the buildings and the grounds. They work in the hotel, in the dining rooms, the library, the kitchens, and the heating plant. They operate the dairy, which boasts the highest milk production of any herd of its size, 175, in the United States. They run the farm and raise garden products for Berea's tables. They operate the cannery, the bakery, the candy kitchen, and the print shop. They make clothing, furniture, brooms, bedspreads. In short each contributes to the support of the school population.

Products of such industries as the candy kitchen and the furniture and broom plants are sold, but school officials say the work program is not operated as a money-making enterprise. William Jesse Baird, dean of the foundation school, put it this way: "There are two main reasons for existence of the labor program. First it has educational values. We believe that learning to work is as important as learning English, that it is character-building, and that it is fundamental to American tradition. Second the program enables the students to maintain their self-respect. They obtain their educations here for almost no cash outlay, some working out even the $150 annual tuition, but they realize they are making their own way."

Berea offers cultural, agricultural, and vocational courses. Its students can obtain Bachelor of Arts degrees in education and arts and sciences and Bachelor of Science degrees in agriculture and home economics. They can learn a trade or study courses leading to medicine, engineering, or law. As nearly as possible the work program is correlated with the curricula.

Berea's endowment is $11,000,000, about $5,000,000 of which has been realized from aluminum. Charles Hall, the discoverer, was a student at Oberlin College in Ohio when Dr. William Goodell Frost was teaching Greek there. Hall later became a professor of chemistry at Oberlin and Dr. Frost became president of Berea. When the discovery was made Dr. Frost went up to Oberlin to talk to his former student. Hall bequeathed to Berea a one-sixth interest in his product.

The annual budget runs in the neighborhood of $615,000. Of this total, $512,000 is realized from student fees and income from the endowment. The remaining $103,000 must be obtained from donors. Dean Baird tells this story of one of Berea's early benefactors:

"Dr. D. K. Pearson, a Chicago physician, was visiting various schools early in the 1900's with the intention of making gifts to the one he considered most worthy. When he came to Berea he inspected every nook and cranny but didn't say much. He stood for quite a while in the kitchen where the students were peeling potatoes. Then he walked over, picked up a peeling, and put it in his pocket. A little while later he sat down in the president's office and pulled out the peeling. 'Any school,' he said as he dangled the strip from his finger, 'that's so thrifty it shaves its peelings this thin gets my money.' He gave $25,000 then to pipe water from mountain springs into the campus. Later he made other substantial gifts, including money that built the men's dormitory."

At one time the school accepted Negroes, but the state legislature made that illegal back in 1904, and since then all students have been white and 90 per cent must be from the mountains. One-half its ex-students return to their home counties, but a study has shown that the higher the education level attained the greater is the tendency to seek livelihoods elsewhere. Berea has produced many outstanding preachers, doctors, lawyers, teachers, and businessmen. It has, moreover, turned out men and women who are better homemakers for their training.

President William J. Hutchins, who was succeeded in 1939 by his son, Francis S. Hutchins, attributed the success of Berea College to its labor system, its emphasis on the home, health, "ancient simplicities and the fine arts," and religion.

"We who serve the mountains," he declared, "are trying to teach the boys and girls that they can play without perverting the most sacred instincts of mankind, that they can heed the golden trumpet's sound while great sacrifices are being offered, that they may live a life of external hardship and at the same time find their way, straight and clean, to the perennial sources of joy which are not destroyed by the ravages of time and circumstances. We are trying to teach the boys and girls how to take their share, their full share, in the economic and spiritual redemption of the South and in the cosmic redemption of which the great dreamers have dreamed and for which the prophets and apostles and martyrs have died."

High sounding words, but Berea is nonetheless a practical school. Even religion is not overstressed. Students are not required to belong to a particular church or to any church at all. Religion is there in abundance, but it is not crammed down the students' throats.

Regulations are strict at Berea. Students are not permitted to smoke, to attend round dances, or to enter an eating establishment not controlled by the college. They can be, and are, expelled for infractions of the rules. Concerning these regulations Dean Baird had this to say: "We don't prohibit smoking because we feel it is wrong but because we feel the boys and girls who come here should not spend what little money they have on tobacco. We regard round dancing the same way. First the students would have to pay for orchestras and then they would have to have tuxedos and evening dresses and corsages. Those things are all right for students who can afford them, but our students cannot. The same reasoning applies to our forbidding students to go to restaurants. We furnish them plenty of good, wholesome food. Why should they spend money in hot-dog joints?" Until recently girls were not allowed to wear silk stockings or silk underwear or high-heeled shoes. "These things were banned," Dean Baird continued, "for the same reason smoking, round dancing, and restaurants are not now permitted, and also because poorer girls who could not afford silks would be made to feel inferior to those who wore them. Now, however, these things can be purchased at no extra cost." All students except juniors and seniors are required to attend chapel programs. Rolls are taken and demerits are given to those who do not attend. Dean Baird explained this regulation by saying that the school obtained the best in entertainment and educational programs and that it believed the students should be made to take advantage of them. Still another regulation, and one that causes embarrassment to outsiders at times, is one forbidding smoking in the dining room of the hotel. "This rule was made," Dean Baird said, "because the majority of our guests prefer that there be no smoking in the dining room."

The great majority of students seem not to mind the supervision of their private and social lives, but occasionally some fiercely independent boy or girl rebels. I do not think it would be an injustice to Berea to quote what one such student had to say, although the school officials contend the criticism was unjust. Perhaps it was. At any rate, James Stuart, brother of Jesse, the author, wrote an article for *American Mercury* in 1933 called "Freshman at Fishbone."

I find the Fishbone girls are rope-walkers (he said). They have to watch each step. They cannot wear silks. They cannot wear high-heel shoes. The authorities raid the girls' dormitories. They get the slippers with the narrow heels. They keep them.

One is fined for stepping on the grass at Fishbone. One is not allowed to smoke at Fishbone. An old man with a bald head—shiny as glass in the moonlight—crawls around our windows at night, hunting the cigarette butts. . . .

I take a course in the Bible. Old Professor Walrus nods. My faith is not secure. Professor Walrus sleeps in chapel. But that is all right. We all sleep at Fishbone. We all sleep and nod and look drowsy-eyed. But we wake in time to clap our hands after the speech is done and the song is sung and the organ played. . . .

I never go out among the girls. I find it is very dangerous. A boy has been fined $25 for kissing a girl. I would be fined too. My fine would probably be twice twenty-five. But I do not indulge. Social life is limited at Fishbone. I clean out the manure and haul it over the grounds. And I work in the dining room. I wait on table. I get plenty to eat and I am growing. I am getting an education, too. . . .

I find Fishbone is not what I expected it to be. I do not fit. I am independent and free. Fishbone doesn't want that type of student . . . They do not want a student who will not handshake the professors for a grade. . . .

All I want is never to be classed as even a once-student from that school, studying Bible and composition. The price is too great.

I shall fight you because you are insincere. You are a thin monument in the air. You are a wind-structure. You are nothing.

VI

Diary of a Ride

THE BAY MARE'S HOOFS whispered through the sand, splashed through the water, clanked against the rocks. The mid-June sun blazed mercilessly. I should have started earlier or worn a hat.

Often when I rode through the hills I had no destination. I liked to look over the back country, talk to the people, sleep where I happened to be at sundown. But today I had a note from a friend at the Caney school introducing me to another student who lived on Beaver. For a dollar a day I had rented the only available riding nag, a bony bay named Nellie.

A quarter of a mile below the school I stopped to see "Big Billy" Jacobs. He was a fortune teller, I had heard. A tow-headed youngster said Billy wasn't at home but that I'd find him "second house down th' crick."

In the doorway of a little plank house sat Billy. I knew him by the handlebar mustache and the length of his angular frame. He unfolded like a jackknife when I dismounted. Out of the door poured four children, a woman nursing a baby, and a man.

"I would like," I said, "to get my fortune told."

Billy squinted against the sun. "I ain't got my cyards here."

"Let's go back up if you don't mind. I'll pay you."

Billy lived in a stable. "It hain't much," he apologized, "but my daughter's lettin' me and th' ole woman stay here agin th' time we kin build."

He untied a rope on a plank door and stooped through. Turning around like a dog seeking a place to lie he squatted on the bed. Over it hung a huge, faded paper Christmas bell. A heap of clothing and rags took what floor space the bed left. A board partition a foot and a half high separated the "bedroom" from the "kitchen." About five feet square, the "kitchen" contained a little wood stove, a table, a stool, and a chair. Old wallpaper had been tacked over the walls and roof of both "rooms."

Billy pulled a frayed and dirty deck of cards from beneath the bed. I sat on the rag pile. From his shirt pocket he took a pair of dime-store glasses, minus one shaft, and slipped them over glasses he already wore. He shuffled the cards, and I cut them into four piles. After studying each pile a moment he took my palm and surveyed it carefully. He shook his head. "I see a heap o' trouble fer you."

"What kind of trouble?"

"Kain't say definite. . . . You an' yer wife—the cyards say ye've got one—seem t' be a long ways apart. . . . Mebbe hit's jest distance, you hyar and she thar. She yaller-haired. Ain't that right?"

I nodded. "She's blond."

"Wal, you're a-gonna have three women." He smiled and glanced up to get my reaction. "They's a dark-complected gal that still loves ye an' they's a real white-lak gal that's after ye. Yes sir, she shore is." He grinned again. "You'll make a heap o' money, but ye'll lose hit—more'n likely on women. You'll have seven children by yer three wives an' five out children . . ."

I laughed. "You mean I'm going to have five illegitimate children?"

"That's about the size of hit."

"Tell me more."

"Thar ain't much more to tell. The cyards don't say no more, an' yer palm ain't plain no further. I'll advise ye though. Trust in th' Lord."

"Thanks."

He keened his eyes and quoted a long passage from the Bible. "That's th' way I heared hit," he declared, "an' that's th' way I believe hit."

I asked him if he could read and write.

"Kain't write none," he said, "but I used t' read a leetle before my eyes got bad."

"How old are you, Billy?"

"I'm sixty-nine, but I'm rite sprightly like. Me an' th' ole woman has raised ten children, seven of 'em still a-livin'. All married now, 'cepting one boy. He's done past twenty-seven, but we kain't do nary thing with him."

"Well, thanks for your time and the fortune, Billy." I handed him a dollar. He looked amazed. He seemed sorry, too, that he had predicted such an unhappy future, and he kept wishing me good luck as I walked out to the fence and unhitched the horse.

I tried to urge Nellie out of a walk, but it was no use. Her joints couldn't stand it for more than a few yards.

Two miles down Caney we turned right, up Hollybush branch. We passed a few houses and came to a small sawmill. Three or four men were at work, sawing oak barrel-heading. Just as we were passing, someone tooted the whistle. If he did it deliberately he missed his fun. Nellie didn't bat an eye.

In front of a general store four men were pitching horseshoes. A fifth, whittling slowly and deliberately, leaned against a tree. I said, "Howdy," and they returned the greeting.

A few jogs further up Hollybush three women were washing clothes near a pool in the creek bed. I drew rein and watched a moment. Creek water and clothes steamed in a metal tub held over a wood fire by two long pokers supported by a couple of sawhorses. The women still used homemade lye soap but employed a washboard instead of the battlin' stick of their mothers and grandmothers.

As I rode on I glanced back, knowing they would be staring at me. They ducked their heads quickly when I turned.

The houses up the creek were newer than those nearer the mouth—patent signs of the move "up the hollows." The new houses looked like camp cottages, only not so neat.

Most of the hillside had been cleared, and on its rocky, perpendicular slopes men and women, boys and girls, hoed the young corn. Always they leaned on their hoes and watched me as I passed. If I waved they waved back.

Hills not under the hoe were covered with a scrubby second or third growth. Few trees were of timber size.

I pulled up in front of a three-room cabin near the creek and asked a bewhiskered old fellow who sat under a shade tree if I might have a drink of water.

"Yes sir, you shore can," he answered pleasantly. "We got th' best well in these parts. Water's what we got th' most of. Git down an' set a spell. . . . Dewey, fetch a cup fer this young feller."

A small boy pattered out the front door. Shyly he handed me a cup with one hand as he held up his overall pants with the other.

I turned to the well close by and lowered the bucket, recalling as I did that I had never seen a pump in the backhill country. The picturesque, long-armed well-sweeps had disappeared, but still there were no pumps. I asked the old gentleman why

"Pumps cost money," he said. "Besides, water's best when the air kin git to hit."

The well was deep and the water cold. I refused to think about typhoid.

The old man wanted to know who I was, where I came from, what I was doing, and where I was going. I told him, and he asked me the question that always comes next. "Air you kin to so-and-so over on such-and-such a crick?"

He told me about the old days in the hills, "when game war plentiful and a man al'ays had a bounty t' eat," when he stood in his front yard "over t'other side of th' mounting" and shot a deer as it moved up the ravine, when he ground his own corn meal and made his own shoes. He pointed out his bee gums, made from hollow gum stumps, and his sugar gourd, no longer used. "Times hain't what they was," he sighed. "Hit's about all a man kin do jest t' git along these days."

A woman stepped to the door and invited, "Come t' dinner. Hit's ready on th' table."

"But I can't stay for dinner," I protested.

"You ain't et, have you?" she asked.

"No-o-o."

"Well then come along. Yer more'n welcome to what we've got."

Six of us ate in the first shift. We had corn bread, eggs and gravy, cooked green onions, beans, hot-but-weak coffee with brown sugar and no milk.

As the woman busied around passing the food and making me at home she suggested that I pour my coffee into the saucer to cool it. I obliged.

"Begone!" she ordered a hound that had his head in my lap.

I knew I must not offer to pay. I slipped fifty cents into the pocket of the boy who'd brought the cup.

At the head of the creek we started the steep climb up the mountain path. The further Nellie went the harder she puffed. There were no sounds except her heavy breathing and the incessant popping drone of the locusts. One alighted on the pommel of the saddle and I got a close-up of its heavy body and gauzy wings, its individual grating. The horseflies were worrisome. They buzzed around Nellie's nose, neck, and legs, drawing blood when they bit. I slapped at one on her flank. She flipped sideways, thumping my head against overhanging boughs.

I stopped on the mountaintop and threw the reins over a stump. Nellie shook herself and snorted contentedly when I took off the saddle. Climbing to the top rail of the fence that zigzagged along the narrow ridge I filled my pipe and looked beyond the divide.

There at the head of Mullins Branch hollow was a scene of rugged beauty. The half-bowl of the hill wall had felt the plow in the spring, and now a choppy sea of young corn and weeds swept downward. Beginning at the left side of the rim a mud road, rock-strewn in places, wound down like a snake's track past a log cabin at the foot and disappeared into a green river of tree boughs rolling away in the distance. The right side of the U-formation was newly cleared, and the twisted dead limbs of girdled trees reared grotesquely. In the center of the headland were the inevitable washes, the beginnings of Mullins Branch.

Resaddling Nellie I let down the bars that served as a gate and led her through.

When I passed the cabin whose roof I had seen from the hill top, four children came out to stare, and a boy of possibly twelve tagged along behind me. I spoke, but he said nothing. A quarter of a mile down the branch he still was following me. "Where you going, partner?" I asked.

"Ain't that Buddy Hall's horse?" he came back.

"Yes."

"What you doin' with it?"

"I rented it."

"Where you from?"

I told him I was from Lexington and was visiting at Caney.

"Where you goin'?"

Amused at his cross-examination I replied that I intended to ride to New York but probably would spend the night at Charlie Breeding's.

He said no more, and when I looked around a few minutes later he was gone.

I had reached the mouth of Mullins Branch and turned up Right Beaver when the skies grew overcast. I was glad momentarily, for I was sunburned. Then I saw it was going to rain. I prompted Nellie into a trot that jarred my very soul. Ten minutes later it was pouring. I dug my heels into the mare's flanks and she actually broke into a gallop. We took shelter in a stable near a schoolhouse. Rain spattered through holes in the shingle roof, but the warm air felt good after the drenching. Climbing up into the loft and pulling hay around me I sat there in a kind of dream as the water pounded on the roof and dripped and splashed inside.

When the shower was over, a rainbow arched the sky. The air, the streams, the hills were fresh.

Splashing on up the creek we came to a store building. "Kite, U. S. Postoffice," the dim letters said on a sign advertising Star Brand shoes. I knew my destination was not far off.

The Breeding home was a neat, white frame house a few yards back from the creek in a grassy yard. A concrete walk led to the porch, where several people were sitting. I dropped the reins over a fence paling and walked up to the porch. "I'm looking for Dalton Breeding," I said.

A handsome, gray-eyed youth stood up and walked to the porch edge. I handed him the introductory note. He read it and smiled. "Come up and have a chair. You seem to have got caught in the shower. We all gathered out here on the porch after the rain drove us out of the crop."

I reclined with a sigh of pleasure into a folding porch chair as the note was passed from hand to hand. The family surveyed me quizzically but politely. I must have been an odd sight. I needed a shave. My overalls and shirt were wet and muddy. My hair was tousled. I knew from the hot feeling that my nose was sun-scorched.

We made conversation. They learned who I was and what I was doing. I learned about the family.

Charlie Breeding, Dalton's father, was a nice-looking man who had taught a one-room school for thirty years. With an eighth-grade education he had obtained a life certificate. He was little concerned with world affairs. He took no newspaper, owned no radio. That he didn't was of his own choosing, for he was perhaps the most affluent man in the community. In addition to his income from the school he had returns from the land and from natural gas wells on his farm.

Mrs. Breeding was a meek but comely woman, not so aged as most mountain mothers of her years. Her hair was done in a tight knot, and gold fillings showed in her teeth when she smiled broadly. She wore a long dress, blue polka-dotted.

Dalton's sister was a full-faced girl whose dark hair was wound in long braids around her head. She was pretty, shy.

Grandmother was the personification of pioneer stock. A toothless, strong-faced woman who chewed tobacco and spat where she pleased, she didn't belong in a neat, frame house that had a gas refrigerator, gas stoves, gas lights. She seemed scornful of the family's prosperity. One knew she felt cramped, useless. She didn't even talk much. She took off her shoes and went barefooted, just for spite, just as if to say, "You may be too good to do this, but I'm not."

The sixth member of the family was a niece of about sixteen. Crippled, perhaps from infantile paralysis, she was chubby of body and sweet of face. She radiated happiness. The family called her "Crippled Girl." She thought nothing of it.

Bloody Ground

I told Dalton I would like to talk to Miles Bates. I had heard, I said, that he was quite a story teller.

He chuckled. "You mean Papaw Bates."

"I've heard they call him 'Papaw.' Why is that?"

"When he was young," Dalton recounted in a voice that moved like sorghum, "a steer threw him into a papaw tree. It broke his leg and drove in a stob that stayed there six months, so they say. I guess it did. He shows the scar on his leg where the stob went in. But everybody teased him so much about it he don't like the name of Papaw. He gets mad as fire when you call him that to his face.

"Yes sir, Papaw's quite a character," he continued. "He tells tales that are half truth and half made up, and he's done so many things it's hard to separate one from the other. Why once he spent a long time, years I think, in jail because he told around every place that he had shot a man. Even explained how it happened. Said, 'When my gun went off he fell like a white oak.' When Papaw got tired of staying in jail, he had an awful time provin' he hadn't really done it."

"Well let's go see him," I said, pulling myself out of the chair.

Dalton and I walked back down the creek and turned up Bates Branch. He told me Papaw's eyesight was poor and that the boys sometimes played tricks on him. "One time," he related, "Papaw and another fellow were riding along on their mules and this fellow saw a tree stump about the size of a man. He thought he'd have some fun with Papaw so he nodded to the stump and said, 'Howdy.' Papaw come along and tipped his hat and said, 'Howdy,' just as big as you please. Well they rode on a piece and then Papaw turned to this fellow and said, 'You reckon that consarned feller back thar's deef. He never made no pretense o' speakin' to ary one of us.' The fellow just laughed and never did tell him about the stump."

It was a couple of miles up the branch to Papaw's, and we

passed the time of day with each family along the way. Subjects were the weather, mules, the corn crop, and gas-drilling operations. During recent summers big trucks had lumbered up Right Beaver, bringing drill tools, cash, and a new subject of conversation.

I laughed out loud at one fellow. He was sitting on the edge of the porch talking to us and chewing tobacco when suddenly he decided it was about time to expectorate. Instead of spitting out into the yard he turned his head slightly and let fly over his shoulder onto the porch. When he asked me what I was laughing at I told him I had just thought of a joke someone had told me. He said that reminded him of one.

"Over on Puncheon," he said, "they was a kid so mean couldn't none of th' teachers do nothing with him. But last year a new teacher come along and he decided he'd learn that youngster a thing er two. So he got him a good sufficient switch an' he said, 'Young man, come here. I ain't gonna whoop you hard this time. I'm gonna give you jest an ordinary, ever'day whoopin'.' Wal sir, he tuk that switch an' he plumb tore th' hide offen that young 'un. And that cyored him. He thought if that was just an ordinary whoopin' he shore couldn't stand no skinnin'." The teller laughed uproariously, and we joined in.

As we left each place the final exchange was the same. Dalton would say, "Well we got to move along. Better come go 'round." The answer, "Nope. Can't. You-all better stay th' night."

We left the branch and walked a few hundred yards through a birch forest to Papaw's cabin. A lonesomey place it was if ever I saw one, nestled there at the foot of the hill among the trees. We seemed somehow to have lost a few decades while walking through the forest, for the cabin was an old-time, rough-hewn log affair of two rooms joined by a dogtrot or porch, and the setting was one of pioneer days.

In a cane-bottomed chair on the dogtrot Miles Bates leaned

against the wall. He was a mustached old man with a great shock of gray hair. Crow's-feet ran to his watery blue eyes as the gulleys run to the branch at the hollow's head.

Papaw's woman came out to greet us and to bid us "have a cheer an' set a spell." She was a thin, erect old lady with the tired face, the toothless gums, the knowing eyes of the mountain grandmother.

The old man was glad to have someone to talk to and in consequence told us many things. As Dalton had warned, some were true, some exaggerated, and some pure fiction.

He told us he was a double first cousin of those two famous mountain bad men, Talt Hall and Devil John Wright. He took us inside to show us a picture of Talt, and as he did he shooed a hen off the bed. She flew out cackling, leaving an egg on the quilt. Letting her nest there, Papaw explained, saved searching for eggs in the brush.

Miles told us of his travels. "I've been," he said, "jest about ever'where thar is to be—in ever' county of this hyar state, in all forty-nine states, and twice across the big waters."

He said his uncle was a giant, "Baby" Bates by name; that this fellow weighed 300 pounds, was eight feet, two inches tall, and married to a woman from Nova Scotia who was eight foot three. "Baby" Bates was with Robinson's circus, Miles declared, and when it toured to France and England, "Baby" took Miles and Talt Hall along. "When the boat pulled up at London," the taleteller recounted, "some fellers standin' thar made some remarks I didn't like. I jerked out my gun and killed three of 'em graveyard dead. But Talt made me quit a-shootin'. 'You'd better be careful,' he said, 'or you'll get us in trouble.' "

He knew all there was, and then some, about the Clabe Jones war, and he told of shootings and killings that lost me in the maze.

He said he had once been a deputy marshal, that he was a Democrat but was "not very keen on this feller Roosevelt."

He rocked his chair forward and looked me over carefully. "I'd a-knowed ye was a Day if I'd met ye in th' dark," he said. "You look pine blank like th' Days over in Letcher." I told him that was remarkable since so far as I knew I had no kin in Letcher. "Yer all th' same people jest th' same," he satisfied himself. Maybe we are.

The old lady came to the door now and then to listen to the conversation and add a word or two. I asked her how long it had been since she had carded wool and spun it into thread. "It ain't been so long," she said. "I was one of th' finalest ones around here t' quit. I was plumb drove to hit by those plagued dogs. They killed my sheep till there warn't nary one fer me t' fleece."

The subject of Swift's lost silver mine was broached and Papaw was really off. He said when he was a youth he had lived eighteen months with an Indian chief who told him that "if the people around hyar only knowed where t' look they could shoe their horses with silver and gold." He never looked himself, he said, but a fellow he knew prospected until he found a silver vein–"mostest likely 'twar that very vein that Swift unkivered"–and sold it for $100,000. After the purchasers had dug five feet, they hit solid rock. Then this wily prospector bought the property back for $100, found another vein "an' made a million dollars if he made a copper."

Pursuing the subject of Indians, Papaw told about a Captain Miles who tracked a band of redskins to a cave. "Then he clum up in a spruce-pine and gobbled like a wild turkey. A Indian poked his head out fer t' spot th' gobblin' fowl, and Miles let him have it squar betwixt th' eyes with his ole hawg rifle. Then he gobbled again, an' he got another scalp. I'll swan to goodness an' hope I die effen he didn't set thar from sunup to sundown a-knockin' off Indians till there warn't ary one o' them varmints left."

We made another trip into the house, this time to see a flintlock "plum like that'n Cap'n Miles foired." It really was a magnificent thing, taller than my head, perfectly balanced, and embossed in silver. "I wouldn't part with 'er fer love ner money," he declared. "I kain't shoot 'er no more, but I wouldn't let 'er go."

I walked across the dogtrot into the "other house," the kitchen-dining room. The old couple's daughter, a shapeless, bedraggled woman of thirty-five, had a pot boiling on a wood stove. She told me she was the only one of the children still at home and that she "tuk kere of th' ole folks, a-raisin' corn and a leetle gyarden truck." She said she had chicken and dumplin's cooking and suggested that I'd better stay for supper. I was hungry enough to sit down and eat then and there, but Dalton reckoned "we'd better get along."

The hollows were filled with dusk when we got back. We watered Nellie at the creek, filled her stall box with corn, and left her munching happily for the night. A cow and a mule were in the stable with Nellie. In the lot were hogs, chickens, several hives of bees. The Breedings lived on the fat of the land.

For supper there were green beans, peas cooked in the pods, boiled potatoes, side meat, pickle, cornbread, buttermilk, freshly churned butter, and gooseberry pie.

Mrs. Breeding alone of the women ate at the table with the men, and she jumped from chair to kitchen and back to chair throughout the meal. Mr. Breeding was master of the household. When he spoke he spoke quietly, but what he said was to be obeyed. The superiority of the male was taken for granted by Dalton too. When he wanted something done he told his sister, and she did it. There was no "Do it yourself" from her as from sisters in outland families.

Supper over, we sat on the front porch and listened to the crickets and the whippoorwills until the women finished eating and did the dishes. Then "Cripple Girl" brought out a guitar and played and sang. She knew snatches of two or three old ballads, but most of her repertoire had derived from neighbors' radios during programs of the "Early Morning Jamboree" type.

At bedtime I was assigned to one bed in the front room and Dalton took the other. I knew that such a disposition of sleeping facilities meant the others would have to double up or spread pallets, but I knew too there was no use protesting. It would only cause embarrassment. When you accept the hospitality of a mountain home you sleep where you're put and you ask no questions. You're extremely fortunate if you sleep alone. Bed space is at a premium, yet there's always room for one more.

I wondered, the first time I slept in a one-room cabin with two women and two other men, how you undressed and preserved your modesty. I learned the process is simple. You take off your shoes. You get in bed. You take off your clothes.

It wasn't daylight when Dalton shook my shoulder and I crawled out of the featherbed. I looked at my wristwatch. Three-thirty.

I walked around to the back porch and doused my head in a pan of cold water. That was better.

For breakfast—eggs afloat on a bowl of grease, enormous but fluffy-light biscuits, bacon, sausage, gravy, apple butter, honey, jelly, butter, coffee, and milk.

Dalton was to take his sister to Caney for a summer session, so just as the sunrays began to force the mists from the hollows we set out. He sat in the saddle and she sideways on the mule's rump.

"Don't you think," I asked after we had ridden a couple of miles, "that it would be more comfortable for her if you exchanged places?"

He looked at me strangely and said he'd never thought of that.

I daresay he'll never think of it again.

VII

Will of God

IT WAS HOT, and great choking swirls of dust rose from the new WPA gravel road. The hill country was dry as a Sunday-morning mouth. It hadn't rained for weeks, and already the farmers were hauling water for their livestock. Wither showed on the grass and even the trees. The corn crop would be ruined if it didn't rain soon.

I thought as I drove along that a swim would be more pleasant than a foot-washing on such a day. But then foot-washings come only once a year for each church, and I'd found one that I could reach without walking a dozen mountain miles. I recalled reading in a magazine a sort of believe-it-or-not to the effect that people in the Kentucky hills still practice foot-washing as an act of literalistic obedience to a Biblical suggestion. Hell's bangers, I'd lived most of my life within a few miles of places where they held foot-washings every July and August and I hadn't regarded them as strange enough to visit. But then if other people considered them so incredible I thought I'd better have a look.

I allowed I'd found the right place all right. Model-A Fords and '31 Chevys and pick-up trucks were strung along the road, and a few horses and mules were hitched to the fences.

There was the church over there on the left, standing on a knoll in a clump of trees. Not a bad looking church, as mountain country churches go. Weatherboarded. Painted white. Tin roof. Spire still standing upright.

I'd thought the main road was dusty, but it was wave-washed beach compared to that 200 yards of churned up clay. The dust filtered into my shoes and climbed up my britches legs, inside and out.

Once inside the grove I could hear one of the preachers shouting. He must have been addressing a small percentage of those gathered for the occasion, because about 150 were making the best of the shade. Many were clustered around a couple of stands where aproned women were dispensing mushy ice cream, lukewarm pop, and shriveled hot dogs. Others were preparing lunch by spreading fried chicken, pickles, whole tomatoes, cold beans, and biscuits on newspapers for the flies, the ants, and the hungry bellies.

The main part of the program came after dinner, so I walked in and took a seat up front. I found I'd gone too far, though, and was forced to retreat when I admitted I wasn't among those who were to take communion.

The outside of the church was deceiving. Inside one saw the reverse side of the weatherboarding, the reverse side of the tin roof. Floors were of unplaned lumber. Benches were of the same. There was no piano or organ. They're scarce as century notes in mountain churches outside the towns. There was, however, a right fair altar, and before it was a table covered with a white cloth.

On the floor in front of the table sat the ubiquitous water bucket and dipper. What would any mountain gathering be without one!

A group of female communicants sat facing one another on one side of the altar. A group of males sat likewise on the other. Onlookers crowded the rest of the room or craned their necks through the windows like so many terrapins.

Had a movie director mustered for a foot-washing scene a bunch of extras like the group of men on the front row he would have been accused of inexcusable exaggeration. One of the brothers had sorrel hair and bushy sorrel eyebrows and under them a face as set and fleshless as a turtle's. Another, dressed in overalls, had the great, sad eyes of a hound dog and a flowing white mustache that straggled forlornly to his jaw bones. A third, a little man with a mere hair of a mustache, reminded me somehow of a French pervert. At his side was a dummy, who appeared demented to boot. When songs were sung he bellowed enthusiastically, his loose mouth wide open at the side, his voice piercing and toneless as a circus seal's.

"A church that doesn't practis feet washin' is not, aye yes, th' church of Jesus Christ." The moderator, a big-bellied, red-faced, heavy-jowled man who feeds logs to a band saw on week days was teeing off.

"Our Baptis' church, aye yes, was started by God. Some got too proud, aye yes, t' keep it. Some says you kin wash feet, aye yes, by doin' good dos, but I says they's feet-washin' Baptists and then, aye yes, they's Baptists what'll put a feller up fer th' night an' then charge him a dollar, aye yes, fer doin' it. Folks is al'ays a-axin' why we practis close communion, aye yes. Well, hit's like this, aye yes. Suppose you was a-settin' on yer porch, aye yes, a-waitin' fer yer woman tew finish dinner, an' I comes up, aye yes, an' sits down alongside o' ye. An' th' woman, aye yes, she calls dinner is ready. An' you says, 'Come on in, aye yes, an' take a bite with me,' an' I says, aye yes, 'No by ginnies, I won't eat, aye yes, th' way yew do; if yew want me, aye yes, to eat, yew fetch th' table, aye yes, outen th' yard.' D'ya think, aye yes, you'd do it? Shore you wouldn't! D'ya think, aye yes, we're a-goin' t' change our ways, aye yes, to suit ever'body? Course we ain't! So we, aye yes, a-practis a-close communion, and them that wants t' practis our way, aye yes, has got to practis our way, aye yes, aye yes. Hain't that right, you Bible readers?"

"Amen," cried one of the Bible readers, and the moderator walked over and gave his hand a firm pump.

"When Jesus came, aye yes, was they ary Baptis' church, aye yes, on yearth? Yes sir! John t' Baptis' started hit, and Baptis' is th' name, aye yes, God observed an' used fer His family, aye yes, aye yes. Now I wanna ax ye somethin'. Did ary one o' ye here t'day everly hear of a man named Baptis'?"

No answer.

"Of course you hain't. Ye've heared, aye yes, of a man named Christian, an' a man named Church an' a man named House, but yew hain't never hear'n tell, aye yes, of a man named Baptis' 'cause that's the name, aye yes, God set aside fer His chosen people."

The fat moderator was warming up to his subject now. Perspiration soaked his shirt and dripped off his jowls to the floor—or into the water bucket when he leaned that way. He swung into a sort of rhythm and, in addition to his "aye yeses," began to shout certain syllables and words between which the connectives ran fast and almost unintelligibly.

"My brethern, aye yes, Baptis' is th' name God CHOSE fer his people. God called JOHN th' apostel and he ESTABLished that church. It SHALL not, aye yes, be left to anoTHer people. Hit's th' ONly church baptism, aye yes, fixed in HEAven. Jesus said to Peter, aye yes, 'You shan't have NO part of me'; so the Baptis' don't EAT er drink, aye yes, with EVER'body 'cause they don't, aye yes, LIVE t' th' ORder of God. Th' good ole feet-washin' BAPtis' church has CLOSE communion an' ther can't, aye yes, be no FORnicators, no aDULterers, no LIars, no THIEVES, no DRAM drinkers commune with us."

As a gesture of especial emphasis he would grab his left ear with his left hand, extend his right hand in the general direction of the roof, close his eyes, and let out a particularly bullish bellow.

"In MOST of these here churches, aye yes, their preachers have two er THREE women. Yew can't DO that in th' good ole

FEET-washin' BAPtis' church, aye yes. MOST of th' preachers in these here OTHer churches gets PAID fer preachin'. I says when ye get PAID fer preachin', aye yes, you're a-preachin' FOR th' congergation. But me, I'm a-preachin' TO th' congergation. Some says, aye yes, feet-washin' is NOT a COMMANDment but an example. But that hain't so. Hit's stampled in th' Bible, th' WORD of th' Lord, aye yes, aye yes. Ain't that so, Bible readers?"

"Hit's writ, brother."

"I had in head tew read a passage, but I hain't got my glasses. Th' good ole BAPtis' church, I say, is like a VIRtuous wife. You AL'ays know, aye yes, WHERE she is. If ye drink o' th' CUP o' th' Devil, you kain't drink, aye yes, o' th' CUP o' th' Lord. Praise BE t' God, I'm a ZION traveler. Brother Eversole, let's have a song."

Brother Eversole, a young, blond fellow, lined out from the only hymnbook in the congregation one of those melancholy ululations one hears rarely except at Baptist footwashings and funeralizings. The exact opposite of the rhythmic songs heard at Holiness and snake meetings, they had their origin in the Gregorian chants of the sixth century but compare only vaguely to orthodox church music of today. They are sung in a minor key. All selections sound alike. Words are accented at varying intervals.

The leader recited rapidly, "I'm a soldier bound for glory." Then the entire congregation wailed, "I AM a SOLDIER bow-OWNED for G-L-O-ry." Then followed:

I'm a soldier marching home,
Come and hear me tell my story,
All who long in sin have gone.

CHORUS

Farther on, yes, still farther on
Count the milestones one by one,
Jesus will forsake you never,
It is better farther on.

As the song ended the moderator and the man of the perverted look stopped three or four dirty-faced kids from playing in the water bucket and removed the cloth from the table. Two tin cups, a bottle of grape juice, and two plates of pie crust were revealed.

As the two men prepared the bread for serving by crumbling it in their grimy hands the song leader started, "I'm glad that I was born to die . . . "

After all had partaken of the crust a cup of grape juice was handed to one of the women and another to one of the men. They swigged, and I don't mean sipped, and passed the cups on. Lips covered lip marks in total disregard of probable disease.

When all had drunk, the moderator cleared his throat. An air of expectancy pervaded the church. "If I then, your Lord and Master, have washed your feet; ye also ought to wash one another's feet," he recited.

Then they sang:

> When Jesus Christ was here below,
> He taught His people what to do;
> And if we would his precepts keep
> We must descend to washing feet.

Two dishpans half filled with water were produced as the song continued. Women and men began simultaneously to remove shoes and stockings. Women wiggled and squirmed to unfasten their garters without showing their legs. The feet revealed might have been washed that morning, but they hadn't been helped by the combination of dry earth and sweat. Some of them, horny as a lizard's back, obviously weren't used to shoes.

The moderator handed one of the pans to a woman on the end of a row. She was a woman of possibly forty-five who had been nursing on a dried-up pap, which had seen better days, a baby old enough to chew sowbelly.

She stood up and tied a towel apron around her waist.

Then she kneeled, and a fat woman with a horrible goiter plunked a dirty foot into the dishpan. The washer scrubbed the foot with her hands for a moment, then dried it on her apron. While washing the second foot she began to cry, and as the tears flowed she blubbered, "Oh, I'm so happy; I'm so happy I can humble myself and give myself to Jesus."

As the washing progressed the hubbub grew. Tears ran, and communicants shouted testimonials of happiness. She of the goiter yelped, "I'm so happy, the Lord has been so kind to me, Hallelujah, I'm so happy." A scrawny little woman with her hair stringing across her face leaped from the dishpan to the bench shouting, "Lord God, I'm so happy–I don't know–why anybody wouldn't–wanna be saved!"

A pale-faced young woman who had sat in silent tears during the other outbursts sprang to her feet, leaped to me, and threw her arm around my neck. "I don't know who you are, ner where you come from, ner where you're a-goin'," she assured me in a sort of wail, "but may th' Lord bless you, 'cause he kin do it."

Everybody started shaking hands. They were still shaking when I left.

I don't wish to convey the idea that all mountain churches, or even all mountain Baptist churches, conduct foot-washings. They're holdovers from the past, and the more "modern" Baptist congregations have naught of them.

Churches in towns like Hazard, Jackson, Whitesburg, Harlan, Pikeville, and Manchester, in fact, differ little from churches found in towns of the same size any place in the country. It is nonetheless true that there are factors that make the religion of the majority of highlanders distinctive.

There are almost as many Baptists in the Kentucky hills as members of all other denominations combined–this despite gains made by the Holy Roller church and by such sects as the snake-handlers and Jehovah's Witnesses.

Will of God

Odd in view of the present-day predominance of Baptists is the fact the mountain people once were almost unanimously Presbyterian—odd, that is, until reasons for the change are considered. The Baptists had begun to make headway on the frontier at the expense of the Presbyterians by the time Kentucky was settled. As Theodore Roosevelt said, the rough democracy of the border welcomed a sect that was itself essentially democratic. To many of the backwoodsmen's prejudices, notably their sullen and narrow hostility toward all rank, whether or not based on merit and learning, the Baptists' creed appealed strongly. Where Baptist preachers obtained a foothold it was a matter of reproach to the Presbyterian clergymen that they had been educated for their profession. Presbyterians insisted upon an educated ministry, and the mountain wilderness could not support an educated ministry. Conditions on the frontier fostered individualism, leading thus to a spirit too democratic for Calvinism with its supreme authority of clergy. Then, too, the emotionalism of the Baptist preachers, who denounced privilege and proclaimed the power of God to act through the most uneducated, appealed strongly to the mountaineers' temperament.

And so today about 6 per cent of mountain church members are Presbyterians, whereas there are in abundance Missionary or Regular Baptists, Primitive Baptists, United Baptists, Free-Will Baptists, Duck River Baptists, Free Baptists, and others—eleven kinds in all. Some of the Primitive or Hardshell Baptists wash feet and some do not. Missionary Baptists are divided into Northern, Southern, and National conventions. When one tries to explain the differences among them he runs into an apt subject for a theological dissertation, for they split hairs on many points of doctrine. Apparently the only point upon which they all agree is that immersion is the only holy, decent, and fitting way to be baptized.

Second in strength is the Methodist church, which has possibly 35 per cent of the total church membership in the mountains. There are a few Christian or Campbellite churches in the towns and villages, but Catholics and Episcopalians are as scarce as Negroes.

Forty years ago John Fox wrote: "He [the mountaineer] is the only man in the world whom the Catholic church has made little or no effort to proselyte. Dislike of Episcopalianism is still strong among people who do not know, or pretend not to know, what the word means. 'Any Episcopalians around here?' asked a clergyman at a mountain cabin. 'I don't know,' said the old woman. 'Jim's got the skins of a lot o' varmints up in the loft, mebbe you can find one up thar.' "

Were John Fox living today, however, he would find the Catholics were after the last man. They have not as yet made noticeable progress in eastern Kentucky, but they have in eastern Tennessee, and they prophesy that in half a century the hill people may be predominantly Catholic.

In the mountains there are preachers and preachers. Ninety per cent of them preach an emotional, hell-fire religion, but the most vehement of them all are the Holy Rollers. They have affected the entire rural church life. There are preachers who entice ladies of their congregations to fornication, and not one one-hundreth of them are ever found out. There are preachers who preach while they're drunk, though they are fewer than formerly. There are preachers, plenty of them, who just open their mouths and let God fill 'em. And some of the things God fills 'em with! There are preachers, too, of course, who are moral, honest, sincere, and self-sacrificing.

True in the case of mountain preachers is the axiom that one gets about what he pays for. There are a few intelligent and educated men, found generally in the larger towns, but the majority of them are men who eke their livings from the soil or the mines and preach because they feel the call. Often they are ignorant, elemental, intense in feeling, tenacious of dogma, prejudiced, narrow, and positive that their interpretations are the only interpretations.

Will of God

I have heard mountain preachers proclaim that their church was the only church and that members of all others were eternally damned. I have heard them maintain that baptisms not performed in running water were not valid. I have heard long and ridiculous arguments on predestination and on the eligibility of suicides for the kingdom of heaven. I have heard them thank God they could not read.

Withal, I doubt whether as many as a sixth of the highlanders are what a preacher would call good church members. Oh they go to services, because usually an entertaining show is presented. And sometimes they go even when the show isn't so good, for the simple reason there's little else to do.

Take the revival for instance. For maybe two weeks there's a regular jubilee of soul-saving. To those far from the cities these meetings are theater, night club, county fair, and church all thrown together. Neighbor meets neighbor in the chief social whirl of the season, and there is shouting, bounding, ecstasy, and catalepsy. There is a great spiritual uplift. Those who have sinned against God and man repent in the fervor of the meeting and are redeemed. They see visions of eternal glory and of the damnation they have barely missed. There is great rejoicing. Then two weeks later it's all just a memory.

A baptizing, too, is quite an event. Usually it comes at the end of a revival. Or it may be held in connection with a funeralizing, or just held. From out of the hollows they come to the chosen point at the creek—on foot, on mules, or standing like cattle in the bed of a truck. The women wear their best dresses, and still look frowzy. The men wear their dress-up suits or clean overalls. Those who are to be baptized generally dress in white.

The waters of the creek are quiet, for it is summer, and a rash of green reaches down to the muddy bank. The sycamores and birches and maples wave green leaves in the lazy breeze. A frog grunts and propels himself from a fallen log. Crawdads, their feelers waving, scrouge back under sunken roots that look like water snakes. A brilliant cardinal trills close by, then flies away, leaving the jar-flies singing in the trees. A snake-doctor skims along the water. There is a clean, earthy smell.

"They's pearch in this hole." The speaker is a blue-eyed, freckled-nosed kid of possibly ten whose towhead has been wetted down for the occasion.

"I've heared they was but I hain't never tried fer to see." The response comes from another youngster dressed in his dad's cut-down pants.

"I have," says the first speaker jubilantly. "I ketched five in here 'fore noon."

Other conversations are overheard as the folk gather at the creek bank. "How's yer corn, Anse?" "Wal, hit's purty tuk up with weeds. Only half through it th' first time." "Look at Maude. She's got nine young 'uns and she shore looks like she's gonna drap another soon."

The preacher ties a handkerchief over his head. His assistant does likewise. The preacher walks out into the creek, stirring up muddy eddies. With a piece of a fence rail he pokes around, feeling for snags, measuring here and there. "Wonder if they's any snap-turtles in here," he mumbles half to himself. "I know they is," whispers the towhead expectantly. "I seen one this mornin'."

The preacher has found a suitable spot, less than thigh deep. The assistant feels his way alongside. Sister Suke Simpson is first. She has tied a cloth around her dress below the knees, and she wades in like a hobbled horse.

The mixed quartet on the bank sings *a cappella:*

Yes, we'll gather at the river,
The beautiful, the beautiful river.
Yes, we'll gather at the river,
That flows by the throne of God.

The preacher places a handkerchief over his fingers and grabs Sister Suke by the nose. Sister Suke looks frightened, but she places a hand on each of the men's shoulders. The quartet sings louder. Splash! Sister Suke comes up waving her arms and heads for the bank as though she had seen a water moccasin. As she hits the bank she begins to shout, "Glory to God! Praise God! Hallelujah!" Other sisters and a number of brethren join in. Sister Suke tries to shout and leap and keep her dress from clinging between her legs all at the same time. The quartet sings crescendo.

Generalizations about anything are dangerous, and it strikes me they are particularly so when they concern what men believe or do not believe. In such a case one can judge only from careful observation of outward manifestations.

"Are the mountain people truly and deeply religious?" Obviously there must be exceptions to any answer to the question. Further, it depends upon what you mean by "religious." If a religious man is one who belongs to an accepted church, who attends faithfully, who believes in a liberal or broad translation of the Bible and who follows in his daily life the tenets laid down by his church and pastor, then the mountain people as a whole are not religious.

On the other hand they are religious in the way primitive men are religious. They believe in the supernatural causation of observed phenomena. They think illogically. They rely upon opinion and dogma rather than upon scientifically ascertained facts. They are fundamentalists. They are fatalists. They are absorbed in the letter of the holy writ to the exclusion of the concerns of their personal lives. There is little connection between their religious ideas and their ethics.

Their hair-splitting doctrinal disputes and their sectarian prejudices have made change difficult or well nigh impossible. Their otherworldliness has been a gigantic obstacle to progress and has prevented wholly or in part the development of a rational control over social conditions. Before each forward step can be taken—in health practices, in living conditions, in education—"the will of God" must be overcome. Hardships are to be blamed on their own or their neighbors' sins; so they sink into an apathy instead of fighting to overcome their difficulties. This fatalism stifles any impulse to change conditions. It is a passive as opposed to a dynamic philosophy. True, it has its advantage in that current misfortunes seem of small concern, and almost unbelievable suffering can be borne without a whimper.

A certain portion of the mountain people have ever been ready prey for emissaries of new cults and sects. Thus it is that Jehovah's Witnesses have gained a considerable following in the hills during the last year or so, although the old-line mountaineers have fought them bitterly and even ferociously.

The Witnesses have proselyted in the mountains as they have elsewhere in the United States—by personal conversations, by phonograph records, by sound trucks, by the distribution of literature—and since their belief is essentially a primitive folk faith it has gained converts in the hill country. Strangely enough the witnesses insist their movement is not a religion, and they condemn other religions, particularly Catholicism, as snares and rackets. They believe they are battling the hosts of Satan, that the great battle of Armageddon is due any day, and that only Jehovah's Witnesses will be saved.

The things for which they are best known and for which they have been the most persecuted are their semi-pacifism and their refusal to salute the flag. In one town after another they have been threatened, beaten, denied the use of meeting places. And this persecution has had about the same effect as the state's law against the handling of snakes in religious services.

In Harlan County six leaders were arrested and held in outrageously excessive bail for violation of Kentucky's sedition law, which provides prison terms up to twenty-one years and fines up to $1,000. Unable to get relief in the state courts they took their case to the Federal courts and won a truce in hostilities. A temporary cessation it was, though, and the U. S. Supreme Court may ultimately be called upon to decide the issue.

Not so new and much more widespread and potent is the Holiness sect or movement, sometimes referred to as the Holy Roller church. Its appeal lies in a combination of fatalism and rampant emotionalism. Its menace, aside from moral looseness sometimes engendered, lies in its gospel that death and disease are entirely acts of God and that it is a sin for a woman not to bear as many children as possible. It has made greater advances in point of membership during the last decade than any other church, possibly than any combination of churches, in the mountains. It has been particularly active in mining communities.

Here is a little church on a dusty byway of a mining camp. It's a rickety frame structure not much bigger than one of the wretchedly furnished miner's shacks that stand nearby. Pulsating tambourines can be heard, but above the medley of sounds from the meeting rise the laughter and strident voices of overalled males lolling outside. Fifteen or twenty of them in all, they're hitting the bottle. One of them cracks wise, and the others snicker or guffaw as the joke demands.

Jammed in a circle around a crude altar on the inside are about forty men and women of various ages, shapes, and sizes. Sitting a little apart from the group are five or six onlooking couples

A song has ended, and a nondescript man in khaki is taking up the breathing spell by reading Bible verses. When he finishes, a gangling fellow with a face like a turkey gobbler's begins to exhort, falling quickly into one of those cadences where an "ah" follows every few words.

"These is quare times-ah. These is perlous times-ah. You've got t' keep on th' narr' road-ah. I say you've got t' stay in th' blood-ah, th' blessed blood o' th' Lamb-ah.

"Now I know a feller-ah who's been married a-seven times-ah, and when he looks at ary woman-ah, he wonders how it would be t' sleep with her-ah. But th' Lord is a-punishin' him fer his sins-ah. He's a-payin' a-$50 t' one woman an' a-$35 to another an' a-$40 t' another. And praise God-ah, he's come t' be a pyore wreck of a man-ah."

"Hallelujah, serves him right!"

"Amen! Amen!"

Then in a more subdued tone, "And now we'll have a song, and while we're a-singin' if they's any of you brothers er sisters who wants to testify, why you jest git up an' testify. Unburden yer soul t' th' Lord an' he'll wash it clean. An' we'll rejoice with ye as ye lift th' load from yer hearts an' souls."

Someone starts to sing "I Know My Name Is There." Nasal voices twang, resonant tambourines thump and jingle, impatient feet drum the floor.

The preacher and the Bible reader start shaking hands with members of the congregation. Pretty soon everybody is shaking hands. Then they are slapping one another on the back. One man drops to his knees and begins to pray, pounding the wall to accentuate his agonies. Gobbler-face has an encouraging arm around one fat sister who is having a tough time comin' through.

One by one the brothers and sisters begin to testify. Words pour out in jumbled streams, but one can hear: "Lord, I done it t' Phronie Johnson." "Fergive me my weakness, Lord, I'm jes' a pore widder-woman." "O God I'm jes' a mizzable sinner."

One of the couples sitting apart from the group gets up and disappears into the night. Another and then a third follow.

Tears flow down the faces of some. Looks of supreme joy shine on the faces of others. The power hits one meat ax of a woman with vibrations that snap her body like electric shocks. She plunks to the floor in convulsions. The man who has been praying against the wall tries to climb it.

Suddenly there is a crash of glass and a rock whops squarely in the midst of the penitents. The crash is followed by a crack of a pistol. Everybody heads for the door.

The drunken bunch on the outside already is pushing excitedly around a man stretched on the ground. "I tol' that son of a bitch I'd lay him on th' coolin' board if he slung a rock through that winder." The speaker leans heavily on the shoulders of a companion, and the whisky in him talks loudly to the world. "He claimed th' Holy Rollers was jes' a bunch o' no-good bastards. I don't think much of 'em myself, but I don't believe in 'sturbin' worship."

VIII

And He Died

A. B. (HAPPY) CHANDLER didn't mean to start a feud; he meant only to succeed to the seat of United States Senator Alben W. Barkley. The Combses, nevertheless, are carrying on one of the liveliest Kentucky mountain wars in several years, all on account of Happy.

Elected Governor of Kentucky in 1935 the energetic, personable, ambitious young Chandler felt ready three years later to leave the gubernatorial chair and try to unseat President Roosevelt's senatorial right-hand man. And so it was that in the summer of 1938 Kentucky was indulging in one of the hottest Democratic primary campaigns in its history. In Breathitt, as in nearly every other county, the party was split asunder. Men who had been fast political friends were enemies now, some supporting the presumptuous young man with the smiling countenance, others the veteran whip hand of the New Deal.

Lee and Bill Combs were distant cousins and had been friends for many years. In 1930, when they ran for office together, Lee was elected sheriff and Bill jailer. But in 1938 Lee was assisting his brother, Lewis, in managing Chandler's campaign in Breathitt, and Bill, still jailer, was as strong a Barkley supporter as there was in all the hills.

The Democratic county chairman was Sollie L. Combs, father of Lee and Lewis. He, like his sons, was a Chandler man, and the Barkley supporters were trying to unseat him. Leading the ouster movement were Jailer Bill Combs, Sheriff Walter Deaton and his sons, WPA Foreman Wardie Jenkins, Circuit Court Clerk Goebel Allen, and Irvine Turner, state senator, county political boss, and husband of the county school superintendent.

Two nights before the great day of the August 6 primary Turner called pro-Barkley precinct workers and election officers to meet in the county superintendent's office in the Hargis Building, across the street from the Breathitt courthouse. Lee, Lewis, and Sollie understood that the Barkley men meant to elect a new county chairman and thus to remove Sollie from his position of influence. They heard a rumor, too, that ballot boxes were to be delivered to the polls the day before the primary. Such a delivery, they figured, would give their opponents an opportunity to stuff the boxes. Consequently Lee let it be known that he and his father and brother were going to the meeting, invited or not.

Trouble was in the air. Townspeople looking for excitement gathered around the courthouse early that summer evening. Those not looking for excitement went home.

At about eight o'clock Lee, Lewis, and Sollie walked down the street to the foot of the stairs leading up to the meeting room. There they met Sheriff Deaton, his right hand in his pistol pocket. According to the sheriff Lewis seized his right arm to keep him from drawing, and Sollie and Lee walked up the stairs. A minute later from the top of the steps came the sounds of voices, the slamming of a door, the crash of breaking glass. Refused admittance, Lee and his father had knocked the pane out of the door, then turned and walked away.

The Combses left, and Sollie went on down to the Chandler headquarters in the Maloney building. But fifteen or twenty minutes later Lee and Lewis returned. This time the brothers and Sheriff Deaton started up the stairs together, the sheriff trying to dissuade the two. They had walked only a few steps when from the second floor came a stabbing flash and the roar of a forty-five. Someone at the bottom answered the fire. A fusillade crashed back from the top. The three men stumbled out onto the sidewalk, and bystanders scattered for cover.

Lee, who had no pistol, dragged himself about twenty-five feet from the doorway, caught hold of a wire fence in front of a vacant lot, and slumped to the pavement. There was a hole in his chest, and he died.

Seriously hit, Lewis staggered to an automobile. He had two bullet holes in him, but he didn't die—then.

Deaton was the most fortunate. His bullet was in the arm.

To the Good Samaritan Hospital at Lexington, Deaton and Lewis were taken, but to rooms as widely separated as possible.

Next day twelve state troopers patrolled the streets of Jackson. All liquor stores and beer dispensaries were closed. But Friday and election day passed without fatalities. Chandler lost his senatorial race.

Meanwhile Sollie Combs swore to warrants for the arrest of five men: Jailer Combs, WPA Foreman Jenkins, and Circuit Clerk Allen for murder; Irvine Turner and Linville Carpenter for aiding and abetting.

At Lexington, Deputy Sheriff Fred Deaton stood guard night and day in his father's room. But there was no trouble there, and Walter Deaton recovered and returned to Jackson.

Lewis Combs went back, too, somewhat later. He rode in a state police car ordered to the hospital by Governor Chandler.

County Judge Pearl Campbell, an uncle of the Combs brothers, held preliminary hearings for the five men Sollie accused. Turner, Carpenter, and Allen were freed. Bill Combs and Jenkins were held for the grand jury. Subsequently the two were indicted and granted a change of venue to Hindman but were never tried. The commonwealth's attorney said he didn't have sufficient evidence to prosecute.

The public will never know who killed Lee Combs, but Lewis and Sollie thought they knew. Jailer Bill Combs, released on bond, decided it might be best for him to take a trip. He went to the Veterans' Hospital at Huntington, West Virginia, so it was said. Lewis and Sollie blamed Irvine Turner too—not for the actual shooting but for calling the meeting that started the trouble.

After Lewis Combs returned from the Lexington hospital someone fired through the transom of Turner's office. Turner wasn't hit. A few nights later Lewis called at Turner's home. Answering the knock Mrs. Turner's mother told Lewis that Irvine wasn't at home.

Bill Combs returned to Jackson, and he and Sollie met by accident in Judge Campbell's office. Both drew, but someone shoved Sollie out the door before either could fire, so neither died—then.

Other brushes occurred from time to time, and it was an open secret that Senator Irvine Turner and Jailer Bill Combs were marked men. Young, one-armed Fred Deaton became a sort of bodyguard for Turner. The state senator has denied that he ever employed Deaton as such, but the fact remains that the twenty-eight-year-old deputy sheriff was with him almost constantly.

At evening-mail time one Saturday in February 1940 Lewis Combs and Fred Deaton met on the main street of Jackson and walked down the hill to the post office together. Passersby looked on in amazement. The men were sworn enemies. The two were talking, but no one heard what they said. A few minutes later the crowd at the post office saw Deaton reach for his pistol with his lone right hand, saw Combs pull his and fire. When the revolvers quit spitting lead, Combs, shot through the breast, was spitting blood. Deaton, wounded in the side, hip, and legs, was stretched on the sidewalk. Martha Ellen Johnson, a young high-school girl who was so unfortunate as to be caught in the range of fire, had a bullet in her groin.

Lewis managed to stumble to the near-by home of Howard Lucas, lie down on a couch, and gasp that he wanted a doctor. But he was desperately hurt, and three hours later he died.

They took Fred back to the hospital where he had stood guard over his father. He did not die, but he never quite recovered either. Indicted for murder, he had not been tried more than a year after the shooting.

Martha Ellen Johnson lay for day upon day between life and death. She still carries the bullet.

Loafing around the Chevrolet garage on a Saturday night two months after the duel were a number of men who represented both sides of the war. Jailer Bill Combs came in with his deputy, Bent Sizemore. Bill was drunk, and he and Boone Combs, a cousin of the dead brothers as well as of the jailer, got in an argument about the previous shootings. Boone, so the witnesses said, had no gun, but Jailer Bill pulled his, waved it threateningly, let fire under Boone's feet. Patrolman Lewis Watkins hurried in and took Bill outside. Watkins said he started to lock Bill up in Bill's own jail but turned him loose when he promised to go home and to bed.

Next day there was a funeral at a little church about a mile and a half out of Jackson on the Hazard road. Boone Combs, his brothers, Pete and Rudell, and Wilgus Terry and Arthur Lee got in Pete's truck and took the corpse out to the graveyard.

Near the church lived Gus Combs, uncle of the jailer. Bill and his wife, Mary, happened to drive out to Uncle Gus's at about the time of the funeral. Bill parked his car in front of Hager Combs' house, about forty feet from Gus Combs'. As the jailer and his wife walked up toward Hager's, a group of men opened fire from the road. Bill and Mary made it to Hager's home, but Bill ran on out the back door and headed for Gus's. He pulled his pistol; its handle was shot off in his hand. He leaped at the door of Gus Combs' house, but it was locked and he was trapped. He fell there on the porch with five bullet holes in him. One, made by a high-powered rifle, was as big as a quarter. Jailer Bill died.

In town, Deputy Jailer Bent Sizemore and Bill's stepson, Jesse Noble, heard what had taken place. They set out afoot toward the scene of the assassination. At the edge of town they met five men in a truck and the shooting started again. Sizemore and Noble plunged into a little ravine and then zigzagged up the hill like rabbits, Sizemore firing back as he ran. Jesse made it to a tree, but Bent didn't. He had a .44-caliber bullet in his back and he died.

Boone, Pete, and Rudell Combs and Arthur Lee and Wilgus Terry were arrested a few hours later. All five were indicted on murder charges, freed on bond, and granted a change of venue. In the spring of 1941 Rudell was tried at Salyersville for the Sizemore slaying. The jurors deadlocked at eight for acquittal, four for conviction.

Five months after Bill and Bent had fired their last shots, Pete, who runs a furniture store, drove his truck to Salyersville to see a mine foreman. As he and the foreman drove back toward Jackson that afternoon a man raised up from the bushes alongside the road and blazed away with a shotgun. A part of the charge caught Pete in the head, but it didn't kill him. Pete and the foreman said they recognized the ambusher as Henry Marshall, a brother of Bill Combs' wife. Marshall was indicted for malicious shooting but had not been tried when this report closed.

Between the war's opening and the ambushing of Pete the Combses and the Deatons starred in two other fatal shootings.

On February 5, 1940, Deputy Sheriff Jerry Combs, only remotely related to Lee and Lewis, was called to the WPA commodities-distribution center, where the Howard brothers, Tom and Brown, were raising cain. They had told the clerk they didn't care whether it was distribution day or not, they had come for their grub and they meant to take it along. Jerry told the two he would have to arrest them if they didn't drop the sacks of food they had collected. One of the Howards shot Jerry through the back of the head and he died.

A month later Mose Bush, Wilson Deaton, good looking thirty-one-year-old deputy sheriff under his father, and a number of others were en route from Jackson to their homes in the Longs Creek section when a bullet whistled through their truck. Getting out to investigate, Deaton and Bush found four men brawling by the roadside, two girls urging them on. Bush and Deaton tried to stop the fight. For their trouble Mose got pinked in the arm, Deaton got a gaping thirty-thirty rifle-bullet hole through his chest. Deaton died.

It is generally agreed that the Jerry Combs and Wilson Deaton killings were not directly connected with the Combs vs. Combs-Deaton trouble. There was an incidental connection, however, in that two of the four men arrested for Wilson Deaton's slaying were cousins of the wife of Lewis Combs, who was killed by Fred Deaton, Wilson's brother.

Of the four arrested in Wilson Deaton's death, one, Woodrow Salyers, has been tried. As spectators filed into the courtroom at his trial in Beattyville they were asked to check their pistols at the door. The officers collected thirty, but there was no shooting and—wonder of wonders—Salyers got fifteen years.

In the fall of 1940 Joe Jordan wrote in the Lexington *Leader* a column that expresses the public's mystification at mountain feuds. The immediate cause for the comment was Sheriff Walter Deaton's latest trouble, an indictment charging him with malfeasance in office, but the writer was principally concerned with the feud. He wrote:

> According to the news dispatches, Sheriff Walter Deaton of Breathitt County is having some more trouble—as if he hadn't had enough trouble, one of his sons having been shot to death, and another of his sons facing trial on a murder charge. I became very well acquainted with Mr. Deaton when he was a patient in a Lexington hospital (being treated for gunshot wounds, of course), and also with one of his sons, Fred, who was there with him. They both seemed to be very nice fellows. In the course of my reporting duties, I visited Mr. Deaton's hospital room every day, and usually sat and talked with him and Fred for 20 or 30 minutes.
>
> In another room at the same hospital, at the same time, was Lewis Combs of Breathitt County, also being treated for gunshot wounds. His wife was here with him, and they seemed to be nice people, too. I visited them every day, and got to liking them and the Deatons equally well. Now Lewis Combs is dead—he's the one Fred Deaton is accused of having killed. You might have thought none of them would have wanted to be bothered by a reporter at such a time, but I was never treated better or received more cordially by anyone than by Mr. and Mrs. Combs and the two Deatons.
>
> The reason I have gone into this at some length is that I have an idea that some of you must think these are terrible people who are always getting into trouble up there at Jackson and shooting one another. But you wouldn't think so if you met and talked with them. The ones I got to know so well were on opposite sides, and they all seemed to be all right. It's a mystery to me why they can't get along.

Jordan was entirely correct in saying "they all seemed to be all right." They are not people from depraved families. They are not wicked, malicious individuals. The Combs family, two branches of which are engaged in the deadly war, springs from as good stock as there is in Kentucky. At the turn of the century Ellen C. Semple wrote that though the mountain people were the exponents of a retarded civilization and showed the degenerate symptoms of an arrested development, their stock was of the best. "They formed," she said, "a part of the same tide of pioneers which crossed the mountains to people the young states to the southwest, but they chanced to turn aside from the main stream, and ever since have stagnated in these mountain hollows. For example, over a hundred years ago, eleven Combs brothers, related to General Combs of the Revolutionary army, came over the mountains from North Carolina. Nine of them settled along the North Fork of the Kentucky River in the mountains of Perry County, one went farther down the stream into the rough hill country of Breathitt County, and the eleventh continued on his way till he came into the smiling region of the Bluegrass, and there became the progenitor of a family which represents the blue blood of the Old South; while their cousins in the mountains go barefoot, herd in one-room cabins, and are ignorant of many of the fundamental decencies of life."

Miss Semple stretched a point in writing as though all the mountain Combses "go barefoot, herd in one-room cabins, and are ignorant of many of the fundamental decencies of life." That was true of some in the early days; it was never true of others, outstanding citizens in the hills since the brothers came in from North Carolina.

It is probable that no words can explain exactly and conclusively why the mountain people shoot one another, but a look into the background and an examination of contributing causes helps toward an understanding.

At least sixteen factors have brought on feuds or perpetuated them. They are: (1) vindictiveness; (2) whisky; (3) women; (4) hot tempers; (5) preoccupation with guns and gun-toting; (6) quarrels over insignificant matters; (7) pure cussedness; (8) a disregard for human life; (9) the Civil War; (10) slow-moving or corrupt legal "justice"; (11) the attitude of nonparticipants toward the feuds; (12) politics; (13) disputes over land boundaries; (14) a code of honor that calls for shooting it out; (15) "social distinction" attaching to gun play, and (16) a scarcity of distractions.

No clear line can be drawn between the factors that start the shooting and those that keep it going. Some have worked both ways, and no single one is entirely responsible for any feud. To understand the part the factors play, each must be examined.

If there is a synonym for vindictiveness it is mountaineer. The highlander never forgets an insult, real or imagined. He feels he has been wronged and he is not content until he has settled the score in his own way. The power to forgive and forget is not in him. This trait perhaps more than any other causes prolongation of the feuds. It is, moreover, in part responsible for the ugliest characteristic of the mountain feud, the shot in the back. When the hillsman seeks revenge he's not particular how he gets it. To the average person it is one thing to kill a man in a fit of anger, another to mow him down from ambush or to "gang" him four or five to one. There was a certain romance, perverted though it was, in the shootings of the Old West. Men met face to face, both drew, and the best shot won. That was the "Code of the West." It is not the "Code of the Hills." The highlanders call a feud a war, and a war it is. The aim is to get your man, and to get him with as little danger to yourself as possible. Yet the mountaineer is not a coward. His "laywayings" and his "gangings" seem to him merely the simplest methods. He is capable of high courage and on occasion can exhibit chivalry. John C. Campbell tells of an occurrence between two young men he calls Brown and English, representatives of opposite sides in a feud and, in addition, participants in a personal quarrel. The two went to the county seat one day, he relates, but chanced not to meet while there. English left in his wagon that afternoon and Brown left a little later astride his mule. As Brown rounded a bend in the road he saw English ahead, fully armed but unaware of Brown's presence. Three courses were open to Brown. He could shoot English in the back and escape without danger to himself; he could turn and ride back to town; or he could pass and run the risk of being shot. Brown happened to be one of those exceptional mountaineers to whom the first idea seemed repellent. He regarded the second as cowardly; and so he chose the third. He rode forward quickly, hands on the reins away from his pistols. From the corner of his eye as he passed he saw English start, reach for his pockets, then pause, pistols half drawn, as he realized he had been at the mercy of the man now in front of him. Without turning or accelerating his pace Brown rode on out of sight. From that time on the two preserved a silent truce. Years later, when the feud had died out, the two worked in civil office together, but they never spoke to each other except when necessary.

The factors of whisky, women, hot tempers, gun-toting, and quarrels over insignificant things are so closely linked that they can be discussed together. Shooting irons have a fascination and a clinical interest for the highlander. When he is a child he looks forward to the day when he can own one, and when he is an adult he is as proud of his pistol as anything he has. He talks about its caliber, its weight, its balance, its pearl handle, its accuracy. Now let two gun-toting mountaineers get full of whisky, let their fiery tempers flare, and there can be only one result. Sometimes they shoot because one makes a jest the other doesn't like. Arguments over cards, horseshoe games, a stray shoat, a horse trade, a girl, or a box at a pie supper often lead to homicide. It is not unusual for good friends to blaze away when they're under the influence of liquor and their tempers, and it is a certainty that trouble will ensue when two men who bear grudges meet under such circumstances. Wars dormant for years have flamed anew after the clash of drunken representatives of opposite sides. Women play a double role in the killings and subsequent feuds. At times they are merely the objects of argument. At other times they play an active part by urging their menfolk to do battle. As Kephart says, "The average mountain woman is as combative in spirit as her menfolk. She would despise any man who took insult or injury without showing fight. In fact, the woman, in many cases, deliberately stirs up trouble out of vanity, or for the sheer excitement of it."

Few mountaineers are actually mean, as city gun thugs are mean, and thus "pure cussedness" is an exceptional rather than a general cause. But the few sometimes start trouble just for the sake of starting it, and among them are men who take advantage of a feud to vent their own meanness. Such persons, for instance, may not be concerned with a feud but will shoot from ambush participants they don't like, knowing the shootings will be laid to the other faction.

About the only thing that can be said of the mountaineer's disregard for human life is that it exists. Possibly it derives from traditions that are somewhat medieval, but much more probably it comes of long association with nature and a subconscious recognition of her rule of survival of the fittest.

Certainly the Civil War has no direct connection with any feud now in progress, but many of the first vendettas stemmed from it, and they provided the precedent for those that followed. The Civil War in the mountains of Kentucky consisted principally of raids by bands of Union men and retaliatory raids by bands of Confederates. Some of these bushwhacking gangs were not recognized officially by either army. Like the official detachments, however, they looted, burned, pillaged, raped, and incited hatreds that led to many private wars long after the national war was over.

Slow-moving or corrupt legal "justice" has played its part in almost every mountain feud. The mountaineer doesn't disregard the law because he doesn't understand it. Rare is the highlander who has never been a defendant, a complainant, a witness, or a juror; rare indeed the man who doesn't know how to obtain or escape a summons, how to get out on bond, how to delay trials for months or years, how to buy witnesses, how to play dumb when the need arises, how to confuse the prosecutor, how to influence the jurors. The mountaineer disregards the law because he is contemptuous of it. To him court procedure is no sacred ritual but a game in which the cleverest man wins. He thinks nothing of perjuring himself. With one hand on the Bible and the other on his gun he'll swear to tell the truth, then lie magnificently to help a friend or relative. The feud participant knows he will not get unbiased treatment, because it is well nigh impossible to find twelve jurors, a judge, a prosecuting attorney, and witnesses who have no connection—politically, economically, or by blood—with any of the principals or their kinfolk. If the feudist has a friendly court he will "come clear." If he has an unfriendly court it's up to him to finagle some way to beat the law.

An old mountaineer once told me, "There's a prejudice in this county against th' court a-hangin' a man." And I'm willing to believe there's a prejudice against punishing a man at all. If there has been more than one death penalty meted out to a mountaineer for murder in the last ten years I've been unable to find any record of it. Time after time I've seen juries "disagree" in the face of evidence that should send a man to the electric chair. And even when a man is convicted, five, ten, fifteen years, life (which actually means eight years in Kentucky) is the limit. Consequently the mountaineer looks at it this way: "This man has killed my father. If I let the law take its course he may not be tried for years, and then he won't be punished adequately. He'll 'come clear' through some legal shenanigans or, if he's unlucky, get five or ten years. I'll just kill him myself. Even if I'm caught and tried I'll get off light."

And He Died

Killings in which the principals are persons who should already have been in the penitentiary are so frequent their number cannot be estimated. I recall one story that is typical. A Leslie County youth shot and killed his brother during an argument over some insignificant matter. The boy who did the shooting had been convicted of murder and given a short sentence, of which he had served only a small part. The brother also had been convicted of murder, and the circumstances were so extreme he had been given the death penalty. But the verdict had been set aside, and on a retrial he had received a life sentence. After serving three years he was pardoned by the Governor. After the fratricide the weekly at Hyden wrote that "the county attorney was unable to procure evidence showing facts other than that the killing was justified."

Active feudists are and always have been a very small proportion of the mountain population, but the nonparticipants are tolerant of the wars and have made no concerted effort to stamp them out. An analogy can be draw between the attitude of the mountain Kentuckians toward the feuds and killings and of Bluegrass Kentuckians toward handbooks where bets are placed on races. The central Kentuckians tell one another how disgraceful is the handbook situation, but they resent any comment from outsiders. When some crusading official starts an anti-handbook campaign, raids the places, and arrests the operators, the people pretend to be "on the side of the law." But then when time for the trial comes the good citizens either refuse to be witnesses, disclaiming any knowledge of the handbooks, or testify as though their memories had completely failed them. As a result the operators either are acquitted or given a slap on the wrist in the form of a $50 or $100 fine. Next day the handbooks are open again. Feuds work the same way. The people tell one another what bad things the wars are, but they get hot enough to start a new one if someone else calls the mountains feuding country.

Crusades are useless. When and if arrests are made and trials are held, witnesses forget everything they ever knew or tell such conflicting tales no juror can determine what really happened, even if he wants to. The reason for both situations is the same: The people aren't actually opposed.

The Combs-Combs war is a good example of one started by a political argument, although the quarrel was unusual in that it concerned a race not primarily of local interest. The mountaineer loves politics as he loves guns, but generally he is only incidentally interested in state and national campaigns. The hottest arguments, and consequently the bloodiest killings and feuds, stem from school-board contests and county officials' races. Politics, moreover, is directly connected with corruption of the courts as a cause of feuds. The duty of an officer to his office all too frequently is secondary to his family ties and political friendships. Thus a political argument may start a war, and political alliances, bringing about injustices in the courts, perpetuate it.

Land-boundary disputes were among the first causes of feuds, and down through the years they have brought more than their share of trouble. In 1776 Kentucky was made a Virginia county. A year later the Virginia General Assembly passed the first of its land laws. The settlement and preemption sections of the measure seemed fair enough, and the law of 1777, as well as a statute adopted two years later, had the desired effect of stimulating immigration into Kentucky. Hunters of land succeeded the hunters of game. Homesteaders were quick to make their claims. Land speculators acquired huge tracts. Many soldiers of the Revolutionary War took their pay in land warrants. But the Virginia laws had one great defect. Instead of specifying that the territory should be laid off in square blocks and subdivided into half sections and quarter sections the laws allowed each warrant holder to locate his land where he pleased and in whatever shape he desired. He had only to survey his land, or pay others to survey it, then make an entry to obtain a warranty deed. The results of such a system should have been foreseen. Men staked out claims in every shape imaginable. In consequence two or three claims often were made to one section, whereas other sections were unclaimed no-man's lands. Surveys and patents were piled on one another, overlapping and crossing in endless perplexity. When the country became more thickly settled, the sour fruits of this system began to be reaped.

After Kentucky became a state in 1792 it took over administration of the land laws. But instead of helping matters it further confused them by permitting the continued filing of claims just as they had been filed under the Virginia measures.

Disputes over land boundaries began almost with the enaction of the Virginia laws, but in the mountains it was not until after the Civil War, when family began to bump against family as the population increased, that the real trouble started. Sometimes three families had settled on the same land, and each felt that it had a just claim. Courts were far away and very slow. The rifle brought quicker "justice."

The land laws resulted not only in feuds but in endless litigation. It is probable that at no time in the last 160 years have the court dockets been wholly cleared of land disputes. Pending before the United States Court for the Eastern District of Kentucky in 1941 was a suit in which the Pen-Ken Gas and Oil Corporation sought $70,466,900 from the Warfield Natural Gas Company for alleged infringement upon 130,400 acres of land in Floyd and adjacent counties. Pen-Ken contended it held title to the land through a patent issued to one Benjamin Haskell and filed at Buchanan, Virginia, before Kentucky was divorced from Virginia. This claim was made after Warfield had held its lands for from fifteen to twenty years.

Not all the boundary disputes of course have arisen from the old patents, and some of the quarrels have been amusing rather than tragic. Not long ago the Breathitt County grand jury indicted two Perry County deputies and eight other persons on charges of corn-stealing. The trouble started when Jim Deaton and Robert Strong got into an argument over ownership of a field on the Perry-Breathitt line. The men agreed that the county line divided their farms, but they disagreed as to the location of the line. (Recent WPA surveys have shown that many county lines were marked incorrectly or inexactly.) They took their case to court, and the circuit judge upheld Strong's claim to the field. Deaton appealed to the Kentucky Court of Appeals, meanwhile planting himself a crop of corn on the tract in dispute. The appellate court upheld the circuit court. Strong got a writ of attachment, and he, his wife, two deputies, and six neighbors proceeded to gather the corn Deaton had planted. Infuriated, Deaton appeared before the Breathitt grand jury and succeeded in having all ten indicted for stealing corn. When Judge Brack Howard, of the Breathitt-Magoffin district, heard what had happened he threw the cases out of court.

One of the mountain weeklies reported in typical style a story along the same line: "A. L. Brewer and James Stacy," the paper said, "are having a hard time in getting their case tried as to who has the right to possession of a piece of land on Hal's fork of Big creek in this [Leslie] county. They have already had two trials before a jury in which cases the jury could not agree and last Saturday the case was called up for trial again in the quarterly court and after much argument of the counsel on both sides the case was then referred to the county judge for trial without an intervention of a jury and up to this time the judge has not been able to determine who is entitled to the possession. It is a hard case."

The "code of honor" is a real and powerful factor both in starting and prolonging feuds. It wasn't so many years ago that a man in any part of the United States felt honor bound to avenge an insult with his shooting arm. This code still holds in the mountains. Suppose one highlander shoots another, not fatally. The shooter is tried, but he has political influence and is acquitted even in the face of conclusive evidence against him. The wounded man then has three courses open to him. He can accept the verdict and make no further attempt to settle the score, but he will be called a coward. He can leave the mountains to avoid trouble, but he still will be called a coward. He can shoot the man who shot him. The "code of honor" says he must choose the third.

The "social distinction" cause is closely related to the "code of honor." If a man avenges himself he is highly regarded. If he does not he is socially ostracized. Moreover a man who has killed others acquires a sort of Jesse James glamour. The lowlander distinguishes himself through accomplishments of an intellectual type, the highlander through his physical prowess and his shooting eye. In other words the mountain man can strut a little more proudly when he has it said of him in a tone of awe, "There goes the feller that blowed hell outta ole Lattice-mouth Jim Day and filled Prig-nose John Callahan so full o' lead he never got up."

In a land where distractions are scarce, feuds take on an exaggerated importance. A personal quarrel is of relatively little moment to the outland man, because he has so many other things to occupy his mind in a world geared to a nerve-shattering pace. His personal quarrel is forgotten or disregarded in the whirl of business and social life, the rapidly moving world events. But the mountaineer, even today, is not so occupied. Only things that affect him directly are important. His life moves more slowly. He has time to mull over his grudges and his arguments.

A number of writers give credence to a theory that the feuds are holdovers from the interclan wars of Scotland. Charles Mutzenberg even went so far as to say, "Scotland had her feuds—those of the Kentucky mountains are nothing more nor less than transplanted Scottish feuds." That statement is exaggeration if not pure fiction. The mountain people were by no means of pure Scottish ancestry. They were a mixture of Scotch, Irish, English, German, French, and a few sidelines. Moreover the mountain pioneers sprang from the same stock as the lowland settlers, and lowland feuds have been so rare as to be virtually nonexistent. Finally there were no feuds in the hills until after the Civil War, sixty years after the "transplantation." On the other hand it is undeniably true that the mountaineers possess a clannishness, inherited or acquired and not always determined by blood ties, that has been a factor in the perpetuation of feuds.

Another explanation, so false it is laughable, is that the mountain people developed from Indian-fighting a bloodthirstiness they exercise through the gentle art of killing one another. In expounding this theory J. H. Combs, a native of the hills who moved to the lowlands, said, "In the pioneer days these people were compelled to bear the brunt of fighting the Cherokee and other Indian tribes, while the people of the plains were molested with comparative rarity." The fact of course is that the hills were not settled until the Indians were all but driven from the state, and it was the earlier settlers on the level land who bore the brunt of Indian-fighting.

So much for the causes of feuds. It might be well now to consider the prevalence of such wars today as compared to yesterday. There are three opinions: that the feuds are extinct, or virtually so; that they are almost as prevalent as ever; that they are passing, but passing mighty slowly. I choose the third. I know of a certainty that they are not extinct. I know on the other hand that there are far fewer feuds and that the vendettas are fought on a lesser scale than in former years. The Combs-Combs trouble, by way of example, is dwarfed by the Amis-Strong, the Jett-Little and the Hargis-Cockrell-Marcum-Callahan feuds of former years in Breathitt, the French-Eversole war in Perry, the Hatfield-McCoy in Pike and across the West Virginia line, the Tolliver-Martin-

Logan in Rowan, and numerous others in various sections of the highlands.

The Hargis-Cockrell-Marcum-Callahan vendetta lasted nearly fourteen years and more than 100 men were killed. It started in 1899 when the Republicans (or Fusionists) contested the election of James Hargis and Ed Callahan, Democrats, to the offices of county judge and sheriff respectively. During the taking of depositions in the law offices of J. B. Marcum, attorney for the Hargises, tempers flared and guns were drawn. No one was shot, but the police judge issued warrants for several men, including Judge Hargis. When Town Marshal Tom Cockrell and his brother, James Cockrell, went to arrest Hargis the judge resisted, and the two, so he said, drew guns on him. He swore they would pay for the insult.

Shortly after this occurrence Tom Cockrell and Ben Hargis, the judge's brother, met in a saloon and shot it out. Hargis was killed and Cockrell wounded. The war was on in earnest.

From that time until Ed Callahan was shot down in 1912 the feud raged with every highlight and sidelight that any feud ever possessed. There were ambushings and gangings, duels and assassinations. There were arson and patricide. There were trials and political intrigues. There was martial law.

Among those who died were:

John Hargis, another of the judge's brothers, who was killed in a duel with railroad detective Jerry Cardwell on a train bound from Jackson to Beattyville.

Dr. D. B. Cox, a kinsman of the Cockrells, assassinated one night while he was making a professional call.

James Cockrell, shot in broad daylight from a second-floor window of the courthouse. (Curt Jett, a deputy sheriff under Callahan, was convicted of the murder. Jett still lives today—in another section of the mountains.)

J. B. Marcum, the lawyer, who was also a United States Commissioner and a trustee of Kentucky State College, now the University of Kentucky. (He was shot in the back as he stood in a corridor of the courthouse one morning shortly after he had returned to Jackson upon receiving assurances that he would be "as safe at Jackson as any place else." Charles Mutzenberg wrote: "Immediately after the assassination of Marcum, and for a long time afterwards, conditions at Jackson were terrible. . . . Many relatives of Marcum, the Cockrells and their sympathizers left town and sought refuge elsewhere. No one dared travel the streets of Jackson at night who was not sure of the protection of those who held it in their grasp. Churches were deserted; for many months no services were held. It was with the utmost difficulty that any person could be brought to even speak of the matter in any way. Everybody was suspicious of everybody else." It was after the death of Marcum that troops were sent to Jackson and martial law was in effect for several months.)

Judge Hargis, the leader, along with Sheriff Callahan, of the Hargis-Callahan side. (He was riddled with bullets by his own son, Beach, and though the son received a life sentence the Court of Appeals wrote that Judge James Hargis was a "savage, cruel man" who "had established in the county of Breathitt a reign of terror.")

Ed Callahan, who was shot from a hillside ambush as he stood behind the palisade he had built for his protection at his store in Crocketsville, about twenty miles from Jackson.

Undoubtedly the feuds are rarer and less destructive today, but guns still take their toll. Comparatively few of the killings in the Kentucky mountains are connected with feuds, but all are prompted by some of the same factors—temper, vindictiveness, whisky, "code of honor," lack of fear of the law, barbaric disregard for human life, exaggeration of minor grievances, and gun-toting.

Just as in the case of the feuds the men who participate in

the individual shootings are by no means all outlaws or degenerates. Within the last year high-ranking private citizens, jailers, postmasters, sheriff's deputies, constables, judges, state legislators, and court attachés have been charged with participating in gun battles. The average mankiller or feudist is no wild man. He ordinarily is a levelheaded commoner, reasonably honest and abstemious. But somebody says something and the shooting starts.

The killings follow the century-old pattern. Only the scene has changed–from saloon and byway to roadhouse and highway. During the course of a year I clipped from newspapers seventy-one stories on fatal shootings in eastern Kentucky. I made no particular effort to get them all. When I saw one I hadn't had before I just cut it out, and seventy-one was the total. The stories were strikingly similar. Contrary to accusations, moreover, they generally were brief and unsensational. For example: "Hazard, Ky., Oct. 4–Constable Ed Combs reported today he had returned Bosie Holbrook, 25, of Big Leatherwood, from Wise, Va., to await trial in Perry County on a charge of shooting to death Bill Adams, 40, Leatherwood logger and father of four, in an argument over a card game."

Just plain, ordinary shootings in eastern Kentucky are as prosaic as mine deaths in West Virginia. They happen every day, rating generally just a few paragraphs. Unusual angles of course make them worth better play. When a woman cut loose with a pistol during a trial at Jackson, killed two men and wounded another, that was a story for anybody's newspaper. But usually the stories aren't worth much as news, and on Mondays the Associated Press rounds up the week-end shootings like this: "Four men and a girl are dead, three persons are in hospitals and three men were arrested as a result of gunplay in Kentucky during a 48-hour period ending last night. . . ."

What about statistics? Well, Breathitt has few if any

more homicides than Perry, Harlan, and some of the others, so it can be cited as an example. In 1935 homicide, with a score of seventeen, was the leading cause of death. In 1936 homicide tied with heart disease at twenty each. In 1937, 1938, and 1939 it ranked ninth, sixth, and fifth respectively. Breathitt's homicide rate for 1940 was 45.94 per 100,000 population. Kentucky's was 13.3.

The good citizens of Breathitt are irked no end by the name "Bloody Breathitt" and by any story that points to the large number of killings. I can't say that I blame them, for they love their county. Unhappily the facts are against them. No amount of argument stemming from civic pride can get around such little stories as this one:

"Jackson, Ky., March 19 [1941] (AP)—Prompted by the occurrence of two homicides in four days, Judge Chester Bach today called a special term of Breathitt circuit court and ordered the grand jury to meet next Tuesday

"Judge Bach's action was taken shortly after County Judge Pearl Campbell issued a warrant charging John Morgan Allen, 22, and James Fugate, 20, with the rifle slaying Friday of Buery Allen, 45, John Morgan's father, in the South Fork section 40 miles east of Jackson.

"Earlier Judge Campbell issued a warrant charging Rufus Roberts, 25, of Woolverine, an ex-soldier, with killing Roy Chapman, 27, Monday night at a roadhouse which Coroner James T. Goff said had been the scene of 10 deaths. Deputy Sheriff Hiram Smith said Roberts was jailed last night.

"Judge Bach's order said he believed 'the occurrence of these tragedies should receive official notice that such a condition exists in this county that warrants the holding of a special term of court for investigation in order to ascertain those guilty, and, if indictments are returned, to try the case or cases.' "

Breathitt County isn't the only offender. In February of 1941 the Harlan circuit court clerk reported with some pride that for the forthcoming criminal term there were only eight murder cases, the fewest in many years on a regular docket in Harlan County.

While I was collecting the seventy-one clippings on shootings I picked up only eighteen on other crimes, not including such misdemeanors as breach of the peace and drunkenness. That's a representative proportion. In all fairness it must be said that whereas the mountains have a maximum homicide rate, they have a minimum rate for other types of crimes. Court dockets generally aren't cluttered with charges of armed robbery, arson, rape, burglary, storehouse-breaking, grand larceny, and counterfeiting. There are mighty few sex crimes. Sex is still simple and easy and unperverted in the mountains. Civilization will fix that.

IX

Jacks in a Jenny-Barn

HIGHWAYS LINKING THE COUNTY SEATS and byways jutting a few miles up the hollows have brought a degree of modernization to eastern Kentucky, but they also have brought roadhouses.

Problems born of the juke-joints certainly are not peculiar to the mountains, but they are newer and deeper there. The mountain people are fun-loving and for years they have been fun-starved. They find in the roadhouses a new and compelling thrill. They are like youngsters who suddenly break loose from overindulgent parents and snatch at life with violence and abandon. Thus whisky-and-dance establishments spring up along each new road, young and old patronize them, morals are loose, and brawls and shootings are frequent. These facts must be understood, else an account of an ordinary evening at one of the places sounds like pure fiction.

I had stopped for the night in one of the smaller mountain county seats. I tossed a grip on the bed and looked around the room. What a room!—rough floors partly covered by ragged matting and a coat of dust; water-stained wallpaper upon which previous guests had scrawled their names; an old dresser from which the veneer had cracked; a crazy-house mirror; a china wash bowl, ringed by dirty water, and a china pitcher; a porcelain slop jar filled with water and floating cigarette butts; two nails on the back of the door and one bent coat hanger; murky windows lined by the last shower; an iron bed with a tattered quilt as a counterpane.

Stretching out on the bed I bounced up and down a couple of times. Not too uncomfortable. What did I expect for fifty cents anyway?

I was hopping around on one foot, trying to get the other into a trousers leg, when the door opened without warning and someone offered, "Let's go jenny-barnin'."

I had never seen the fellow before, but there he was in my room and evidently addressing me. "You mean what?" I asked.

"I mean let's you an' me go to one of the jenny-barns and have a little fun."

"Jenny-barns. That's what you call the roadhouses?"

"Sure."

"Not a bad name for 'em at that."

He grinned, showing two big front teeth. They were set so widely apart you could have stuck your fist in his mouth and never touched a knuckle. About thirty, he was tall and angular. His mouth was enormous, and when he grinned he looked like a jack-o'-lantern. His hair had receded to the very top of his head, where a thin tuft stuck straight up. "Wanna go?" he asked.

"Why, I don't care if I do. Might as well see what you've got around here in the way of entertainment."

"They're plenty tough, but ever'body has a helluva time. I was out the other night with a bag old enough to be my mother, but was she ready! Man alive! Ever'body goes. Young an' old an' middle-sized. They drink an' dance an' shoot an' you know what, but they have the damnedest time you ever saw."

"Nice respectable places."

"You know it! Say—what's your name?"

"Day."

"Day—lots of Days up here."

"Yeah. They're all over these hills. Must have bred like jack rabbits.'

"Ever'body breeds like jack rabbits up here. What's your first name?"

"John."

"Is that what they call you?"

"It's as good as any."

"Where you from?"

"Lexington."

"What th' hell you doin' up in this Godforsaken country?"

"Oh, I like the hills."

"I like 'em too—I'm from Whitley County—but at least it's civilized down there."

"What's your name?"

"Just call me Blackjack. I work for the state highway department. Me and the rest of this gang been up here about six weeks now I reckon. We're cuttin' a new road through."

"How did you happen to ask me to go jenny-barnin'?"

"I seen you drive up and thought you might like to have some fun. These suckers around here ain't got no car. Besides, ever' time they get drunk they get in a fight. I figger they're goin' to get me killed one of these times. You don't get fightin' drunk, do you?"

"Nope. 'Specially not in this country."

"I'm glad of that. I'm goin' to have to stop hornin' around with these rascals here. I don't wanna fight when I get drunk. I just have a big time. Ever'body's my pal and all that. Near time for supper. You ready?"

"Just about. Soon's I shave and put on a shirt."

"Don't get too cleaned up. Nobody else does."

Jacks in a Jenny-Barn

After supper Blackjack and I walked out on the porch. "Let's go," he said.

"Now? It isn't even dark."

"They start early and go late around here. Besides, we'll have to get the girls before somebody else does."

"Aren't there plenty of them?"

"Sure, but if you don't want leavin's you'd better go now. I know a couple I want to get tonight."

"All right. Which way?"

"Drive out to the Happy Landing. It's only about three miles."

We pulled up to the roadhouse a few minutes later, and Blackjack announced, "There's one of 'em."

A buxom blond was standing in front of the place talking to a boy. Blackjack stuck his head out the window and called, "Hi, Agnes." She turned around and waved, said something to the boy, and he walked inside. Agnes sauntered over to the car and put one foot up on the running board. "Hi'ya, Blackjack. You on the loose again?"

"Yeah, I'm always on the loose."

"Who's your friend?"

"This here's John Day."

"Glad to meetcha."

"Thanks. Same to you."

"What are you two tryin' to stir up?"

"What d'ya reckon?" Blackjack grinned.

"I don't have to reckon, knowin' you. Which way you headin'?"

"Truth is we were looking for you."

"Well here I am."

"We thought maybe you and Dot 'ud buzz around with us for a while tonight."

"I don't know about Dot, but I about halfway had a date with Pete."

"Aw to hell with Pete! He's littler than I am anyway."

"Yeah, but Pete's mean when he gets drunk. I don't want him on my tail."

"Pete won't do nuthin'. Come on."

Agnes looked down at her bright red fingernails for a moment. "O. K. Lemme in."

"Where's Dot?" Blackjack asked as he let Agnes in the center.

"I don't know. Home I reckon."

"Let's go get her, John."

"Which way?"

"You turn off the big road right up here a piece. It's about a mile over from there I guess."

"Can you drive it?"

"Yeah. It's been graveled."

Ten minutes later Agnes pointed out the house. Standing in a hollow about fifty yards from the road it was respectable-looking if a bit misshapen by the addition of a frame structure to a two-room log. The yard was clean, and flowers grew from old iron kettles on either side of a path. Rambling rose vines clung to the porch railings.

Two mongrels yapped a warning, and a girl appeared at the front door.

"Come on out, Dot," Agnes shouted.

"Be right with you."

A brunette, pretty in a forthright way, came down the path.

"Hi, Ag. . . . Well, if it ain't old long, brown, and ugly!"

"Never mind the wise cracks. Get yourself in here."

She climbed in on Blackjack's lap and turned toward me. "Hi, Red. Where d'you hail from?"

"He hails from Lexington, and his name's John."

"I prefer Red."

"Call me anything you like. Where do we go from here?"

"Let's go back where we picked up Agnes and get some

licker," Blackjack suggested. "This county's supposed to be dry, but that don't cut no ice. I've set down there and drank beer with the deputy sheriff in th' next booth."

We went back to the Happy Landing, and Blackjack and I bought a pint of whisky.

"Now where?" Agnes asked.

I said, "Let's drive over to that place—what do they call it?—the Wander Inn."

Blackjack turned and looked at me. "Are you crazy? Any of these dives are bad enough, but those places around that coal camp are the toughest joints in eastern Kentucky. Somebody gets shot or cut over there almost ever' night. Why just the other night . . ."

"I know. Two people got killed and another one got run down by an automobile. I've heard of it. I want to see if it's as tough as they say it is."

"You're nuts, but it's your funeral. . . . What d'you say, girls?"

"If you can take it we can," Dot answered.

"Atta boy, Dot! I can see we're going to get along famously. Let's be off."

We had driven about five miles when Blackjack unwrapped the pint. "Pull over to the side of the road and let's take a drink. Might as well get started."

He uncorked the bottle and handed it to Agnes. She tilted it and drank fully a fourth without even making a face.

"Holy Moses!" I exclaimed. "You must have been raised on a bottle."

"Born with one in my mouth," she laughed.

"I can do better than that," Dot boasted. And she did.

Blackjack took his share and passed the bottle to me. I took about three swallows.

"Don't be a sissy," Agnes teased.

"Sissy nothing. You don't want to land down in one of those hollows, do you? I've got to drive."

"Well, give it to me. I'll finish it." She drained it, and Blackjack threw the bottle out.

"We oughta got a gallon the way you fishes drink," I said.

"Plenty more where we're goin'," said Blackjack.

Dot began to sing.

"You are my sunshine,
My only sunshine.
You make me haaupy
When skies are gray.
You'll never know, dear,
How much I looove you.
Do not take my sunshine away. . . ."

"Do you know 'Barbara Allen'?" I asked.

"Naw. I've heard granddad sing it, but I never learnt it. Too many verses."

We arrived at the Wander Inn about eight o'clock and parked the car on the cinders beside seven or eight others. The blare of the juke-box and the hubbub of voices sounded through the open door.

We walked past the bar, located in an anteroom, and seated ourselves in one of the dance-hall booths. The main room, low-ceilinged and dimly lighted, was perhaps sixty feet square. Scarred booths sat around three sides, and a gaudy nickelodeon squatted against the fourth between two doors leading from the barroom. There were three other doors among booths along the back wall. One said "Ladies," one said "Gents," and one didn't say anything.

The air was close and hazy with smoke. Five or six couples, one of them a pair of girls, danced to a Bing Crosby record. Several men in shirt sleeves and women in sleazy dresses strolled around between the barroom and the dance hall.

A waitress meandered over. She was well-constructed. Her starchless apron-uniform was tight across the hips and open at the neck. She leaned over the table and gave it two or three swipes with a damp cloth, showing in the process a goodly portion of her ample breasts. "What'll you have?"

"Whisky," said Blackjack.

"What kind?"

"Bring us a pint of Cream of Kentucky, some ice, and some 7-Ups."

"We ain't supposed to sell nuthin' but beer here, so keep yer bottle off th' table. It bothers th' sheriff to see it settin' out."

"O.K."

She left, brushing against my knee.

"Why do these God-damn waitresses figger they gotta show everything they got?" Agnes stormed.

"Jealous, Agnes?" Blackjack bantered.

"Jealous? Hell no! I got as much as she has, but I don't go around waving it in everybody's face."

"Aw well, they gotta make a livin', ain't they? And they don't do it slingin' beer. How about it, John?"

"Right!"

"Trouble is most of 'em are burnt. You gotta be mighty damn careful er you'll end up with something you didn't ask fer."

The waitress returned with our order. She set the glasses and bottles out on the table, paying no attention to Agnes' glare. "Anything else, boys?" She rested her hand intimately on Blackjack's shoulder.

"That'll be all right now, thanks," I answered.

The girls and Blackjack each poured a Coca-Cola glass full of liquor, swilled it, chased it with a gulp of 7-Up. I poured half a glass, stirred in some mixer and ice, and drank it.

My three companions already had that hazy look about the eyes. They were going to get stinking drunk, but I didn't care. I felt a warm glow. Everything was rosy.

"Let's struggle, Agnes," Blackjack offered.

They joined other couples on the floor.

"Well, Dot, let's you and I have a try at it."

The juke-box was playing "Stardust." Funny place for "Stardust." It was Glenn Miller too. Sounded good.

Dorothy danced clingingly, pressing her lithe body against me and resting her head on my shoulder. "You dance swell," she said.

"Thanks. You do all right yourself."

"You know," she said, leaning back a little and smiling. "I kinda like you."

"Swell. I like you too."

"Do you? I hope so. You're kindly diff'runt from th' rest of these mules. You ain't tried to paw all over me. You ain't even tried to kiss me yet."

"Judas priest, I must be slippin'! I've known you all of two hours too."

She laughed. "Look at old Ag tyin' on to Blackjack, would you! She sure has herself a big-eye time. . . . How old you say she is?"

"Oh, about twenty-five, I guess."

"She'll never see thirty again. She's been married twice and has two grown kids. But she ain't never done a lick of work in her life. That's why she looks as young as she does. Look at me, all freckled. I'm only twenty, an' look at my hands. Look like I been fightin' a blackberry bush. That's what livin' on a farm'll getcha. My ole man gives me hell all th' time fer runnin' around, but I wanna have some fun. Ain't nuthin' up there in that holler. Till two year ago you couldn't even git up there except walkin'. Nuthin' to do all th' time but work er set around. I got sick of it. Plenty o' people got sick of it. That's why they raise so much hell now they've got a chance to git out a little."

"I guess that's right. Roads surely have made a difference."

"You betcha they've made a diff'rence. Least you can find

somethin' to do now. Let's have another drink. I feel like howlin'."

Agnes and Blackjack were sitting in the booth with their arms around each other. We sat down opposite them and ordered another pint. When the waitress came back with it Blackjack ran his hand up under her dress. She squirmed away a little—but not much. Agnes smacked him. "You keep your hands to yourself, big boy, er I'll whittle you down to my size." She wasn't mad now though. She was feeling too good to be mad. "Come on, my red-headed friend. Let's dance." She climbed up in the seat and crawled over Blackjack.

"Yippee! Let's swing it!" Her big breasts felt like pillows against me. She wiggled her hips to the music. She started to hum. Her feet weren't keeping time and she was hard to hold up, but she didn't care. She was having fun.

When the piece ended we went back to the booth, Agnes snapping her fingers to a sort of Charleston step. "Wanna go with me, Dot?"

"Yeah." Dot stood up unsteadily. " 'Scuse us, boys. We'll be back if we don't fall in." They weaved toward the back of the dance hall.

"Let's go see what they got in the back room, Blackjack. People been goin' in and out of there all evening."

"O.K."

We walked to the unmarked door. I turned the knob. The door was locked.

"Try knockin'."

I rapped and the door opened. A brute of a fellow with a cauliflowered ear sized us up, then pushed back the door. We walked from a little hallway through another door.

The back room was small and even more smoke-laden than the dance hall. Six or eight men were playing cards. Another group of men and two women stood around a dice table. Under a steep stairway were two slot machines.

We walked over to the crap table and watched for a few minutes. The players were mostly miners, rough-handed, seamy-necked men. Some were dressed in their Sunday best, others in overalls. All were drunk or getting that way. They played as though they had plenty of money—two bits, four bits, a buck, five bucks a roll.

I felt an arm around my waist and turned quickly. A girl had come from some place and was glued against me. She smiled. "How about a little fun?"

"No thanks—I guess not."

"Aw come on. Whatta you got to lose?"

"Nope. Nope."

She turned toward Blackjack, and he grinned that pumpkin-faced grin. I caught hold of his arm. "You know what you said out there a little while ago." He was drunk, but for some reason he didn't go with her.

I moved over to the card table. The men were playing draw poker. A pretty good pot was in the center, and all the players had laid down their hands except a sandy-haired fellow and a hump-shouldered man who sat next to the banker.

"I'll call," said the sandy-haired man, tossing the last of his chips in the center. "Whatcha got?"

"Full house—kings and treys." The other player spread his cards on the table.

"I gotcha." As he leaned forward he knocked his discard to the floor with his elbow. He reached down and picked up the cards, then tossed his hand on the table. "Four jacks."

The banker jumped from his chair and grabbed Sandy's wrist. "You took one of those jacks out of your discard!"

"I'll be damned if I did!"

"You gonna argue about it?" The house man scowled.

"Sure I'm gonna argue. I'm hooked fer eighteen bucks an' you wanna gyp me out o' this pot so's yer friend over there kin have it."

"I got no more interest in this fellow here than I have in you, but what I say goes. Get that?"

"Not this time it don't!"

"Hey, Buck!" The bouncer already was on his way from the hall.

"What's th' matter here?"

"This guy wants t' argue."

"All right, buddy, let's go." He grabbed Sandy by the collar.

Sandy's face was flaming. "By God, I won that pot fair with the best hand I've had all night."

"You comin' out quiet er am I gonna have t' toss you out on yer ear?"

The cauliflowered bouncer propelled Sandy through the door into the dance hall and half led, half dragged him out through the front door. The ousting stirred only momentary interest in the crowd.

Blackjack and I went back to the booth. Agnes was hanging over the back jabbering with somebody at the next table. Dorothy was in a daze, one hand around a glass and the other around the bottle.

Blackjack spanked Agnes across the rump and she whirled around and slid to the seat. "Where you guys been all night?" She ran her hands through her hair and giggled.

I sat down beside Dorothy and she flopped over on my shoulder. "What's the matter, Dot?" She made a feeble attempt at a smile but didn't answer.

Blackjack was pouring drinks when someone slapped me on the shoulder. "Hi, pal," he greeted.

I turned to see a tall, beaming fellow whose knees seemed about to buckle under him. "Mind if I sit down?" he asked.

"Not at all." I scooted Dorothy over against the wall, and he hitched in beside me.

"I ain't drunk–very. My leg's been this way a long time."

"I thought you were just before folding up."

"Naw. I got all crippled up with the jake-leg."

"Th' hell you say. Pour yourself a drink. I haven't seen anybody with the jake-leg since the early thirties. I thought everybody either died or got over it."

"I damn near died. In bed flat o' my back fourteen months. Damn Jamaica ginger anyway! That's what Prohibition done for you. I like t' never got so's I could walk."

"Does it bother you much now?"

"Doesn't hurt none, but I can't get around to do much good. Can't dance or nothin'. Doctor said I'd be jerkin' around the rest of my life, so I've tried to get used to it. Where you from?"

"Lexington."

"Sure 'nough? I'm from Cynthiana. I ain't been up in these hills long. Come up and got a job in th' highway garage, fixin' trucks and the like. Name's Bill Kokomo. Say—look at those jennies stomp, would you!"

The juke-box was booming "Tuxedo Junction," and a dozen couples were doing a jitterbug that for sheer carnality would have put Harlemites to shame.

"These gals up here sure got broad transmissions, ain't they!" Bill chuckled and choked on a drink.

"Must be from climbing hillsides," I said.

"Quit makin' cracksh about th' girlsh. They're all-l-l right." Agnes waved her arms and knocked a glass to the floor. She laughed wildly. "Yow-e-e-e, lesh throw dishes."

Blackjack got a strangle hold around her neck. "Calm down," he said, "before I sit on you." Both laughed and started kissing, rocking back and forth in the seat.

"Look over yonder," Bill indicated with a nod of his head.

In a booth across the dance floor a girl and a boy were oblivious of the crowd. Their lips were pressed together. He had a hand down in her blouse, and she had one leg over his.

"Really goin' t' town, ain't they?" Bill agreed.

"You said it!"

Our attention was drawn from the couple by the sound of a violin above the phonograph music. Cocked up against the wall near the nickelodeon and sawing away vigorously on a fiddle was a gray-haired man well in his cups. He grinned and spat a stream of tobacco juice as eyes turned toward him.

When the record ended, he sawed louder than ever, patting his foot to the rhythm of "Pop Goes the Weasel." The crowd joined in with hand claps. Then somebody shouted, "Let's square dance." Couples ran, slid, and stumbled to the center of the floor to form a circle.

"Lesh square dance," Agnes squealed, climbing over into Blackjack's lap

"I can't," he protested.

She grabbed my hand. "Lesh square dance!"

"I can't either."

"Aw yesh you can. Come on. We'll show 'em how ish done."

I propped Dorothy against the wall and joined the circle with Agnes. The old man changed his tune to "Cacklin' Hen," and someone started calling the set. It was a wild dance. I didn't know what I was doing, but nobody seemed to care. Everybody laughed and clapped and skipped and skidded. We got about halfway through the set before Agnes' feet flew out from under her and she fell so hard she jarred the floor.

"Oh my God, I'm killed!" she yelped, her dress half up to her thighs.

The dancers laughed louder and kept on gliding and skipping as I dragged Agnes to her feet and led her back to the booth.

"Oh my fanny, my fanny," she moaned.

"Aw hell, it's well padded," Blackjack laughed, bending double with mirth.

She groaned, rubbed herself gingerly, then suddenly forgot

all about it and announced, "I'm hungry. Why don't somebody feed little Agnes?"

I called the waitress.

"I wansh a bowl of chili, a hamburger with onions, and some pickleshed pigsh feet," she ordered.

"My God, that's enough to kill a horse!"

"I ain't no horsh."

I turned to Dorothy to ask if she wanted anything and saw tears streaming down her face. "What th' hell's the matter with you?"

"Ever'body leavsh me," she blubbered. "Nobody wansh me. I'm not a bad girl. I jush wanna have fun."

"Aw, don't pay no 'tenshun t' her," said Agnes. "She gets on them cryin' jags."

I patted Dorothy's shoulder, "Come on, snap out of it. Everybody loves you. Try something to eat."

"You think I'm bad?"

"No, course not. You're swell. Come on, perk up."

But Dorothy was not to be pacified. She covered her face with her hands and bawled. I was still trying to quiet her when a scuffle began in front of the phonograph. Before we knew what was going on, half a dozen fellows were slugging and cutting at each other. Then somebody let go with a pistol. I didn't know who started it. I didn't know what it was about. I didn't know whether to sit still, climb under the table, or try to get out. Blackjack decided for me. He grabbed Agnes by the arm and they made for the door like rabbits for a thicket. I followed, dragging Dorothy and fully expecting to get a bullet in the back every step. As we piled into the car we heard another shot. We sat and listened for a minute. Loud voices came from the dance hall, but the fight seemed to be over. I turned to Blackjack. "Wanna go back and see what happened?"

"Hell no, you damn fool. I told you not to come here

in the first place. When th' shootin' starts that's when it's time to go home."

"Suits me." I was curious, but I figured Blackjack was right.

Next day, though, I found out what started it. Two young bloods got in an argument over what piece to play on the nickelodeon. Nobody was killed. It was just a minor shooting.

X

"—The Damnedest, in Kentucky"

THE GRIZZLED FELLOW next to me in the Leslie County courtroom leaned forward, laid his hand on my shoulder sort of friendly like, carefully dropped a mouthful of tobacco juice on the floor between his feet, and listened intently. Apparently a friend of his was being questioned. There was little other reason for interest at the moment. The other spectators—both sexes and all ages, sizes, and shapes—had grown restless or drowsy. They had come to be entertained by the "lie-swearing" trial, and though two hours had passed, only eight jurors had been seated. The lawyers droned along, asking repetitious questions of one prospective juror after another

The courtroom was a high, square place with plastered walls and ceiling, cracked and dull. Two tall coal stoves towered in corners, and four big windows opened from each of two sides. In the center of the third side were the main doors, knot-holed for hallway spectators like the fence of a baseball park. Opposite the entrance and under an arch was the judge's high desk. In front of him, in the very center of the room, was a low enclosure containing jurors' benches, lawyers' tables, and the witness chair.

The spectators sat or lounged on rough wooden benches placed like seats in an arena around the enclosure. Some of the men wore overalls; others, cotton trousers and blue or white shirts open at the throat. Women, wearing gingham, dimity, or rayon, were in the minority, but among them were several young girls who had come with their beaux as though to a circus or ball game. A number of the men were whittling nonchalantly. One old fellow with a drooping mustache peered through little gold-rimmed glasses at a newspaper he rattled loudly from time to time. Another had fallen asleep and was amusing the group around him with his snores. Yet another sprawled at length upon a bench within the enclosure, his feet upon a railing and a cigar jammed in his mouth as though he owned the place. He was John L. Dixon, a hook-nosed, bright-eyed old man who had retired recently after practising law at the Leslie County bar since it was established back in 1878. He liked to tell about the old days when court was held in a dwelling and the host would furnish the liquor; when the clerk would write in his order book toward the end of the day, "Everybody else is drunk and I'm getting that way, court's adjourned"; when a jack started braying while a lawyer was speaking and the judge rapped for order with the declaration, "One at a time, gentlemen; I can't hear you both at once."

Judge Guy L. Dickerson of Knox County, a distinguished-looking gentleman with a full, red face, pompadoured gray hair, and beribboned glasses, had asked that there be no smoking, but the men didn't take him seriously. Pipe, cigar, and Bull Durham smoke floated lazily in the humid, odor-laden air of the courtroom. His honor himself chewed tobacco during the proceeding, expectorating with considerable finesse into a brass spittoon at one end of the bench.

The ever-present water bucket sat on a little table at the judge's left. To it spectators and principals kept walking.

At the judge's right stood the sheriff, Curt Duff. I had

talked to him, among others, about the background of this case that was so typical of mountain political mix-ups.

Sophia Sizemore was on trial today. She was accused of perjury, or "lie-swearing" as the people chose to call it. The trouble had started several months previously when Judge Sam M. Ward sought another term in the Perry-Leslie circuit. On the face of the count he lost a hot fight for the Republican nomination, but he charged both his opponents with having violated the corrupt practices act—and he won the contest. But in the final election the circumstances were reversed. Ward lost Perry County by 398 votes but carried Leslie by 811, winning on the count for the circuit by 413. However, his Democratic opponent, Dr. K. N. Salyer, Hazard bank president, doctor, and lawyer, accused Ward of having violated the corrupt practices act by intimidating some voters and bribing others with money, whisky, and promise of official favors. He also accused Ward's supporters of having tampered with the ballot boxes in Leslie County, and he asked that Ward be disqualified on the first count and that he, Salyer, be declared elected on the second. After hearing 194 witnesses at a contest hearing in Hyden, Judge John Noland of Madison County ruled that Ward had bought votes and thus could not be seated, but that ballots in Leslie had not been altered and thus Salyer could not be seated either. Ward prosecuted an appeal and Salyer a cross-appeal, but the state's appellate court upheld Judge Noland and declared the office vacant at the expiration of Ward's current term. Even before the hearing before Noland was completed, Ward, still judge of his circuit, caused several witnesses against him to be arrested on perjury charges. He let it be known that he was still a candidate for re-election and that he wanted his name cleared. He summoned a grand jury and obtained indictments against ten of those arrested, among them Sophia Sizemore. Six of the ten already had been tried, with the score tied at three convictions and three disagreements. Those convicted had taken appeals. Kentucky's dockets would not be cleared soon of the Salyer-Ward case.

Twelve jurymen, all from without the circuit, were at last agreed upon, and Sophia Sizemore's trial was ready to proceed. The spectators quit whittling, talking, and reading to give their undivided attention to the proceeding. The commonwealth's attorney made an opening address in which he declared the state would prove that Sophia Sizemore had maliciously lied when she testified against Judge Ward and that she had lied because she had been paid by supporters of Salyer, who, he said sarcastically, so righteously accused Ward of corrupt practices. A defense attorney then took the floor and denied vigorously that the state would prove any such thing. He was a wiry little fellow, deaf as the table he rested his hand on. From time to time his assistant, a heavy-set man with a rumbling drawl, tried to tell him something, ending always by scribbling the information on a bit of paper and handing it to him. The oration on each occasion was interrupted as the speaker took his glasses from his pocket, rested them on his nose, read the note, handed it back, and replaced the glasses.

During the opening statements Sophia Sizemore, fat and freckled, chewed gum and looked about at the audience. She was a middle-aged woman, mother of six children. One gathered the impression that she was merely an unfortunate incidental in this fight for political office. She seemed a bit bewildered, though not greatly concerned.

The first witness was Ward himself, a slender man with a harassed look on his wrinkled face and with long, straight hair that refused to stay slicked back. He recounted Mrs. Sizemore's testimony against him at the hearing before Judge Noland. He stated: that she, Mrs. Sizemore, said she overheard Ward and Jay Feltner, a Leslie farmer, talking in the courtroom on election day about voting; that Ward told

Feltner to go see Sheriff Curt Duff (a Ward supporter who had himself won office on a contest); that Feltner then went into the sheriff's office, and that the sheriff handed Feltner something "that looked like money" and said, "I'll make it all right." That Mrs. Sizemore said also she had seen Ward whispering to Malcolm Feltner, Jay's brother, and that after the whispered conversation Ward handed Malcolm something "that might have been money."

Ward did not talk rapidly, but the court reporter, a fleshy, chinless woman who wore immense horn-rimmed glasses, had difficulty in keeping up. She interrupted several times to ask the witness to repeat.

Having set forth Mrs. Sizemore's assertion Ward proceeded to impeach her with categorical denials that any such incidents took place.

Malcolm Feltner was called to the stand. His overalls were so muddy and wrinkled he looked as though he had waded recently through a quagmire. He testified that: "I didn't even talk to th' judge on 'lection day, and he shore didn't hand me nuthin'." The prosecuting attorney seemed satisfied and turned the witness over to the defense. The heavy-set lawyer walked over with a look on his face like a cat who'd just caught a mouse. He produced a piece of paper. "Here," he declared, "is an affidavit you signed with your mark, Malcolm Feltner." He read it. It said in effect that Feltner HAD talked to Ward and that Ward had paid him for his vote.

"What about this?" he demanded, waving the paper in front of Feltner's bearded face.

Malcolm's eyes darted around the room as though he were looking for an exit.

The lawyer repeated his question.

"They read me a paper . . ." Malcolm began at last.

"They! Who's they?"

"I dunno–some o' Salyer's men, I guess."

"Go ahead."

"They read me a paper like that and said they'd give me $3 to put my mark to hit."

"Did you?"

"I don't jest remember."

"Did you or didn't you?"

"I don't jest remember."

"Well, did you talk to Judge Ward?"

"I can't say as I did."

The lawyer stood and glared at Feltner for a moment, then turned around and walked away. The judge waved his hand, and Malcolm slunk out of the chair and back into the witness room.

The prosecution called Jay Feltner. He was even more unkempt than Malcolm–and more equivocal, too. Through answers to questions phrased simply and carefully by the prosecuting attorney Jay testified that he didn't talk to Ward on election day, that Ward didn't tell him Curt Duff would pay him for a vote, that he didn't go to see Curt Duff, and that Duff didn't give him anything.

But then the defense took hold of him.

"Now, Jay," the big lawyer drawled. "Do you remember the trial before Judge Noland?"

"Yessir."

The lawyer turned the pages of a transcript. "Now you said during that hearing that you talked to Judge Ward on election day, that he asked you if you were going to vote for him and you said, 'Yes sir.' Then you were asked if Judge Ward promised to pay you $1 for 'your day' and you replied, 'I couldn't remember.' You admitted that you knew Curt Duff and that you were in his office on election day. You were asked whether you got any money from Duff that day and you answered, 'I couldn't say pine blank now since I thought the matter over.' Then you were asked if you hadn't made an affidavit stating that Judge Ward agreed to pay you $1 'for your day's work' and that the money had been paid to you in the sheriff's office. You admitted that you had put your mark to such an affidavit. Then you were asked, 'Was it true?' and you replied, 'I thought it might be true.' Is what I have been reading you here correct?"

"Yessir. . . . I mean nosir."

"What DO you mean?"

"I dunno." Jay was lost. His eyes popped out and his Adam's apple jumped up and down.

"You don't know!" the lawyer shouted. "Of course you don't know. You make an affidavit to one thing, say another at a hearing, and still another at this trial. Now what I want to know is did you or didn't you make the affidavit?"

"I could have. . . . They offered t' pay me $2 fer it."

"Were the statements in it correct?"

"I couldn't say pine blank lessen I thought th' matter over."

The lawyer dropped his hands to his sides and asked resignedly, "Well, did you or didn't you talk to Judge Ward on election day?"

"Come to think of it I don't think I did."

The lawyer shrugged his shoulders and turned to the jury with a look that said, "What's the use?" Then swinging back to Jay as though to pop another question he said calmly, "You can go."

Jay looked tremendously relieved. A titter ran over the crowd. Judge Dickerson rapped for order and called a recess.

I didn't go back after the recess. I knew there'd be more of the same, and I'd heard enough. I had to smile though. Here was Sophia Sizemore being tried for perjury and before her trial was over a dozen-odd witnesses would perjure themselves and nothing would come of it.

Next day I heard the jury had been unable to reach an

agreement. Small wonder! I marveled that three juries had convicted in the six cases tried previously.

Judge Ward's term ended on June 21, 1940, a couple of weeks after Mrs. Sizemore's trial, and on July 13 Governor Keen Johnson appointed Oxford graduate Roy Helm to serve until November. Helm found the docket jammed with more than 1,000 cases. Ward had been too busy with the contest to keep the regular work up.

There was to be a special election in the fall; thus political finagling wasn't over when Johnson appointed Helm–not by a long shot. Dr. Salyer decided he'd had enough, but Ward was going to see it through to the end. Moreover John Asher and J. A. Smith, convicted of violating the corrupt practices act when Ward contested the Republican primary of the previous year, were still trying for the judgeship.

Since the court of appeals decision barring Ward and Salyer came too late for candidates to file for the August 1940 primary, Republican and Democratic committees of the judicial district were called upon to name their candidates for the special election in November. Ward, Smith, and Asher made their approaches to the Republican committee, but in response to a question by the committee chairman the attorney general ruled that all three were disqualified from holding the party nomination. The Republican committee then named Calloway W. Napier, and the Democratic committee chose Johnson's appointee, Helm. Ward, Smith, and Asher immediately filed as independent candidates. The situation was further complicated when two members of the Republican district committee, one of whom had voted for Ward and one for Asher, filed a circuit-court action declaring that Napier had not actually obtained a majority vote of the committee and asking that the secretary of state be restrained from placing Napier's name on the ballot.

The field was reduced when Smith withdrew in October, but Napier retained the nomination, and he and the other three fought it out bitterly through election day. Helm won, and for some strange reason nobody contested his victory.

This case is not remarkable. It isn't even unusual. I have told of it in some detail only because it is so typical of Kentucky mountain politics. It reveals how bitter and involved a race for local office can become. It shows how vote-buying, perjury, and personal likes and dislikes enter into a campaign.

I don't know whether or not Judge Ward bought votes, bribed with whisky, and promised favors. I do know it would have been strange if he hadn't. Everybody else does. I don't know whether Sophia Sizemore and the other 193 witnesses at the original contest hearing told the truth or lied like sinners. I do know that in nine out of ten cases they would help their friends, by truth or lie.

Back about the turn of the century Dr. William Goodell Frost, president of Berea College at the time, wrote: "The politics of the mountains are complicated. Fundamentally the people are Republicans, because they were 'fer the guverment' in the Civil War. And the more pronounced policies of the Republican party since the war have been understood and approved by the mountain folk. . . . Like other Southern men, however, they show the lack of the training of the 'town meeting.' Their exaggerated individuality is only offset by a spirit of clannishness with which they gather around a leader in the old feudal way. County politics are usually a barefaced scramble for the offices, though the counties which are so fortunate as to have a few able and high-principled men often keep them in the public service with commendable fidelity. Many mountain men 'expect something' from their leader at election time. This is not, in their eyes, a bribe. They would on no account so demean themselves as to sell their vote to the opposite party. But they will stay at home on election day unless their leader shows

“They shall take up serpents” (Russell Lee)

Photographs courtesy Photographic Archives,
University of Kentucky Libraries

At home in a mining community (Russell Lee)

A mining camp lines a hollow (Jennie Darsie collection)

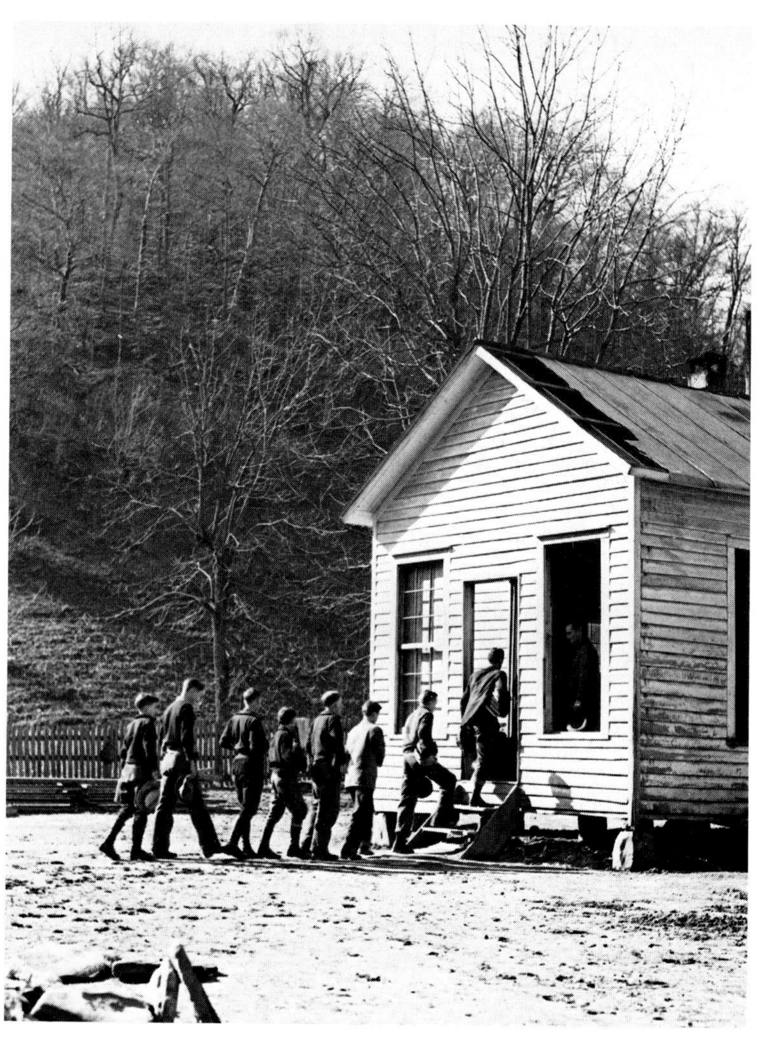

Children enter a schoolhouse (Marvin Breckinridge)

A family reunion (Russell Lee)

Miners in Harlan District, 1932 (Herndon Evans collection)

Loading coal (Russell Lee)

House call: Frontier Nurse enters a mountain home
(Marvin Breckinridge)

himself 'a generous feller.' If they fight and vote for their chieftain he owes them some feudal largess in return."

A part of Dr. Frost's observation still holds, and a part does not. He knew of course that the mountain people were "fer the guverment" at the time of the Civil War because they had been for it from the time of the Revolution and because, for the most part, they were not slave-holders. He knew too that they continued to vote the Republican ticket because their fathers before them had voted it. He could not have known that in the 1930's a man by the name of Franklin D. Roosevelt would come along and make Democrats out of a host of them. Yet, F.D.R. and his WPA notwithstanding, many of the mountain counties still are predominantly Republican. Dr. Frost's statement about the "barefaced scramble" for offices is still apt, and so is his comment about the people's tendency to gather around a leader. But certainly it is no longer true that "they would on no account so demean themselves as to sell their vote to the opposite party." Thousands of them are so poverty stricken they will sell their votes to the highest bidders—and that's the principal reason unprincipled men are able to hold mountain counties in their grasps year after year.

The mountaineer's love for politics in general, his interest in local races in particular, and the manner in which these two lead to shootings are discussed in the chapter on feuds. One thing should be added. The intense interest in local contests sometimes is due to that first law of nature: self-preservation. It's a good thing to have a sheriff, a judge, or a jailer who'll be of assistance in time of trouble.

All the impulses and intrigues of the political campaigns reach a climax of course on the one big day, election day. That's the time when plots grow thickest, money moves fastest, whisky flows freest, and guns shoot quickest. A Kentucky election day that passes without trouble in the hills is no kind of an election day at all. Here's a newspaper report that appeared the day after the last general election:

"A shooting affray and ballot-box thefts in Breathitt County, absence of the Johnson County sheriff, who was investigating another shooting, and an error in Perry County's tabulation sheets have delayed the vote count in these three (mountain) counties.

"Deputy Sheriff Ballard Watkins said three men were shot, one perhaps seriously, at the Elkatawa polling place in Breathitt. One of those wounded was a candidate for the county school board. . . .

"Deputy Watkins said the ballot box at the Taulbee precinct was taken yesterday morning after a 'disturbance over the school board election,' but that later it was returned and put into use. . . .

"Subsequently, however, seizure of the Leatherwood precinct box containing 435 votes was reported by Lester Combs, George Blanson, and Lewis and Ike Watts, who said the truck in which they were taking the box to Jackson was stopped by a log laid across the road

"Some eight masked men carrying pistols and rifles then seized the box, they said, and disappeared into the woods. . . . Leatherwood usually produces a Democratic majority. . . .

"Watkins and two others guarded remaining Breathitt County ballot boxes last night. . . .

"In Johnson County, near Paintsville, Johnny Trimble, 24, was shot and wounded seriously last night. . . . Because the sheriff's presence is required at the central ballot-counting location, tabulation of votes was postponed until today. . . .

"Perry County's election commissioners decided to limit the count last night to five of the 54 precincts after it was found that tabulation sheets bore the names of Franklin D. Roosevelt and Wendell L. Willkie and listed the Socialist and Prohibition parties by name but failed to carry the names of the presidential electors of any party.

"A stormy dispute arose over the sheets after five of the boxes had been opened and their votes removed. The election commissioners . . . ruled at first that these votes must be replaced in the boxes and all counting deferred.

"Further protests were entered that votes could not be put back into the boxes, and after another consultation, the commissioners ordered the names of the presidential electors written on the backs of the tabulation sheets and said they would allow counting of the five opened boxes and defer counting of the others. . . ."

Some of the other election-day maneuvers are a bit more subtle than stealing the ballot boxes and shooting candidates. They include such practices as the old chain vote, the voting of dead men and mythical persons, and the double or triple counting of ballots—practices that are by no means peculiar to the hills. A checkup after the last general election revealed that in several precincts in Harlan, Bell, and Pike counties the number of ballots marked was larger than the number of registered voters and that in at least one other precinct the number of votes counted was six times the number of ballots actually marked.

The irregularities were called to the attention of the Senate Campaign Expenditures Committee, but as usual it did nothing except set forth, in a report released five months later, facts that already were known. Tom R. Underwood, chairman of the Democratic state central committee, forecast the action, or rather inaction, of the senate committee when he stated a few days after the election: "The smoke is fast clearing away from the general election of November 5. Although Harlan, Bell, and Pike counties are included in the territories listed by Chairman Gillette of Iowa for investigation by the Senate Campaign Expenditures Committee, no charges affecting the possible result of the election are included. As a matter of fact, the 'ballot box stuffing' reports turned over to the committee were handed in by Senator Alben W. Barkley of Paducah, the Senate floor leader, and there isn't a man in Kentucky who was better pleased with the results of the election."

In March 1941 the committee released its report. It voiced the naïve hope that its investigation of corrupt election practices in Kentucky had "contributed materially to the elimination of vote-buying, coercion, and 'repeat voting' in counties in which committee investigators were active during the 1940 election."

Contributed materially, my eye! The committee knows, if it knows anything at all, that it can't improve Kentucky politics by saying, "Now you've been bad boys and you musn't do it again."

After the campaign with its plots and counter-plots, after election day with its shootings and ballot thefts, and after post-election days with their contest suits comes actual service by those finally seated. It is true, as Dr. Frost said long ago, that "the counties which are so fortunate as to have a few able and high-principled men often keep them in public service with commendable fidelity," but unfortunately many of the officials can't qualify as "able and high-principled men." It's a rule of thumb that men who gain their offices corruptly will run them the same way. Such men have two purposes: To pay, through favor or otherwise, the debts incurred in the campaign (so that they can remain in office) and to get as much for themselves as possible. Within the last year no less than a dozen officials in mountain counties have been indicted for malfeasance. Generally speaking, things have gotten pretty bad by the time indictments are returned.

Withal, politics in the mountains varies only in the degree of corruption from politics in the rest of the state. Politics is, indeed, "the damnedest, in Kentucky," and there's little likelihood that it will improve soon.

XI

Farmer in the Dell

JOHN FOX PORTRAYED the Kentucky mountains as picturesque, the hill people as quaint. The idea caught on, and the vast majority of writers ever since have seen only picturesqueness and quaintness. As a result the average American knows little if anything of the truth beneath the surface.

After reading one of Jesse Stuart's pieces I feel like shouting, "But damn it all, these people are more than quaint characters! They are desperately poor, bewildered human beings who need a lot of understanding. This country is more than picturesque! It is stark and worn and crowded. The quiet, primitive life of John Fox's day is gone. Misuse of the land, the industrial age, and population pressure have brought a new life, one fraught with tremendous economic and social problems."

After reading one of Jean Thomas' books I feel ill. Everything is so lovely and quaint; so damnably, sickeningly quaint. And scattered about are such gems as these: "There are not many tenant farmers in the mountains, or even those who make a crop on shares. . . . They [the mountain people] have neglected time-saving and labor-saving devices of this machine age, yet they have preserved a precious heritage and a freedom from the economic ills of the machine age."

I do not mean that all color has gone from the mountains. I rail at a romanticism that sees only color, that ignores changes and refuses to recognize facts.

During the nineteenth century the economy of the mountains was almost closed. I say "almost" because from the earliest times the highlanders bartered for necessities they could not produce at home. In a broad sense, though, the region—and in fact each family within the region—was independent. This economy worked very well. There was game in the hills and there were fish in the streams. There were plenty of grazing room and mast for sheep, hogs, and cattle. There was bottom land for garden truck and corn, and when it wore out there were hillsides. The people were not rich and they did not have luxuries, but they had adequate food, clothing, and shelter, and they had a free, full life that was not without charm.

But as farms were divided and subdivided for the ever-increasing population, as fish and game were exhausted, as trees were destroyed and the soil washed from the hillsides, self-sufficing farming—farming in which the value of products used by the family is greater than that of the products sold or traded—became bare existence. With the construction of railroads and subsequently of highways a twentieth century industrialism was superimposed upon the simple economy. For a time it seemed the new industrialism would solve the problem. The coal mines, the gas and oil fields, the lumber mills, the railroad shops, the brick yards supplied the supplementary income that was so badly needed. More, thousands of mountaineers migrated to industrial cities outside the region. But the supplementary income did not offset the loss in farm resources, and the migration did not counterbalance the birth rate. When the depression struck, moreover, income from industries dwindled or stopped, and migrants returned to the hills to try once more to eke a living from shrunken, eroded farms. Most of those who returned have remained, even through the "national defense" boom of 1941. The government's spending of billions on armaments, as a matter of fact, has done little to help the Kentucky mountains. A few new mines have opened, some of those closed during the depression have reopened, and all have increased their production, but the number of men employed through increased activity has been in large part offset by the number released through mine mechanization. Many men have found jobs outside the area again, but the number has not been large enough really to alleviate the difficulties.

Although self-sufficing farming no longer affords a good or even a decent living, a vast majority of mountaineers still practise it. Breathitt County's products, a study has shown, are consumed largely within its borders, and comparatively little is brought in from without. The spinning wheel no longer spins, but the county nonetheless is still largely on a subsistence basis. And the crux of the problem is that three-fourths of the people are farmers in an area poorly adapted to farming. There are other issues of course, but none so important, and other problems grow out of it. Breathitt's difficulties in this respect are the difficulties of the entire region.

As Molly Clowes has pointed out in writing of the self-sufficing farm, 36,000 of the 86,829 mountain farmers are tenants, but some of the poorest farmers are owners. "Baffled possessors of forty acres of 'heired land,' " she said, "they plow halfheartedly in the thin, sand-colored dirt, farmers not from choice or training but because they were 'borned on the land,' without any real hope of making a living at farming, but equally without hope that any other occupation would bring them a better life. There are just too many farmers in the mountains for the land to support. Every valley with its strip of bottom land capable of supporting two or three families must maintain ten to fifteen. Mountain farming is more a matter of subsistence than of cash earnings. There is neither room nor fertility for the cash crops that provide the substantial incomes of the Bluegrass. The mountain farm must produce potatoes and pork for the table, sorghum and corn, cabbage, turnips, peas and beans and milk. The mountain family lives fairly well during the summer, when the garden is bearing, and just after butchering in the early fall, when fresh hog meat is ready. It is the long winter and the spring, when vegetables have given out and the cow is dry, that mean lean days for the family. Throughout this bleak time, when cabin doors are shut and windows are tight, the fire flickers in a draft that means perpetual colds and sniffles for the children, and the road outside is a solid barrier of mud or snow between them and the outside world of school or village. The woodlot, the wagon mine or the little digging in the hillside provide the winter's fuel and even a little work that can be bartered for food."

Knott County is as nearly "typical" as any in the mountains of Kentucky, and facts concerning it apply, with only slight variances, to the whole region. Thus a confusion of figures can be avoided by examining Knott individually. It is a county of some 227,840 acres in the center of the most precipitous section of the hills. It is a land of creek-bottom settlements; since the streams have cut deeply, the hills are steep and ridges narrow. Agriculture is the principal occupation of its people, but it has coal mines, oil and gas fields, and some timber. The soil is a stony, unproductive, clay loam that erodes badly and does not hold moisture. The county's birth rate is high; its population immobile. The population increased by 31.4 per cent in ten years—from 15,230 in 1930 to 20,007 in 1940. During the last several years never less than one-third of the population has received WPA assistance, either through work or the receipt of commodities. One person in fifty has an automobile. Telephones outside the county seat of Hindman, a village of about 650, are rarities.

The county government, like that of other mountain counties, went in debt to float road and bridge bonds and has never been able to pay out. Its indebtedness of approximately $170,000 compares with $102,000 in Leslie, $300,000 in Clay, $68,000 in Owsley (where the annual income is only about $9,000), $210,000 in Magoffin, $800,000 in Floyd, $359,000 in Breathitt, and $543,000 in Perry. The counties incurred the debts before the state budget law, which prohibits the making of debts beyond the limits to pay, was enacted in 1934. Eight already have defaulted and at least eleven others will default within a few years unless they increase the amounts set aside for debt service. The State Revenue Department reports, by way of example, that Harlan and Pike are not building up reserves to meet heavy bond maturities due within a decade. All the debtor counties face a well-nigh insurmountable problem. They have levied the maximum tax rate, and during the last ten or fifteen years assessed valuations have been decreasing. Blanket increases on realty ordered by the State Revenue Department for eight mountain counties in May 1941 may help to a limited extent.

Knott has no railways and it had no roads except the creek bottoms until 1928, when an eleven-mile stretch was built across the southern tip to link Hazard in Perry County with Whitesburg in Letcher. A traffic-bound road, later block-topped, was completed from the Hazard-Jackson highway to Hindman in 1931, and three years later it was extended on through the county toward Prestonsburg. These three stretches, totaling thirty-seven miles, still represent Knott's highway mileage.

A few years ago the Department of Agriculture made a study of Knott County–Knott where the ridges are narrow and the slopes are steep; where homes are small, one-story houses, unpainted or shabbily painted, with interior walls often covered with newspaper and worth an average of $343; where modern conveniences are lacking and food is scarce.

The average money income from a farm in Knott, the department pointed out, is just $56 for each family each year. The county not only has poor roads but poor schools and limited sanitary and medical facilities. Yet the inhabitants are immobile. They like Knott County. They have always lived in Knott County. In Knott County they hope to die.

Of the grown sons of the families interviewed, more than 73 per cent were still in Knott. Less than 20 per cent of the men and only 6 per cent of the homemakers had ever been in all their lives beyond Kentucky or some adjoining state. Some of the men had been away to war. Some had gone looking for work. One girl had been on a honeymoon. Three had gone to funerals. Those who had lived away from Knott County had come back because they were homesick or because they "couldn't do no good" away from home.

Commenting upon the government report *Scientific Monthly* wrote that "in these modern days of loose home ties, wandering youth, drifting childless families, trailer residence and transient camps, population experts, psychologists and sociologists urge attention to the 'immobility' of the Kentucky people before plans are made to move them from their submarginal acres."

Let's take a look at these submarginal acres through the 1940 census. A trend toward smaller and smaller farms is shown in the fact that in 1930 the county had 1,951 farms averaging 78.3 acres, whereas by 1940 it had 2,645 farms averaging 55 acres. Of Knott's 227,840 acres, 63.9 per cent was classified as farm land. The classification is apt to be misleading. In 1939 only 20,282 acres actually were productive. Ten thousand ninety-six acres of so-called cropland lay fallow, whereas 27,820 acres were in pasture and 78,099 were in woodland. In 1930 the average value of a Knott County farm and the buildings upon it was $1,582. By 1940 it had dropped to $883. The value of farm lands and buildings per acre was $20.21 in 1930; $16.04 in 1940. Of the 2,645 farms, 555 included only from 3 to 9 acres each, whereas 711 boasted between 10 and 29 acres; 417 between 30 and 49; 347 between 50 and 69. Only 209 included the 100 to 139 acres considered a fair-sized farm. The proportion of tenancy increased from 34.9 in 1930 to 39.6 in 1940. Tenant farmers harvested 6,335 acres of the total of 20,282.

The livestock census revealed further pitiable conditions. Approximately half the farms had neither horse nor mule. Four hundred and seventy farms didn't even have a cow or a calf. The other 2,175 farms reported a total of 4,636 head of cattle, only 324 of which were kept for beef production. Just sixty-five farms had sheep—a total of 648 head. Hog meat and mountains can hardly be disassociated, yet 786 farms had not a single sow or pig, and the total for the other 1,859 farms was 6,661.

I can't speak of hogs without turning aside for a moment to say something about these remarkable mountain razor-backs. They can't roam as widely as they used to, and mast is no longer plentiful, but they still are the most independent animals on earth. They pick up their own living when and where they please. Horace Kephart did an admirable job when he wrote: "In physique and mentality, the razorback differs even more from a domestic hog than a wild goose from a tame one. Shaped in front like a thin wedge, he can go through laurel thickets like a bear. Armored with tough hide cushioned by bristles, he despises thorns, brambles and rattlesnakes alike. His extravagantly long snout can scent like a cat's, and yet burrow, uproot, overturn, as if made of metal. The long legs, thin flanks, pliant hoofs, fit him to run like a deer and climb like a goat. In courage and sagacity he outranks all other beasts. A warrior born, he is also a strategist of the first order. Like man, he lives a communal life, and unites with others of his kind for purposes of defense. The pig is the only large mammal I know of, besides man, whose eyes will not shine by reflected light—they are too bold and crafty, I wit. The razorback has a mind of his own; not instinct, but mind—whatever psychologists may say. He thinks. Anybody can see that when he is not rooting or sleeping he is studying devilment. He shows remarkable understanding of human speech, especially profane speech, and even an uncanny gift of reading men's thoughts, whenever those thoughts are directed against the peace and dignity of pigship. He bears grudges, broods over indignities, and plans redresses for the morrow or the week after. If he cannot get even with you, he will lay for your unsuspecting friend. And at the last, when arrested in his crimes and lodged in the pen, he is liable to attacks of mania from sheer helpless rage. If you camp out in the mountains, nothing will molest you but razorback hogs. . . . The moment incense of cooking arises from your camp every pig within two miles will scent it and hasten to call. You may throw your arm out of joint; they will laugh in your face. You may curse in five languages; it is music to their titillating ears."

But to get on with the census—the poultry count was but little more encouraging than the livestock tally. Of the 2,645 farms, 2,367 reported they had at least one chicken, turkey, duck, or goose. That left 278 farms without a single fowl, and the 2,367 had a total of only 61,056 chickens, 51 turkeys, 1,025 ducks and 709 geese. The average number of fowls for a Knott farm, then, is twenty-three.

A few decades ago almost every farmer had his "bee gums," but in 1940 only 482 had them. The total number of hives was 2,384.

In the matter of farm crops Knott's story is truly that of the rest of the region. Corn not only is the principal crop, it is practically the only crop other than garden products. In 1939 Knott farms produced 340,131 bushels of corn on 14,448 acres. Not a single farmer grew wheat, rye, or barley, and only two grew oats. Ninety-two farms produced some sorghum cane for syrup, and ten farmers raised a total of four acres of tobacco. Although the county agent has advised, asked, and begged his farmers to plant more cover crops, only 607 had any hay at all on their farms in 1939. The total acreage was 1,787, of which 976 acres were in annual legumes such as cowpeas and soybeans, 24 in alfalfa, 10 in sweet clover, 563 in lespedeza, 125 in timothy, and the rest in other hays.

A natural question for one to ask is, "Why does corn remain the predominant crop?" There are several reasons, first and foremost of which is the fact that it is a grain that serves as food for both man and stock. If a man has a good corn crop he will have roasting ears, he will have corn bread, he will have hog meat, and he will have milk and butter. Moreover corn gives larger yields than the small grains and it yields fairly well with careless cultivation and on poor land. No machinery is required for planting, cultivating, or harvesting. Corn is easily stored. Used directly on the farm, it does not have to be taken to market—an important factor in a land of poor roads. And so corn is another one of those endless chain problems. So long as it remains the dominant crop, hillsides will continue to wash away; yet any other crop would not support so many people.

The Knott County agent has worked for twelve years to improve farm conditions, and although his efforts have shown some results he feels the agricultural situation is rather hopeless. "The hill land," he said, "can't be successfully cultivated, and you can't raise crops to support an ever-growing population unless you do cultivate."

But as I have indicated, Knott is no worse off than a number of the other mountain counties. After making a study leading to a Ph.D. degree, Mary B. Willeford drew a statistical word picture of an average or typical family in Leslie County. "Such an average family of five persons," she said, "has a yearly modal total family income of $416.50; a yearly modal per-capita income of $85.70; a yearly modal money income for the family of $183.53, which is $36.70 in cash for each individual in the family for the year. Such an average family lives on a modal size farm of 10 acres, of which 7 are improved. During the year under consideration, not quite 6 acres of the 7 acres capable of being planted were put in cultivation, and only 3½ acres were harvested. This average family is struggling under adverse conditions at a pitifully low economic level."

The Bureau of Agricultural Economics has found that in the entire Appalachian area the small, strictly mountain farm usually returns little more than a bare living for the family, which generally includes six or more persons. Only small acreages are in cultivation on the slopes, the bureau reports, and these slopes often are so steep or rough that hand cultivation is practised. Of the field crops, corn occupies the greater part, and frequently all, of the acreage. Usually small gardens and a few fruit trees are found on the farms, and truck patches (in which beans, potatoes, etc., are grown to supplement the garden products) are not uncommon. A horse or mule, a cow, from one to three pigs, and a few chickens, often not exceeding twenty-five in number, is the livestock combination common to many of the farms, although frequently there are farms without a horse, a cow, or pigs. The pasture furnished by these farms is often scant, and purchases of small quantities of feed are not uncommon. To maintain a fairly good standard of living on the small mountain farm, even with a few acres of land comparatively easy to cultivate, is next to impossible without an appreciable amount of income from other sources. Earnings from work off the farm by the farm operator and other members of the family in many instances increase the family income in limited amounts. Usually these earnings are less than $100 a year, but in not a few instances they amount to $500 or more. Probably more than half of the mountain farms are under fifty acres in size, and the farm families on possibly less than half of these farms receive income from work off the farm

Homes in Knott are like those in the rest of the region. The "box houses," those made of upright planks with narrower strips covering the cracks, predominate, but there are many log cabins, a number of the better frame dwellings, and a few—a very few—brick or stone residences. The story is about told when one states that their average value is $343. However, details are worth considering. The houses can be divided into four classes: Good—those constructed of frame, brick, or stone that have at least three rooms, plastered or boarded walls on the inside, solid foundations, coats of paint, and the general appearance of having been kept in repair; fair—those of box or log construction that are sturdy, have three rooms and don't leak; poor—those of box or log that have two rooms, rough stone or post foundations, and roofs that don't leak if it doesn't rain too hard; dilapidated—those one-room, sometimes windowless cabins that look as though they will collapse if you sneeze hard. I don't know the exact proportion of each of these, but I would say that fully 50 per cent of the houses belong in the last two classes. After studying 228 houses of all types in Knott County the Department of Agriculture's Bureau of Home Economics reported that 2 per cent had plastered walls, 17 per cent had walls of tongue-and-groove boards, 6 per cent of planed boards, 66 per cent of rough boards, and 9 per cent of odds and ends. In 59 per cent of these houses the rooms were covered with newspapers and in 9 per cent with torn or dirty wallpaper. Twenty-eight per cent of the residents reported that the roofs leaked. Only about 5 per cent of farm homes in eastern

Kentucky have electric lights, piped water, telephones, and radios.

Furnishings of mountain farm homes have changed greatly in the last few decades. About the turn of the century a "typical" mountain home contained a couple of double beds in each of the two rooms. These beds were homemade wooden affairs with laced cord that supported shuck mattresses topped by featherbeds. Cane-bottomed chairs, a table, and possibly a chest of drawers and an iron stove were about the only other pieces of furniture. Gourds along the walls held salt, sugar, and soda, and hollow logs served as meat and flour barrels. Churns, washtubs, and many of the kitchen utensils were homemade pieces that stood or were hung about the cookstove or fireplace. In a corner or over the fireplace was the old, long-barreled rifle. Today the homemade furnishings have given way to cheap "brought-on" articles. They include iron beds, a "good" chair or two in addition to the cane-bottoms, a marble-topped dresser, a "safe" or cabinet and a stove in the kitchen, a couple of tables, a Winchester rifle, and calendars and grimacing photographs.

The work of the county agents in making the best of a bad situation should not go unnoticed. The fact that the mountain farms are still able to care for the population at all is due in large part to the agents' efforts. These trained men are working in each of the counties with and for the farmers, urging them to spread more superphosphate and lime, to cultivate their bottom lands intensely and plant trees and grass on the hillsides, to grow more hay crops and less corn, to start berry patches and orchards, to increase livestock and poultry production, and to replace scrub with purebred stock. Their work has had its effect, but these men find themselves in much the same position as the county health officers. The more they do the more there is to do. Their problems are almost unsolvable.

The WPA too has aided materially. Many persons of course

condemn it on the ground it has destroyed the people's initiative, but I doubt that it deserves as much blame as it receives on that score. Conditions already had destroyed initiative before the WPA came along. F.D.R.'s WPA has provided food when food was mighty scarce and in addition has spent in the last eight years an average of more than a million and a half dollars in each of the mountain counties of eastern Kentucky. That money has provided jobs, roads where there would have been no roads, clothing, books, school buildings, courthouses, and jails. Through the fiscal year 1940 the WPA spent $1,071,097 in Knott County. It built twenty-five miles of roads—not highways, but at least passable roads—seventeen bridges and viaducts, three school buildings, one other public building—and 274 sanitary privies.

XII

To Dust Returneth

Tom picked up a piece of shale and whipped it underhanded so that it skipped along the narrow, shallow waters of the Betty Fork of Troublesome Creek. "Looks just like any other branch in the hills, doesn't it?"

"Yeh."

"With such a euphonious name, seems somehow like it ought to be different."

Troublesome. How peaceful looking this little creek, and yet how apt the name. If all the men slain along its branches in the last 100 years had been killed at one time, Flanders Fields would have had a peer.

Tom is a university professor, but I found out long ago his profession shouldn't be held against him. Good old easy-spoken Tom from the Mississippi mud flats, he's got more energy and horse sense than half a dozen ordinary college professors. Tom was writing his fourth book about Kentucky. That's why he and I and two mountain girls were heading for a funeralizing on Little Carr.

Emma, willowy, fair, and keen-eyed, had been a student of Tom's. Now she was teaching a one-room school. Dumpy little Catherine, her sister, had one more year at Caney Creek

Junior College. Then maybe she too would go down to Lexington to the university. The girls were natives of Knott County. Their father owned a farm and kept a store.

It was a beautiful early summer morning, so beautiful I didn't even mind the prospect of an eight-mile walk. The air was rain-fresh, and the sunlight fell slantwise on the red-brown of the worn hills and the green of the oaks and maples and shank-high corn. Bees worked the blossoms along the edge of the road. Betty Troublesome was unusually full for the time of year, and click beetles scurried around puddles in the road, which crossed and re-crossed her. A titmouse whistled somewhere overhead, and a sapsucker hammered on a dying beech. Above all other sounds came the metallic cadence of a million locusts.

"Those confound locusts make a lot of noise, don't they?" Tom remarked as he looked for a place to cross Betty again without getting his shoes muddier.

"Yeah," I answered, "but I guess they don't do much harm. They don't seem to hurt the trees."

"I've heard it said," proffered Em, "that they ruin the blackberries by layin' their eggs on the blooms."

"I've heard they poison spring water too," Catherine chimed in.

"I've heard that," I said. "I ran across some people the other day who were carrying water nearly a mile because they said the locusts had poisoned their spring. But I don't think there's much to it. I know I read somewhere that they don't hurt blackberries."

"A woman told me the other day that the locusts brought the bean beetles sixteen years ago and took them away this year," Emma said.

"Beetles are fewer this year," I agreed, "but I guess maybe the cold winter had something to do with that. I imagine the idea that the beetles are brought or taken away by the locusts is just another superstition."

"Well, course I don't believe in superstitions," said Catherine, as her short but sturdy legs carried her up a sharp incline, "but some of them work out awfully funny. You know, people up here believe that if a granny-woman hands a new baby to a woman who's never had one and says, 'Within a year you'll be holding one of your own,' she'll have one. And I've seen it work too!"

"You haven't had one handed to you, have you?" I teased.

The blush showed between her hair and her collar as she trudged along in front of me.

"Well, I guess there's more that don't work than do," said Emma. "I had some of my older children write out the superstitions their parents told them, and you ought to see some of the lists!"

"What were some of them?" I queried.

"Well, let's see. If a baby's first trip is upcreek, he'll be upheaded, and if it's downcreek, he'll be downheaded."

"Upheaded mean smart?"

"Uh-huh—and strong willed."

"What are some others?"

"If a rooster comes up to th' kitchen door and crows with its head toward you somebody in th' house will die before the same hour the next day."

"A lot of them are about death, aren't they?" I interrupted.

"Yeah. Let's see, I ought-a know some more along that line. If you step on a new grave you'll die within a year. . . . I can't seem to think of any more o' those. They're a good many about babies. If you let a baby see itself in a lookin' glass it'll have a hard time cuttin' teeth. To make teethin' easier get a willow stick and make as many beads as the baby is months old; string them and hang them around his neck. T' keep a baby's hair from fallin' out wash it in camphor. A stranger kissin' a birthmark can make it go away."

"How about some of the old ones about witches?"

"Oh, they's plenty of those all right. I think this is a pretty good one. . . . If someone is a seventh child and born on th' seventh day of th' month they can make a knockin' spirit. T' do that they go on top of th' highest mountain, curse God, and say, 'I give myself up to th' Devil.' Then they have control of a knockin' spirit."

"Whatta they do with it after they've got it?"

"Well, they make tables walk an' chairs jump and. . . . I knew an old woman once who claimed she had a knockin' spirit she could make knock on people's teeth an' scare th' daylights out of 'em. 'Knock ole hell,' she'd say."

"An old preacher over in Magoffin County told me about a man who must have had a knockin' spirit or something after him," I commented. "He said this fellow swore he was bewitched and that the witch would get on him and ride him various places every night. One night this man decided he'd mark the place where she rode him to—and the next morning his bed was soiled!"

"Say, that's getting pretty bad," cautioned Emma. "But my face was kindly red at one of those lists I was tellin' you about. You know the old superstitions about if you drop a knife a woman's comin' and if you drop a fork a man's comin' and so forth. Well, one of my seventh grade boys brought in one that said, 'If you drop a dishrag, a bitch-whore's coming.' I asked him what that meant, but he just said, 'I donno; Mammy tol' me hit.' "

"That's not bad," I laughed. "That old preacher told me his mother had believed in witches. He said she thought his aunt was a witch and that a witch-doctor told her she could be protected from the spell by not lending anything to this aunt."

"There are a good many ways to break a witch's spell," said Em. "For instance people use to think that witches kept th' butter from churning. To kill the witch so th' next batch would churn they'd take nine witch hazel switches an' switch through the milk as they poured it into a fire. Another way to kill a witch was to draw a picture on a tree of the person thought to be the witch, then shoot th' picture with a silver bullet."

"A lot of the superstitions have to do with bad luck, don't they?"

"Oh yes, they's thousands of those. Why, it use to be considered bad luck even to have a woman visit you on New Year's Day!"

Our conversation was interrupted by the deep-throated baying of three hounds.

"Howdy," Catherine sang out.

"Howdy," came a reply from the dogtrot of a two-room cabin.

"Goin' to th' funeral-preachin'?"

"Nope, guess I kain't," answered the bearded man on the little porch. "Quin's gone an' I reckon I'd better stay home an' keep house. You-all come up an' rest a spell."

"Thanks, guess we'd better be gettin' 'long though. More'n likely they'll start early."

"Guess that's right."

"Quin and Zach there aren't much above the eyes," Catherine told us after we'd walked on. "They're brothers. Never have got married. Live there just the two of 'em, and Zach does the cooking."

"Look at that little old granny-hatchet go, would you!"

"What's a granny-hatchet?" Tom asked.

"Lizard."

"See that big rock and that hole over there in that slate bank?" queried Catherine. "A man got mashed all to pieces there."

"How?"

"Groundhoggin' coal and th' rock rolled down on him. Remind me to show you when we go back where a man got shot. There's a little tree markin' it. They say the tree started to grow there the night he was killed."

"O.K.—say, Emma, have you ever heard of a dumb supper?" I asked.

"Oh sure. I even attended one once."

"It's sort of a way to catch a man, isn't it? How does it go?"

"Well, when several girls around a neighborhood figure they're gettin' to be on the cull list they sometimes plan one of these dumb suppers. They all meet at somebody's house at night and set a meal. While they're getting things ready they walk backwards and nobody can say a word. If anybody walks forward, or looks behind her, or talks, or laughs, or even smiles, then the spell is broken. They set two places at the table for each girl, and they carry the plates, knives, forks, glasses, and so forth one at a time. Everything's supposed to be ready before midnight, and if nobody has broken any of the rules, then they all sit down at their places. At twelve o'clock if any of the girls are going to get married within a year their husbands-to-be will walk in, sit down, and take a drink from their glasses. But if there are any of the girls who will never marry, their coffins will show up beside them."

"Does it ever work?"

"Well, in a way. The girls always let it out there's going to be a dumb supper, so if there's a boy who's been talkin' to a girl some time and is about ready to ask her the question, he may show up. Sometimes even two or three show up. Then sometimes maybe some of the girls' brothers will fix up t' scare them by slippin' a coffin into the room."

"By George," observed Tom, "I believe it's going to rain."

Dark clouds were gathering along the ridge tops, and it was growing blacker over toward the head of Betty Troublesome.

"We'd better step on it," Tom warned. And we did.

We'd walked possibly another half mile when there was a rumble behind us I thought at first was thunder. It was a truck, rumbling and rattling and lurching from side to side as first one wheel and then another plunged into a rut or struck a boulder. Fifteen or twenty men, women, and children stood or sat in the bed among Coca-Cola cases and ice-cream freezers.

"Wanna ride?" the driver invited. We had climbed a bank to get out of the truck's path.

"You bet!" I couldn't see room for four more, but we piled on somehow, and a little farther along we picked up two more.

A skiff in a heavy sea couldn't have bounded and rocked more than that truck did. I grabbed a siderail with one hand, the tailgate with the other, and stood as spraddle-legged as I could without stepping on somebody. When we'd hit a particularly deep rut the siderail would grate against the bank, and occasionally we'd have to duck to keep a limb from knocking our heads off. Still everybody laughed and joked as we pitched against one another or barked our shins on a row of pop cases.

The graveyard, as are all mountain burying grounds, was located well above the creek's highwater mark. It was on a rounded knoll 200 yards from the roadway, and most of that 200 yards was sharp acclivity. In the very center of the little plot towered a massive oak, a virgin tree that seemed to look down proudly upon its lesser brethren.

The oak evidently was to be used as a pulpit, for scattered in a circle around it, sitting or standing between the graves, were the people who had come from along Little Carr, from Defeated Creek, from Spider and Amburgey and Bath and Irishman, and even as far away as the upper waters of Left Beaver to hear the funeral-preaching for a man who had been dead more than a year.

On Blinky Shade Anderson's grave was spread an embroidered counterpane. Over it were scattered brilliant red, purple, yellow, and green crepe-paper flowers, and from the bushes near the grave floated gay paper streamers—a touching, pathetic tribute. Unlike many of the graves in the little burying ground Blinky Shade's was marked by a headstone. It was a flat piece of sandstone, planted upright. On it was scratched, "Shade Anderson–Born Jan. 4, 1894–Died March 11, 1939." Fastened to it by a piece of wire was a small photograph of Shade, fading already despite its protecting frame.

A gaunt, sharp-nosed man, sallow of face and long of neck, began to read haltingly, his Adam's apple working up and down like an elevator. It was Blinky Shade's obituary he was reading, and here's the way it was written:

Shade Anderson known to one and all as Blinky Shade borned Jan. 4, 1894. Departed this life March 11, 1939 age 45 yrs 2 months & 7 days he was the son of Solomon and Rachel Anderson. He was married to Octavia Slone June 5–1912 to this Union was borned 9 children. 2 of them proceded Him in death oh What a happy meeting I believe they had and seven still with their mother to mourn the loss of Father together with Sister Octavia his wife but we hope our loss is his eternal gain. The people that Knew that he was a good morial citizen and was loved by all. he had been a praying man ever Since he lost his children and had made many confession to his friends. to that effect he was a changed man. He joined the Old Regular Baptist Church and was baptized and lived a faithful member and devoted christian until shot down in the middle of the Road in the prime of life by a dirty coward from ambush. to his family he said a few days before he got killed that when he died not to worry over him for he didn't think there was anything but Death between him and His God. His wife was with him in the Hospital When he called for his children and told them to pray. Sweet Jesus had come and he had to go home with him. when he met with this sad hour of Death all was well with him. As he grew weaker he would talk of seeing the heavenly companys coming to convey him Home. We will not write all Of the sweet words that he left but we feel shure that the Lord did come and took him home so we would say to the children not to forget the council that father gave them to pray and meet him in Heaven. This is getting lengthy so it must end.

He had just finished the obituary when the threatening clouds began to drop great pellets of water. Soon they were falling so thick and fast the oak no longer afforded shelter, and the crowd dispersed down the hillside. The few who had come in automobiles hurried to them; others crept under the trucks; still others tried to make a tent out of a tarpaulin, but the majority wandered around in the downpour like a bunch of turkeys. A frightened mule reared against his bridle, jerked a fence rail loose, and galloped off, tripping now and again over the rail. A woman with a baby in her arms tried to leap the branch. She slipped and sprawled in the water but never let go of the baby.

The shower ended as abruptly as it had started, and the sun shone again. But what the drenching had done to the courtin'-age girls! Cheap crepe and satin dresses had shrunk inches, and they clung to buttocks, thighs, and breasts despite determined pullings fore and aft.

The ground was too wet for sitting, and so the meeting was adjourned to a schoolhouse a mile down the road. Off we straggled, the girls still yanking at their clinging dresses or trying to rearrange disheveled locks.

When the men and women had tucked their knees under the low, two-seated desks of the one-room school and the children had found places in the aisles or on tops of desks, the mourners filed in and arranged themselves along the recitation bench in the front of the room. There was buxom Sister Octavia, Shade's widow—yet no longer a widow. Only last month she had found her a new man to help hoe the corn and scythe the weeds and do other things a man is good for. There was Sister Octavia's wizened aunt, her long-bearded grandpappy, her in-laws by the first marriage, and her seven living children.

Brother Lem Miller, he of the galloping Adam's apple, kneeled in front of the mourners' bench and led off with a prayer. "Ohhhhmmmmm Godddd [rising inflection] be merciful unto Sister Tabia in her lonesome hour. Ohhhhh mmmmm Godddd I pray you to go with us t'day. Ohhhmmm Goddd remember Sister Tabia's children. Throw an arm o' protection 'roun' them an' guide them on their way. Ohhhhhh mmmmmm Jesus Master, be with Sister Tabia an' her family on their way home this evenin'. Ohhhhhmmmmmm Father Father cause them to realize without Thy grace they can't be saved. Let us die in th' right mind that we may call our chil'ren in an' warn them of everlastin' eternity. Ohhhhh mmmmmm Lorddd when our souls and bodies separate, take us home. . . ."

He prayed thus for twenty minutes by the watch, and when he at last arose, wobbling, from his knees, tears were flowing along the mourners' bench. His prayer had been successful.

A tall, bronzed man took over as Brother Lem sat down and mopped his lean face contentedly. "Jest as shore as we're a-settin' in this hyar room t'day we'll all meet th' same death as Brother Shade. Not mayhaps by 'ssassin's bullet, but we'll meet it one way er t'other. But let God's will be done an' not ourn. I'm God's servant sent out t' tell th' dyin' world of th' life t' come fer them that lives His word. Jest one man kin preach th' gospel, an' that's th' man, uh yes sir, God has called and sent out to th' field. I, uh yes sir, knowed this, uh yes sir, man fer many years, an' I, uh yes sir, see his face in this church, uh yes sir, and I seen it in th' graveyard, uh yes sir, uh yes sir, but I know he's gone over thar where pain won't tetch him no more."

The "uh yes sirs" came after every few words as he worked himself into a frenzy. Then he'd halt the rigmarole and talk quite calmly for a while.

"These ole bodies of ourn will molder back to dust, but th' inward man will go back to God from where hit came. I'm a man what tries to please. Sister, you can go an' tell that grave up thar on th' hill, 'Grave, you can't hold th' body of my husban' forever.' In th' sweet bye and bye he'll come out o' thar an' he'll have a body what'll know no pain, a body what'll know no thirst, a body what'll know no hunger. Hit don't make no never mind how many rocks er how much dirt er how much wood you pile on him, you can't keep him down. But them that don't repent this side o' th' grave shore won't have no chanct on t'other side.

"Hit may be afore th' goin' down of th' sun this evenin' that we'll be deprived of th' priv-lege to repent, fer th' pale horse and th' rider er a-comin'. There's a-comin' a day when you'll find no shelter. There's a-comin' a day when th' young boys will be a-goin' to th' battlefield and when that day comes, uh yes sir, uh yes sir, put your faith in Him [pointing to the roof]. Oh I've been left without a father er a mother, uh yes sir, but I wouldn't ask them to come back into this troubled world. A man what raises up his arm and says, 'I believe in th' Father, th' Son, and th' Ghost,' he'll go to Heaven if he never seen ary hole o' water in his life. A man what hain't been reginerated and reborn don't know nothin'. What sin you have committed that's th' one you're a-goin' to pay for, uh yes sir. Brother Shade was here, but he's moved out. He's gone to another shore unknown to us. I've heared them that stood at th' grave and said, 'Farewell, farewell, I'll never see you again.' Oh I, uh yes sir, wouldn't say that fer nothin' on this yearth! I expect, uh yes sir, t' see my loved ones over thar in th' sweet bye and bye."

Tom and I went outside to listen to the conversations of the groups scattered around the schoolyard, at the ice-cream-and-pop truck, and on the stone wall along the creek bank. Two others took our seats. The preaching would go on for maybe three hours, and during that time there would be a complete turnover of audience—all except the mourners. When it looked as though the last bit of emotion had been wrung from them somebody would pass around a photograph of Blinky Shade in his coffin, Blinky Shade lying there so white and still and natural-like

To Dust Returneth

Odd things, these delayed funerals; yet there's good reason for their origin. When a man dies in the wintertime far back off a passable road it more than likely isn't convenient to hold a funeral then. There may be no preacher available; arrangements for a big funeral can't be made quickly; many people can't attend because of the weather and the condition of the roads. So the body is laid to rest quietly, and the real funeral, a memorial service, comes later.

Funeralizings are not as common as in days past, and town residents and those of some means living in the country have funerals as people do elsewhere, fancy caskets and all. But often when an average back-country dweller dies, a homemade coffin is fashioned from whatever lumber is available. It may be bought at a near-by sawmill. It may be jerked from a barn loft. Usually the coffin is lined with white muslin and covered on the outside with black muslin. The corpse is dressed in new clothes or in such manner as may have been requested. At times strange requests are made. One man may want to be buried barefooted. Another may wish to be laid away in an old suit he liked. Seldom is the body embalmed, and generally it is kept in the house just one night. On the next day the crude coffin is carried to the little graveyard and placed in the hole dug by members of the family or friends. The box is opened for the last look and there's some weeping and moaning. Maybe somebody says a few words, and maybe there's a song. Then the coffin is closed, boards are laid over it and the dirt is piled on.

Next summer, perhaps the summer after or maybe even several years later, the real funeral services will be held. Often they are held for several people who have died since the last funeralizing at the burying ground. Sometimes the family of the deceased puts on a big party and feeds all those who come. I know of a widow who saved for two years to stage a funeralizing and dinner she felt did justice to her dead husband. Not all of them are sad. I attended one at which an afternoon ball game followed the morning preaching.

The mountaineer is singularly callous toward death. Frequently, during the death watch, a jug or bottle is produced and everybody drinks and swaps yarns. The only real emotion is manifested at the brief committal services. That displayed at the funeralizings the preachers manufacture through their hellfire sermons or the pictured corpses in coffins.

XIII

Trees of God's Rough Acre

A FLOOD STRUCK Breathitt one February night in 1939. Great walls of water thundered down the hills and swept the hollows clean. Fifty-one human beings and 1,000 head of hogs and cattle were engulfed by the swirling waters and crushed against the rocks. Hundreds of homes, sturdy log cabins and fragile board shacks alike, were smashed and rent like fiber crates. Acre upon countless acre of the precious top-soil was torn from the scraggy hills and washed away.

It was not the first flood in Kentucky's highlands. Nor was it the last. Flash floods they call them, because, unlike the stealthily creeping inundations of the great rivers, they strike in the night and are gone in the morning, leaving desolate farm and urban communities that are miles from streams of any size. Flash floods they are, but something else too. They are a part of the price for the forests' destruction, that tragedy of tragedies in God's rough acre.

When first the hill dwellers looked out from mountain peak upon the deep-troughed waves of tree boughs they knew they had never seen more magnificent forests. In summer the swelling sea was varied, feathery green; in autumn a glow-ing mass of sunset beauty. Even in stark winter the boughs were a network of silver majesty, melting into the blue haze that forms the highland sky.

Along the river banks grew papaw thickets, and with them over the foothills were giant sycamores, red and white elms, lindens, ash, buckeyes, lynns, beeches, liriodendrons, swamp alders, hemlocks, pitch elders, red oaks, ironwoods, amelanchiers, sweet gums, golden alexanders, red and black haws, and hawthorns. In the ravines were hickory and walnut and chestnut trees. On the higher hills reared post oaks, black oaks, scarlet oaks, mountain oaks, black locusts, pines, holly, white oaks, laurels, poplars, black cherries, cucumbers, cedars, persimmons, spicewoods, dogwoods, white ash, black gums, and chestnut oaks. Tops of the hills were crowned with black oaks, rock maples, hickories, and pines.

Virgin white and yellow poplars, white oaks, and mountain chestnuts were six to ten feet through their mighty trunks, and they rose as straight toward the sky as cathedral spires.

Here, it seemed, was a forest illimitable, inexhaustible.

For the first fifty or sixty years after the white settlers made their way up the creek beds the forests were not seriously damaged. The hillsmen cut trees to make their homes and to cook their meals; they girdled them and burned them to make way for the corn, but they did not make serious inroads in the great preserve.

By the middle of the nineteenth century, however, population pressure began to be felt. Families of ten children produced 100 grandchildren, and there had to be more room for more corn. Trees were a nuisance when food was the aim. The up-the-hollow trend started, and steeper and steeper slopes were cleared for the crops. The hills balded like an aging man.

Then in the 70's and 80's American and foreign markets turned to Appalachia for hardwoods. Trees became something more than things of beauty or obstacles to cultivation. They became a source of cash income. But there were no roads in Kentucky's highlands, and since it was next to impossible to take sawmills into the forests, the forests were taken to the sawmills. The creeks and rivers furnished the means.

In the summer the mountain men worked their crops as usual, but in the winter they turned loggers. At first their broadaxes rang against the trunks of the big poplars and oaks and walnuts near the creeks. Then they felled those farther back and snaked them down the hillsides with chains and oxen or mules. What matter if young trees were crushed in the dragging? There were plenty more.

Most of the creeks were too shallow to float huge logs, but in the spring there were tides, rushes of water from rains and melting snow. Of these the loggers took advantage. Choosing places along the stream where the banks were high, they built square pens on either side of the creek bed, and they filled the pens with rocks. Between these piers they built log dams, gated in the center, and behind them they rolled the logs bound for the mill. All winter they worked, cutting and building and rolling and snaking. Then at spring equinox the tides came, forming lakes behind the series of dams. When all was ready the triggers on the dams' gates were pulled, and the avalanche of logs pounded down the hollow.

The men worked furiously to keep the logs from jamming or swirling off on the bank. Gorge locks were near catastrophes, for if logs piled so tightly they could not be loosened immediately, the tide was past and there would be no pay check that spring. The men then had to work through another summer, tearing loose the jam and building new splash dams. But stranded logs were not so serious. They were left to rot along the banks.

From Sprucepine, Bad, Greasy, and Lovely, from Bent, Marrowbone, Cutshin and Grassy, Bull, Turkey, Old Buck, and Hell-for-Certain the logs swept down into the Middle

Fork of the Kentucky River. From Goose Creek, Cow, Buffalo, and Red Bird they floated into the South Fork, and from Fishtrap, Leatherwood, Lost, Quicksand, and Frozen they found their way into the North Fork.

Out of Perry and Breathitt came great squared timbers of white oak, bound for Liverpool and the shipyards. They were so big a man could ride a single timber, and so long he had to keep it endways, even in the river.

As Western cattlemen had their brands, each mountain logger had his mark. But logs, like Texas longhorns, sometimes were rustled. On April 17, 1891, the now-extinct Jackson *Hustler*, weekly paper in Breathitt, deplored:

> It is a great shame that rights of property in the State of Kentucky are not more sacred. These lumber enterprises at Ford that are scattering so much money in the mountains and giving such a steady market for timber ought to be regarded with more consideration. They are unmercifully preyed upon on the Kentucky River by men who rob them of their logs. On every tide, logs are stolen and their ends cut off to get rid of the brands of the owners. These logs are sometimes carried up little creeks and manufactured into shingles and lumber. In some places on the river this stealing is going on to such extent and is so tolerated and encouraged by the people regarded as respectable that it is almost impossible to arrest or convict those engaged in this nefarious business.

Once out of the hollows and into the larger flows, from 40 to 120 logs, depending upon length of tree and width of stream, were lashed together in rafts. For buoyancy the lighter poplars, pines, hemlocks, lynns, and ash were tied to the heavier oaks, walnuts, hickories, beeches, and maples. Then long sweeps, one fore and one aft, were fastened to the rafts with knee poles and dowel pins. Bow hands and steersmen manned the sweeps, and the rafts were off for the journey down the river.

At Beattyville, if it was into one of the three forks of the

Kentucky the logs had been splashed, the rafts were made into great booms and towed or floated on down through the palisades, through the rolling Bluegrass region, and into Frankfort, the sawmills' home in early lumber days.

A rowdy, hard-drinking, hard-shooting lot were those raftsmen. For them the annual trip to Frankfort was an adventure that paid off in gold at the journey's end. With that gold they could buy excitement—and they did. It was not unusual for members of the clan to spend in a few days of drinking, gambling, and carousing all they had collected for their year's efforts. Some among those thus financially exhausted, plus others who took a liking to the level country, decided not to go back, and, having come by the river, they settled by the river. Along the Kentucky's banks grew a colony known as the Craw. A strange settlement it was, a settlement of beachcombers with the fierce independence of the mountaineers. As the years passed it became a world unto itself, a place where men did as they pleased and defied the law to change them. But after the sawmills left Frankfort and moved closer to the timber the Craw gradually passed into oblivion. The last remnants were swept away by the Kentucky's 1937 flood.

The majority of the loggers of course went back home when the logs were sold, but the celebration didn't end when the return trip started. This fact was so well recognized by the Louisville and Nashville Railroad that it chartered coaches to the lumbermen. The men then paid their proportionate shares for a coach instead of buying tickets. In this way the L. and N. segregated the men with the axes and guns from the less boisterous passengers.

One day as the conductor was about to give the signal for the start toward Lexington a bearded logger staggered up to the door of the loggers' car. "Lemme in," he shouted.

"The car's full," the conductor answered.

"By Gawd I paid my share an' I'm a-gonna ride!"

"The car's full," the conductor repeated. And he closed the door.

A minute later he threw it open, and this time he begged, "For the Lord's sake, come on in!"

The logger was hewing himself a door in the side of the car.

At another time a timberman stumbled through the station and tried to make his way to the coach. "You can't ride that train," growled a Frankfort officer. "You're too drunk."

The logger just mumbled something and staggered on. The officer made a leap and grabbed him by the collar. "I'm going to arrest you."

"Go ahead," said a voice from the coach.

The policeman looked up into a muzzle of a long-barreled rifle. Behind it was a steady, cold eye.

"Go ahead an' arrest him."

The officer turned around and quickly walked away.

All the way back to the end of the line at Jackson, or to Irvine when that road was built, the men continued their spree. Usually there was nothing the trainmen could do, but in desperation one day Conductor Bradshaw uncoupled the lumbermen's coaches and left them standing on the track between Lexington and Winchester.

That part of the trip that could not be made by rail usually was made afoot. The men walked 25, 50, 70, 100 miles on the last laps of their journey. It took about ten days to run a raft to Frankfort from Hyden and about four days to travel back. The men sometimes rode the train back to Lexington, a wagon to Irvine, and walked in two days the last sixty-odd miles to Hyden.

Many are the anecdotes told of days when logs were snaked by oxen and splashed into the streams. Here is one related by A. B. Combs, a former sheriff of Perry County:

"Shade Combs was quite a fellow, but he came in for a lot of kidding. One day Shade was snaking a tremendous log toward the North Fork when he got too close to the edge of a cliff. The dirt started to slide a little, one of the oxen lost its footing, and then the whole shebang–oxen, log, Shade, and all–went a-tumblin' and a-bouncin' down through the rocks and bushes. It nearly killed Shade–broke his leg and cut and bruised him all up. He wasn't able to get about for several months. When he finally did get out he came into Hazard, and while he was walking around on the street he ran into White Jim Combs. Jim asked him where he'd been so long. Jim of course had heard about Shade getting hurt, but he just wanted to kid him a little. Well Shade told him what had happened. 'I'll tell you,' he said, 'if that damn clift hadda been one inch higher hit shorely would've kilt me graveyard dead.' Jim laughed. 'I al'ays knowed,' he said, 'that th' clifts in this hyar country wasn't high enough.' "

At about the turn of the century, sawmills were established at Jackson, Beattyville, and West Irvine, and fewer booms were taken on to Frankfort. The Jackson *Hustler* tells, in somewhat unsteady language, about lumbering operations in Breathitt from about 1900 to 1910:

> The Swan-Day Lumbering Company, had one of the biggest mills in the world located here at Jackson. Ford Lumber Company also had a large manufacture of lumber. These concerns dealt in ties and staves which were brought down the river by tens of thousands when the river was said to be tided. This was called tie and stave drives. There were large booms made of logs chained end to end, for miles up the river. At points they were separated by shares. Hundreds of men were employed at these points with spike poles bringing inside of booms that which they wanted that was branded or marked. The others were let float on. They worked day and night. By night they had pine torches and large fires made of cannel coal. This work lasted until the tide left or the end of the drive. Log drives were similar to stave and tie drives. . . . At points there were telephones along the river owned by different concerns, connected with telegraph offices along the railroad, where the river was in

view. They kept each point advised as to the stage of the river and approximately the number of material floating by per minute. Jackson was the principal point for this figure. Observing from the old bridge a float per minute, which ran into the thousands. Occasionally some man working on the boom lost his life. Jackson was equipped with a loading hoist and long docks. Materials were taken from the river and inspected later loaded into railroad cars. This industry furnished enough cars for three or four trains daily.

During the years just preceding the first World War, railroads branched farther into the hills, and the heyday of river logging passed. However the streams were still employed to a certain extent for several years after the war, and in Leslie County, which still has no railroads, logs were floated down the Middle Fork until 1932.

In 1910 E. O. Robinson and F. W. Mobray established a mill at Quicksand, three miles up the North Fork from Jackson in Breathitt. Operations of the Mobray-Robinson mill during the next fourteen years were typical of the intensive lumbering by big concerns during the first two and a half decades of the twentieth century. The railroad was extended from Jackson to Quicksand, and narrow-gauge tracks were jabbed into the hills in all directions. The company bought land—15,000 acres—it bought timber rights, and it bought logs from others. It continued in Breathitt County the boom the Swan-Day company had started. It employed 500 men, and Quicksand grew to a town of 2,000. Sawing the great trees into boards at a rate of 100,000 feet a day, Mobray-Robinson became the biggest hardwood producer in the world. At its main office in Cincinnati it took orders for lumber from all over the nation, and it opened a branch in Liverpool to handle the export trade.

By 1924 Breathitt and the adjacent sections of Perry, Knott, and Magoffin were stripped. Mobray-Robinson moved out.

Today there isn't even a ghost town at Quicksand. Even

the course of the railroad was changed so that it no longer runs through there. With the closing of the mill the people scattered back to their hill farms. And it was only then that they realized that their greatest resource was gone and they had nothing to show for it.

When the big band mills move out of a section the little portable mills begin their scavenger work. Small trees and stumps are hauled in trucks to these steam- or gasoline-powered mills and sawed into low-grade lumber or barrel heading. This work, largely the kind being done today, represents the last stage of decline of the lumber industry.

After Mobray and Robinson finished their job they turned their 15,000 acres over to the University of Kentucky, and the school's College of Agriculture set about to reclaim the despoiled land. It is unfortunate that all the lumbered land could not have been turned over as was this tract. The university established an experimental substation at Quicksand. During the first two years the principal tasks were razing the lumber shacks, hauling away tons of sawdust, and building a headquarters. Then began the tedious process of reforesting the stripped land and of carrying out experiments in agronomy, animal husbandry, and horticulture in an effort to make the best of a bad situation.

Extension forester for the university is W. E. Jackson. During the last four years he has been in charge of reforestation work on the Quicksand holding, and before that time he served twelve years in the Federal forestry service and ten years as Kentucky state forester. One day he and I sat in a swing on the broad veranda of the substation lodge. "Tell me," I requested, "just what you think of forestry in the mountains today and what you expect in the future." Here is what he said:

"Much of this hill land has been cropped so long and then grazed so long that the soil is too thin even to grow trees. Land that is not too thin will reforest itself if given a chance, but it will reforest in the poorer species, because they are the ones left standing in the cutover tracts. To avoid a growth of undesirable, or at least second-rate, trees some planting must be done. There is one great factor in our favor. Timber in the hills of Kentucky grows back true to type. I mean by that that Southern pine land, for instance, reforests in scrub oak, but trees indigenous to the Kentucky hills, and there are few worth-while hardwoods that are not, come back in as hearty and valuable form as the virgin growths, provided of course that the right species are given a chance.

"Another point in our favor is that lumber companies are beginning to cut on a sustained-yield rather than a strip basis. The breakdown of our reforestation work lies with the small farmers, who own their land and feel they can strip it if they please. There are perhaps 10,500,000 acres of land in Kentucky classified as forest land, but nine million of this is pitiful in its forest inventory. Heavy cutting, fires, and continued grazing have made conditions what they are, and usually an inventory shows that there is by no means as much worth-while timber on a tract as appears at first glance. Of the 10,500,000 acres eight million are in farm holdings. We've got to educate those farmers in some way to the point where they will not strip their land. By intensive farming of bottoms they can get along without breaking the slopes, for the slopes don't produce anyway. I would like to see the government place a restriction on the degree of slope that can lawfully be broken. It's got to be that or outright government ownership. I really despair of the individual farmer. I had hoped that the opening of this country by highways linking the county seats would bring enlightenment and a change in idea about handling land, but the situation is as bad as ever."

Through five steps, then, the hills have been denuded, and all five have been accompanied by uncontrolled forest fires. The steps are these: (1) clearing land for crops; (2) splash-logging to mills outside the highlands; (3) splash-logging to mills within the region; (4) rail- and wagon-logging to such great bandsaw mills as Mobray-Robinson; and (5) truck-logging to numerous small portable mills.

The rapidity with which the hills were stripped is shown in the fact that the original hardwood stand of approximately forty-five billion feet had been reduced by 1910 to eighteen billion feet and by 1922 to five billion. And the most tragic part is this: the exploitation has been of only incidental benefit to the local populations.

At the present time saw-timber in the mountain counties of Kentucky, West Virginia, Virginia, North Carolina, and Tennessee is being cut or destroyed by fire, insects, or disease at a rate of three billion board feet a year—six times as fast as the trees are growing.

A few years ago Ronald Craig, forester at the time for the Kentucky Agricultural Experiment Station, made a careful study of timber in Knott County. His findings are of interest, since Knott is just about a median county in timber stand.

Sixty-three per cent of the timber left in the county, he reported, was oak and hickory. Fifteen per cent was beech and poplar, and the remaining 22 per cent was red maple, sugar maple, hemlock, basswood, black gum, black locust, and cucumber magnolia. The valuable walnut had all but vanished. A blight had brought extinction to the chestnut. Many other trees that once had flourished on Knott's hillsides and ridges were gone.

Moreover he stated that 58 per cent of the existing stand was defective, largely because of devastating forest fires that blighted but didn't kill. "The causes of past fires," he said, "were brush-burning, smoking, and deliberate incendiarism. No attempt was made to extinguish a fire once started, and so burned areas frequently totaled thousands of acres."

Craig pointed out that 75 per cent of the county's land was good for forests and nothing else, and that yet the strongest objection owners raised to devoting the land to timber was that they needed it for corn. "The answer," he asserted, "is that the farmer will make more money in the long run from timber than from corn. He must get his cash income from sources other than 40 to 80 per cent slopes. He can get it from intensive cultivation of bottom lands and lower slopes, from mineral leases, and, as he does now, from labor off the farm, for which he would have more time if crop acreages were reduced. Meanwhile returns from the farm in timber will be gradually increasing, whereas returns from land in crops would be gradually decreasing."

On Red Bird River in Clay County lies the Ford camp, headquarters for the timber holdings of Henry Ford. They include 115,000 acres in six counties—45,000 in Clay, 61,000 in Leslie, and the rest in Perry, Letcher, Bell, and Harlan. Although 100,000 of the 115,000 acres are in merchantable hardwoods and include almost the last of the hills' virgin stand, Ford's land is not being lumbered. Thus it is a liability to him, since he must pay taxes and receive no income. But the holdings are a sort of legacy for coming generations of mountaineers. As long as that land is held as it is the timber is safe, and in all probability when lumber operations are begun they will be carried out on a sustained-yield basis.

The mountain people continue to live on the Ford property. Some pay a little rent in cash or labor. Others give nothing more in return than their services as fire watchers. "We'd be better off," said Ford's manager, Chris Queen, "if we had just a fourth as many people on the land as we do. But they won't leave, and most of the few who do leave come back. We let them clear enough land to get along on and use enough timber to repair their homes. But they are seldom satisfied with having the forests as they are. Always it's, 'Can't I clear this hill or can't I clear that ridge.' "

In 1933 the Federal government had under consideration the purchase of land in the most mountainous region of the state for extension of the Cumberland National Forest. Long interested in forestation because of a belief that in it lay the salvation of the hill country, Mrs. Mary Breckinridge, head of the Frontier Nursing Service, prepared a petition to the National Forest Reservation Commission asking that land still in timber be purchased rather than land already despoiled. She pointed out:

"A national plan for conservation of timber and flood control should include the virgin forests on the watersheds. To allow the few existing stands of such timber to be ruthlessly destroyed, after the fashion of typical American lumbering, and then to take over the land and reforest it, is costly and wasteful in the extreme. In many thousands of acres of timber land in the region (Laurel, Clay, Owsley, McCreary, Whitley, Knox, Perry, Leslie, Bell, and Harlan counties) there is a 60 per cent stand of white oak. It would take seventy to one hundred years to get a new stand. It would take forty years to get a new stand of poplar, the most valuable of the softwoods in this area. The custom of allowing the forests to be destroyed and then replanted, obviously costly in money and time, has a further disadvantage. When the forests are gone the uncontrolled waters rush to the Mississippi, carrying the soil with them, before the forests can be replanted."

She stated that, "while the initial cost of acquiring virgin timber lands is of course higher than the cost of buying cutover lands, the ultimate cost is less." She submitted a list she had compiled of the owners of the largest tracts in the area. Concerning these tracts and their owners she said that the assessed valuation averaged $12 an acre but that the land probably could be purchased for even less. The reasons: (1) the owners were hard-pressed at the time, and since they had bought at low prices they probably would sell low; (2) the precious bottom land need not be included in the purchase.

"This virgin timber," she said, "can be bought at the present time more reasonably than it could have been bought five years ago and probably more reasonably than it can be bought again. In buying this timber land the government will not only be saving the watersheds from destruction and providing an economic outlet for the population but will furnish a yardstick by means of which can be determined the feasibility of scientific forestry to replace wasteful lumbering before the last stands of virgin timber on the watersheds are destroyed."

The forest commission did give serious consideration to Mrs. Breckinridge's suggestion, and it made a survey of the territory. But in 1935 Regional Forester R. M. Evans wrote: "I am sorry to tell you the time does not seem ripe to extend the Cumberland Forest eastward. By that I mean that while forest conditions are such as to lend themselves admirably to national forest purposes, and opportunities for public service accruing from national forest ownership are abundantly present, the majority of the landowners are not now willing to dispose of their holdings at prices which the government would consider equitable."

So the commission passed up the last of Kentucky's old timber stand and continued to add to the submarginal acres it began acquiring in 1930 in the Red River section of Powell, Wolfe, and Menifee counties. Acre after worn-out acre was purchased at an average price of $3.78 until today the boundaries of the Cumberland National Forest include 1,338,221 acres in sixteen counties—Rowan, Morgan, Bath, Menifee, Powell, Wolfe, Lee, Estill, Jackson, Owsley, Rockcastle, Laurel, Pulaski, McCreary, Whitley, and Wayne. Of the 1,338,221 acres within the boundaries, however, only 425,629 have been acquired by the government. The Cumberland National Forest is largely a forest in name only. Seventy-five per cent of the timber considered merchantable stands on 165,000 acres, and even these acres are in second growth. The remainder of the 425,629 support for the most part a scrubby growth that will be of no value for years.

With a capital investment of $1,610,766 the forest is a liability now—to the National Forest Service for upkeep, to the counties through loss of tax revenues in the change from private to public ownership. But it is a potential asset, and a great one. In years to come the counties will realize far more from 25 per cent of timber-sale receipts than they did from direct taxation. It is estimated that the 165,000 acres actually in timber can produce on a sustained-yield basis 12,000,000 board feet each year for the next twenty years. Maximum production from the entire forest, sixty to eighty years in the future, is estimated at 50,000,000 board feet. And the forest not only will provide income for the counties but work for the residents. About 3.5 man-days of labor are required to turn 1,000 board feet from standing timber to lumber. Concerning work opportunities afforded, Forest Supervisor H. L. Borden said:

"We sell timber to big and little. No operator is too small or too big. We sell timber in amounts as low as $10 and as large as $40,000. We make a great many small sales to provide work for the small operators in the mountains. For example within the last year one mountain inhabitant purchased sufficient timber in small lots to make 1,200 railroad ties. He hired help to cut the timber; hewed the ties himself; skidded them to the roadside with his own mule; hired trucking of his product to the point of acceptance. He cleared about $600 on his operations. He has fourteen children. This $600 was probably more money than the family had seen in the last eight years."

From Washington in 1941 came word that the government planned broad legislation providing for public regulation of more than 300,000,000 acres of privately owned forest land to prevent wasting of forest resources and "to require private owners to observe cutting and replanting practices which would keep the land reasonably productive."

Progress made by the Cumberland Forest and news such as that from Washington are at least encouraging, for in the forest lies hope—however slight—for eastern Kentucky.

XIV

They Still Distill

BRRRR-iiinnnnn-gggggggggggggggggggggggggggggggg!

"Good Lord! What's that thing doing going off here in the middle of the night!"

I groped for the alarm clock. Crash! "Damn, there goes the ash tray."

Finally the alarm was off and I lay back in bed a moment and tried to collect my senses. "Now I remember. I'm supposed to go on a raid."

I snapped on the light and looked at my watch. "Two A.M.—better get out of here—long way to drive before daylight—Julian'll probably be still asleep—brrrrr, must be zero outside—better put on plenty of clothes."

Still groggy, I pulled on underwear, two pairs of wool socks, shoes, shirt, three sweaters, trousers, overalls, and corduroy jacket.

Outside the air was cold and crisp. The stars were bright. "Won't rain anyway. Ought to be all right for pictures when the sun comes up."

Beep-beep, Beep-beep, Beep-beep. No signs of life. Beep-

beep, Beep-beep. Still no signs. "Guess I'd better go in and get him. Can't wake up everybody in the neighborhood."

In answer to the bell a light in a room off the hall, a shrinking feminine figure in a nightgown, a crack in the door. "Yes?"

"Is Julian here? I was supposed to pick him up at two-thirty. We're going on a raid."

"He's upstairs. Probably didn't hear his alarm. Wait till I get back in the bedroom and then you go up and get him."

Sprawled across the bed was Julian, fully dressed, even to heavy galoshes. A bedside light burned on the table. An oversized alarm clock, set for two-fifteen, ticked away. It was two thirty-five.

I grabbed Julian by the shoulder and shook him.

"Huh? Oh!" He gazed blankly first at me and then at the clock. "Didn't that thing go off?"

"Yeh, it probably went off all right, but you just naturally didn't hear it."

"No wonder. Didn't get in till nearly two. Thought I'd just doze a little. Lordy, of all nights for that bunch to throw a party. Where's my hat?"

"Here's your hat. Come on. Grab your cameras and let's get going. We can't keep Champ waiting."

"Holy fright! Why must we go still-raiding at this ungodly hour?"

"You wanted to go yesterday."

"Yesterday wasn't in the middle of the night."

"Quit griping and come on."

Outside, Julian began to shiver. "Wow, it's colder'n a vestal virgin out here. We'll freeze to death in the bushes."

"Aw, we'll be all right once the sun comes up."

At Mt. Sterling we found Champ, the Federal revenue man, a deputy sheriff—and a restaurant. Scrambled eggs and bacon and toast and coffee never tasted so good!

"You two can leave your car here," said Champ. "We'll go

in Hank's Ford. We have some pretty bad road after we get to Frenchburg."

"Think she'll make it?" I inquired as I peered at the deputy's mud-covered 1929 jalopy.

"You're damn well tootin' she'll make it," Hank defended quickly. "She ain't much to look at, but she's been over roads a mule would shy at, and in my opinion she's got a good bit o' go in her yet."

"Can't beat a Model-A for still raiding," Champ agreed. "They can all but climb trees."

"O.K.," I apologized. "Let's be off."

We piled in and the Ford roared for the take-off. "Clutch slipping a little," Hank explained as he got her into high with difficulty. "Have to get that thing tightened before I go out again."

Hank started to sing: "Oh I got a gal in Sourwood Mountain, she won't come and I ain't a-goin' t' fetch her. . . ." We all joined in, and the raiding party was off in a holiday mood.

As we drove along through the night the roar of the car was broken only by a snatch of song, a request for a match, or a bit of banter. The highway was abandoned except for an occasional truck. Beyond the glow of Hank's headlights we could discern cultivated fields rolling off from the road. Then as the land grew bushier and knobbier we could see the dim outline of the hills, like great black clouds on the horizon. Soon those clouds were on either side of us. We were winding along through a valley.

"Hank," said Champ, "stop right up there at the next house on the left. That's where I get a little information."

Champ shouted "Hello!" three or four times, and presently there was the glow of a lamp inside. We heard a door open, voices in conversation; then Champ was back in the car and we were on our way again.

"That fellow is a pretty good source," Champ volunteered.

"He told me almost the exact location of a still we'll get this morning. He used to bootleg—and for that matter I'd bet my suspenders he still sells some."

"He bootlegs? Then how does it happen he's willing to be an informer?" I asked.

"I don't know the exact reason in his case, but a lot of our best tips come from men who are dealing in liquor themselves. Sometimes one moonshiner will inform on another because of the competition. Sometimes a bootlegger will tell on the fellow that's doing the making because he thinks he's been overcharged or because he's gotten hold of a bad batch, rot-gut you know. Then there are some who squeal just to save their own hides. They're the worst of the bunch."

"Pretty rotten business to deal with guys like that, isn't it?"

"Yep, I guess it is. We haven't got any more respect for them than the Germans, say, have for Frenchmen who sell out their country, but it's all part of the game. We'd have a tough row to hoe if we didn't have spotters. Of course not all tips come as a result of grudges. Some come from people who are honestly interested in seeing the law enforced."

"I guess you have to rely pretty much on tips in order to find stills."

"Well, not so much to find stills as to catch the distillers. We could strike out through the woods and by a lot of hard walking find stills all right, but the 'shiners would be gone. If we caught any of them it would be luck, because they generally post lookouts. When you use that method you're firing blind. The easiest and best way is to know where you're going, then get there before daylight and wait for the men to come in."

"I remember though," Hank chimed in, "that during Prohibition it wasn't nothin' to get eight or ten stills a day just by taking several men and fannin' out through the woods."

"That's right," Champ agreed. "Back in the days when 'shine was selling anywhere from $8 to $20 a gallon stills were as thick as gnats, and the makers took a lot of chances. Lordy, I've seen Federal court terms at Jackson when there were 700 liquor cases on the docket. But now with whisky selling around $2 or $2.50 it isn't worth risking much on. They hide their stills pretty well, and you can't catch many of them just hit or miss."

Hank wheeled his flivver off the highway onto a dirt road, and pretty soon we were jolting first in a creek and then alongside it. On the first steep grade the old bus started to wheeze asthmatically, and Hank ground her to a stop to fill the radiator. "Hope this clutch holds out." He showed anxiety for the first time. "She pulls so hard she gets to boiling."

"Champ, do you run into many spots where you have to use your gun?" I asked as we bounced along again.

"Naw. The only thing I'm afraid of is a 'shiner running over me trying to get away," he grinned. "Say, Hank, we'd better park this buggy up here a little ways and strike out on foot. We don't want to scare 'em off with this threshing machine."

"Threshing machine, hell," Hank remonstrated. "You said yourself . . ."

"Oh, I know. I was only kidding. Pull her right over there. We'd best walk the rest of the way. It's only a couple of miles."

Hank drove the car onto a little level spot at the side of the road, and we dismounted. I slung the Speed-Graphic case over my shoulder, and Julian picked up the big Graflex with the telephoto lens.

"Looks like you boys are well prepared," Hank remarked.

"Yeah, and it looks like you-all are too," I answered.

He and Champ were loading their forty-fives, and Champ had tucked a piece of tarpaulin under one arm.

"What's the canvas for, Champ?" Julian asked.

"That's for sitting. Time that frost soaks into your rear end you'll wish you had one." He chuckled.

As we picked our way along the rocky road Champ took up the conversation where we'd left off when we parked.

"Nope. Raiding isn't as hazardous as it used to be. There's a lot less shooting than you might think. For my part I don't intend to shoot anybody. If a man gets away from me I generally get him later. And the 'shiners–most of them don't figure it's worth while to shoot a revenue man. If they get caught they won't get but maybe thirty to sixty days if it's their first offense, and not more than a few years if they're old offenders. But if they kill a revenue man they know they'll get the chair, or at least life in the pen. Of course it wasn't always that way. Back in the old days–I mean before the World War, before my time as a raider–a 'revenooer' just about had to shoot a blockader on sight to keep from being shot first. It was a deadly war in those days. The mountain people had made whisky since the time they moved into these hills. They figured it was their right and that it wasn't any of the government's damn business to come messin' around. They'd fought excise taxes from the time of the Whisky Insurrection you read about in history. To them a tax on whisky was like a tax on bread, and I can see how they felt. Yes sir, they were belligerent as hell in those days, but they've calmed down a lot. Guess they felt it was kinda useless. Most of the shooting anymore is not done by your old-type mountain blockader but by some of the tough guys working for operators of big whisky rings."

"Jumpin' Jehoshephats, it's dark," Julian complained, stumbling over a rock.

"Yeah," Hank agreed, "but that means it's gonna start gettin' light before long. We'll make it just about right."

"Here, Julian," I said, "let's switch cameras for a while. What have you got in this case? Your enlarger? This thing must weigh fifty pounds. Holy mackerel, it's cold. My feet are numb in spite of two pairs of socks."

"Oughta have galoshes like mine," said Julian. "They're the stuff."

"Yeah. Say, Champ, I've known several moonshiners and they seemed like pretty decent fellows. Outside of making whisky they were law-abiding citizens and as good friends as you'd want."

"That's right. Mountain moonshiners aren't a bad sort at all. They're a lot better than the fellows who do the transporting and selling. I don't blame most of them for making whisky. It's more of an economic question than a moral one. There's not much stigma attached to making whisky, or even to being sent to jail as a result for that matter. Like I said a while ago, mountain people have always regarded it as their right to make whisky if they want to. Before the roads were built in here about the only way they could get their corn crop to market was to take it in jugs. And right now you take a man with a family living on a little old scrub farm of fifty or seventy-five acres, it's mighty hard diggin' to raise enough to live on. It's natural for him to turn to about the only other thing he knows how to do. Course some of 'em are good-for-nothings who'd rather make moonshine than work—although the Lord knows making whisky isn't play. It was particularly bad during Prohibition when every son-of-a-gun and his brother had a still. All in all though they're a pretty good bunch. Lot of them, sorta like bartenders, don't drink their own concoctions. . . ."

"Shhhh," Hank warned. "There's a light in that house up there."

Our heavy breathing and the crunch of our shoes on the frosted mud road were the only sounds. But a hound bayed, and a man's figure was outlined for a moment in the doorway. We crunched on past.

"Do you think he suspected who we are?" I asked, worried.

"I doubt it," Champ replied. "I hope though that he isn't connected with this still."

They Still Distill

"How much farther is it?"

"Not very much. We'll cut over in the woods right up here a piece. We'll have to go over the hill to avoid that house in the hollow. What's-his-name said the still was at the head of the second hollow beyond a big oak that stands almost in the road. That was the tree back there, so I guess we've found the right hollow."

We started the climb, silently at first, then with heavier and heavier breathing.

We paused a few minutes at the top to catch our wind before Champ struck out along the ridge. We followed Indian fashion. Soon we struck a road—no, not a road, a wagon trail. But it was better walking.

"The hollow branches up there a piece," Hank pointed out. "Which fork'd we best follow?"

Champ pondered a minute. "Looks like this wagon trail's been used. We'll follow it. Seems to go along the ridge up the left hollow. See over there. Tree's been cut down, probably for fire wood. It may be a good sign."

Atop the hill it was getting light quickly. Stars had faded, and though mists and the shadows made the hollows still dusky-dark, a glow from the rising sun touched the ridge.

"The still shouldn't be far from here," said Champ presently. "You-all can sit down and I'll scout around a little."

"No thanks," I objected. "I'll set this camera down—and gladly—but I'll join the scouting party."

"Me too," said Julian. So we spread out a little and proceeded toward the head of the hollow.

We hadn't walked more than a hundred yards when Champ announced, "Here she is, boys! You have to get right over it before you can see it."

It was a pretty layout.

Picture the head of a hollow where the hills, rocky and covered with scraggy pines and leafless ash, beeches, and oaks, form a horseshoe like half a great stadium. The first rays of sunlight are just beginning to cast their shadow-patterns through the trees that fringe the top and to sparkle in the mists rising from the valley. At the base of the stadium where the curve is sharpest is a little basin, the beginning of the valley, lined with giant moss-covered boulders. In this nature-formed cup is a spring, the white body of a sycamore–and the still, a rustic contrivance that so blends with the landscape it is barely visible. Along the walls formed by the boulders are two oblong pens made of poles. In them are the mash barrels surrounded by leaves and covered with burlap sacks to keep the mash at the right temperature for fermentation.

Champ clambered down into the depression, lifted a sack carefully, sniffed, then tasted the "beer." "She's ready to run," he observed, "and the still's set up. We'd better get under cover in a hurry. They're liable to be here any time."

"Where'll we go?" I asked. "Cover seems to be a little scarce around here with no leaves on the trees."

"Wonder if I can get up there on the hill and shoot 'em with the telephoto before they know we're around," Julian asked, half to himself

"Hell no," I answered before Champ had a chance. "They'd spot you in a minute, and they wouldn't shoot you with a telephoto."

"I think the only place we can hide to do any good is in the ravine below the still," said Champ. "We really ought to surround it, but I don't see how we can. They'll probably come up the same road we did, and we can see them from the ravine. We'll let 'em get to the still. If they run off to the left there they'll be in plain view, but if they run toward the other branch of the hollow that won't be so good. However the most important thing is to keep them from seeing us first."

We scattered out along the ravine, Champ nearest the still, Hank about twenty-five yards down from him, then Julian and I around a bend and under a little bluff.

We waited for what seemed an eternity, shivering and shifting uncomfortably from one rock to another.

"Damn," said Julian under his breath. "I sure wish I could have got a shot of those boys in action. Not knowing we were around, you know. That would have been a honey. Might've sold it to *Life*."

"Don't worry. We'll get some pictures. All I hope is that those guys don't decide to wait until tomorrow to make a run. I'm half petrified already."

We waited impatiently for about fifteen minutes more. Then I heard a rustling along the wagon road. My heart beat faster as I whispered, "I believe they're coming."

"Shhhhhhhhhh!"

The rustling came closer. I climbed a few feet cautiously and peered over the edge of the embankment. About twenty-five yards away and headed in the direction of the still were two men in overalls and mackinaws. Between them and me were only a few bare trees and bushes. I ducked and slipped around the bend of the ravine. Hank was standing with his gun out. I barely could see Champ, but he too was standing and apparently ready.

Julian eased up behind me and whispered excitedly, "What's Champ waitin' on?"

"I guess he's going to wait till they build a fire under the still."

"What for?"

"No alibi that way. Can't say they were just passing by and stopped to look at the still."

"I sure hope they make it snappy. This waiting's gettin' me down."

A few minutes later Julian exclaimed, "Look! Smoke!"

"Yep. Guess they've got her goin'."

"Hank's moving up. Come on, we got to see this."

We picked our way up to the point where Hank had

waited, and Champ waved us down. He whispered something to Hank, then left him and crawled carefully up the bank. I caught hold of a little bush growing out of the bank and by straining could see Champ walking slowly toward the still like a bird dog approaching a covey. He was almost to the point where you look down at the still when I heard a faint "crack." He stopped dead in his tracks. Almost instantly two forms bobbed up from the still basin on the opposite side from Champ and headed toward the other branch of the hollow.

"Stop!" Champ shouted. Then "Wham" his forty-five roared, echoing and re-echoing down the valley.

The two only hastened their mad scramble.

"Stop 'em, Hank!" Champ yelled. "They're headin' right toward your hollow!"

It worked. The two cut back and ran hell-for-breakfast toward our ravine.

I saw Hank crouch against the bank, and Julian and I fell over each other doing the same.

It was all over before I realized it. The men slid down the bank almost into Hank's lap. He stood up, pointed his gun at them—and that was all there was to it.

Julian and I hurried to the captives. For a moment nobody said a word. The men just breathed heavily and glowered at Julian and me like "what the hell are you doing here!" Both men were tall, lean, and lantern-jawed. The older had a gray stubble; the younger was clean-shaven. Their features were strikingly alike.

When Champ slid down the bank beside us the older man announced, "Yer a gover'ment man. I knowed ye th' moment I seen ye there on th' bank. I've seed ye at court."

"That's right," Champ agreed pleasantly. "I'd have saved you a run if it hadn't been for that confound limb I stepped on."

"Guess somebody tol' ye where th' still was at."

Champ didn't answer.

"Dirty bastard!"

"Now, now—take it easy," Champ soothed.

"Aw, I got nothin' agin ye really," the man fumed, kicking a rock. "I guess you're jes' doin' yer job. But if I could catch that grass-gutted son-of-a-bitch that informed—I'd feather into him with a club and then finish him off with a shotgun!"

"That'd be too good fer him, Pap." The younger man spat on the ground.

Champ addressed the bearded man. "What's your name?"

"Rance Johnson. This hyar's my boy, Jim."

"Well, come on. Let's go up to the still. You two want to promise to tag along or do you want to be handcuffed?"

"We'll go."

"It's really a shame to mess up a pretty layout like that," I said as we looked down at the still again.

That seemed to please the old man.

"Never seen a finer place," he said proudly yet sadly. "Spring right there so we don't have to pack no water. Rocks keeps th' wind from blowin' out th' fire."

"That fire's burning right along," Julian observed.

"We'd a had her cookin' in a bit."

"I've seen a good many stills," I said, "but I've never seen one before that was what you might say operating. How about showing me how it works?"

He looked at me questioningly. "What d' you follow anyhow?"

"Oh, me?—why, I—this fellow here and I—we're just—I mean we just came along for curiosity. We wanted to get some pictures of a still."

"I didn't think ye was revenue men. You didn't have no guns and ye had them kodaks."

"I just brought them along with me," Champ explained. "Go ahead and tell them how the still works."

"Wal, this hyar's the mash. We got seven barrel."

"How do you make it?" I asked.

"Course diffrunt people has diffrunt ways of makin' their mash, but ginerally speakin' it has 'bout th' same make-up. You take an' sprout you some corn. Have t' keep hit warm and wet and ye have to be kerful not let it rot. When hit's sprouted good you grind it up. Then yer ready t' make yer mash. Use t' be people used all corn, but now'days they use mos'ly sugar. Need some sprouted corn, though, to make hit taste like anything a-tall. Thar hain't hardly nothin' people don't use 'stead pyore corn. I've knowed 'em to use this hyar layin' mash. Mos' any kind o' ground meal'll do. But me and th' boy hyar, we been a-makin' good whisky. We don't make no pizen.

"Wal, ye take yer meal an' yer sugar an' ye make mush outta hit in th' barrel with b'ilin' water. An' ye put yeast in hit t' make hit 'work' fast. Then ye let 'er set."

"How long?"

"Oh, three er four days ginerally, dependin' on th' weather. Ye have t' keep hit warm. That's why them leaves air aroun' thar. Now stick yer finger in that there 'beer.' "

I did, and the liquid felt hot in contrast with the sharp air.

"When my pappy made whisky, and his pappy afore him, he mos' ginerally niver had no yeast. So hit tuk mebbe a week er ten days to git ready t' run. But they niver used nothin' to hurry it up an' give 'er a sting lak some does now. Why, I've knowed 'em t' put lye an' soda in hit an' mebbe poke root berries an' a plug er two of terbaccer t' give it a bite."

"When the mash is through 'working' you're ready to cook?"

"Yep. Ye carry hit in buckets an' pour it right in th' still thar."

"Why, this is just an old oil drum."

"Yessir," he admitted shamefacedly. "But hit don't do no harm. A man can't hardly git him a copper still no more lessen somebody comes along an' steals hit er cuts hit ep."

"Why is it about half buried?"

"Oh, you make sort of an oven-like out o' th' rocks an' dirt, with th' fire in front an' the smoke comin' out behind. That makes hit git hot an' cook faster."

"What's this keg on top of the oil drum?"

"That thar's th' still cap. Ye see, after you pour in th' mash, ye set that cap over th' hole and ye take flour an' water an' make a paste t' put around th' crack. Then yer ready t' start yer cookin'. Now nex' to mixin' yer mash proper, cookin's the most important thing. You kain't let 'er git too hot an' you kain't let 'er git too cold. Effen it's too cold, th' vapors won't come off, an' effen it's too hot, ye bile off a lot o' water. Ye see, th' whole secret of 'stillin' is that alkeyhol boils 'fore water does. Hit rises up in a vapor into that thar still cap, and if ye get th' mash too hot, a lot o' water-steam goes up with hit. Course there's allus some water, and that's what that thar thumpin' keg's fer."

"That's this keg that connects with the still cap?"

"Yep."

"What's it got in it?"

"It hain't got nothin' in it. Hit's empty—'ceptin' what water drains t' th' bottom. Ye see, th' vapor hit comes from th' still cap over through this pipe into th' thumpin' keg. Wal, th' keg's cool, so most o' th' water-steam goes back to water and draps down to th' bottom, but th' alkeyhol-steam hit goes on out through this other pipe in th' top of th' keg an' into the worm, this hyar quiled copper tube. Now this here worm, as ye kin see, runs through this barrel o' water. Hit's th' condenser. Th' cold water on th' worm turns th' vapor into alkeyhol, an' hit runs out th' bottom hyar into this pail. That's yer whisky."

The old fellow ran his tongue along his lips as though he were tasting the whisky. Then a film came over his eyes, and he turned his head and hunched his shoulders.

"Isn't it run back through or something?" I asked quickly.

"Nosir, not when yer usin' a thumpin' keg," he answered, forgetting again his despondency. "Now if ye don' use no thumpin' keg hit's shore best t' run it through agin, 'cause 'singlings' kin be moughty rank. Some sells hit right lak that though. But others runs it through agin. That's 'doublings.' "

"Why do you call that thing a 'thumping keg'?"

"If you heard her go 'thump, thump, thump' when th' vapor's a-movin' you'd know why."

"This bung down here, is that where you let the water out when it accumulates?"

"Yep."

"Well tell me–I know that in distilleries they have instruments to measure the alcohol content, or proof, of the whisky. How can you tell when the whisky is right?"

"By th' bead. You shake her a bit, not hard ye know, an' if them bubbles rise to th' top and stays there, she's all right. Course some kin fool ye on that. I've knowed 'em t' put soap in hit to give hit a bead. And some even puts buckeyes in hit fer t' make a bead, an' them things is pizen as sin!"

"Where do you sell your liquor?"

He looked at me sharply and didn't answer.

"No, no. I don't mean to what person. I mean where is the market? Legal whisky isn't very expensive."

"Oh, they's allus somebody to buy. Lot o' fellers up here says they'd rather drink good mountain dew, effen they know hit's made right, than gover'ment whisky. Then a lot o' people in towns buys it. You kain't buy no gover'ment whisky fer forty or fifty cents a pint, an' that's about what this sells fer, retail."

"Well, pal," said Champ, "I guess you've asked about enough questions. We've got to cut this outfit up and get back to town."

"I hate to see it torn up," I said a little sadly.

The old man and his son looked dejected.

But we set to work with an ax and a grubbing hoe that had been used at the still, and in about five minutes no two barrel staves were together. Everything was broken or cut up except the copper worm. This Hank slung over his shoulder. Champ kept a little pail of the "beer" as a sample. I picked up the crude stirring fork—used to stir the mash—as a souvenir.

"Would you mind goin' past th' house before we go to town?" Rance asked. "Hit's right almost on th' way."

"Sure, we'll go past," said Champ obligingly.

The six of us walked down the hollow silently, this time approaching the house we had avoided so carefully before by climbing that devilish hill.

I had intended to ask the old man why he took a chance making whisky for $2 a gallon, but when I looked at the ramshackle, three-room cabin in the hollow, the sad-eyed, bedraggled, stoop-shouldered old woman who peered out the back door, the young girl with a dirty baby on her hip, the seven—eight—nine children, I knew such a question was superfluous. Wood smoke curled lazily out an old stone chimney, but it must have been cold inside. The board shack was not in keeping with the chimney, which evidently had been left standing when a fire razed the original log structure. The yard was barren and ugly, strewn with old automobile parts the children used as playthings. A pathetic little garden spot, bare now, was the only sign of tilled earth. There must have been no cow, no chickens, no hog, for the usual log lean-to was missing.

The old woman gazed first at her husband, then at us. She understood. She didn't even appear angry—just resigned. The children stared. The older ones stood off. The younger ones approached us in curiosity, ready to beat a hasty retreat if we made a move toward them. A couple of hounds "woofed" once or twice, then brushed against us like cats, thumping our legs with their tails.

Rance and Jim went up to the back door and talked to the

sad-eyed woman for a minute. They looked at us from time to time.

"Mister," the old lady addressed us in a voice astonishingly soft. "D'ya think Rance an' th' boy kin git out soon? I don't know what we-all'll do without 'em."

"They can get out on bond," Champ replied. "Course I've got to take them to jail now, but they will be arraigned before the commissioner right away, and he'll set bond. After that it's up to the judge when the next court term comes."

"How much will th' bond be?"

"Well, I can't say for sure, but it's usually $500 in such cases."

"Five hundred apiece."

"Yes."

Rance and the old lady looked at each other. A shadow came over his face and he shook his head. "Thousand-dollar bond—moughty hard t' git—ye better try Todd Howard, Susan. If he won't sign it—I don't know."

"I'll try."

"Wal, good-by, Susan."

"Good-by."

"Good-by, Ma."

"Good-by, Son."

XV

Parade Before Justice

"JURORS AND WITNESSES INSIDE, please. All jurors and witnesses only—are you a juror or a witness?—all right, take a seat—all jurors . . ."

The marshal separates the men and women he wants from the overall-and-gingham-clad crowd that pack-jams the halls of the Federal Building. Soon the small, neat courtroom is filled, and the Jackson term of the United States Court for the Eastern District of Kentucky is ready to begin.

The judge, in a long black robe, enters from a door behind the bench and starts up the steps to his seat. The marshal brings his gavel down with a sharp rap. "Stand up please. . . ."

His brief opening recitation completed, the crowd reseats itself noisily, and court is in session.

The grand jury is impaneled—thirteen white men, a light-skinned Negro, and two women. The judge presents his charge, speaking carefully, earnestly.

Federal Judge H. Church Ford is a youthful-looking man, short, chubby, but not fat. His face is round, his cheeks pink, his grayish-black hair thinning. His blue eyes behind rimless glasses bespeak intelligence, kindliness, and good humor. As he talks to the jury he leans over the desk and seems to address each member personally. His voice is firm, but not petulant or irascible.

When the charge has been delivered the jurors retire to consider the true bills prepared for them. During the hour or so that elapses before they return with some fifty indictments, the civil docket is called, and criminal cases carried over from the last term are cleared away. The parade of the accused begins.

The first is a gaunt old man of sixty-five or seventy charged with distilling. His right hand is off at the wrist.

"Guilty or not guilty?"

"Guilty, Yer Honor. But give me another chanct. I got a big fambly at home."

"How are you going to get along without making whisky?"

"I don't know, sir, but I made up my mind I ain't gonna make no more."

"Your record indicates it's taken you a long time to make up your mind. How have you been keeping your family in the past?"

"Makin' a little and night-watchin' a little."

"Do you still have a job as night watchman?"

"Nosir. I was workin' fer a lumber company, but hit's done moved on."

"How old are your children?"

"Well, I couldn't say offhand."

"How old is your oldest?"

"I don't know eggsackley."

"Well, is your oldest daughter grown?"

"Oh yes. She's grown all right. She's got fourteen children."

The judge sighs. "Probated three years."

Next is a youth of nineteen.

"You're a son of the man just before me?"

"Yessir."

"Were you making whisky?"

"Yessir."

"Do you go to school?"

"Some."

"Why don't you work?"

"Couldn't get no job."

"Thirty days."

Three young men, two of them brothers, step forward.

"Do you plead guilty to distilling?"

"Yessir," they chorus, hanging their heads and shuffling their feet.

The judge looks at the record on the desk before him, then back at the three.

"My information is that you three have been making more whisky than anybody in this part of the country and that there is no reason why you couldn't work if you were of a mind to—a year and a day each."

Stepping forward now is an emaciated old fellow wearing a blue shirt and a pair of trousers that remind one somehow of flowered wallpaper. He clicks his false teeth and rolls his tongue from side to side.

"You're charged with possessing. Are you guilty?"

"Wal, Yer Honor, th' law says they found five pints and a piece of a pint. I plead guilty t' th' piece of a pint."

Laughter. The marshal raps for order.

"Well, you haven't been up before. I'll probate you."

"Thank ye, sir."

A wiry old mountain farmer eases up toward the bench. As the judge starts to speak the hoary fellow cups a gnarled hand behind his right ear and squints his eyes.

"You are charged with endangering a government forest by starting a fire and leaving it untended. Are you guilty or not guilty?"

"Not guilty."

"Not guilty—then why haven't you hired a lawyer?"

"I hain't got nuthin', no land er no stock. A feller kain't hire no lawyer like that, kin he? I don't aim t' give no trouble. I was a-burnin' on my own rented premises."

"I know you were burning brush on your own land, and I don't believe you intended to cause trouble, but the law says you can't start a fire near a government preserve and then go off and leave it. Such carelessness can destroy thousands of acres of timber. Do you understand that?"

"Yessir."

"All right. I'll dismiss the charge this time. But you remember what I've told you. And you tell your neighbors about it."

"Yessir. Thank ye, sir."

A pale, nervous young man steps before the bar. He is charged with distilling.

"Guilty or not guilty."

"Might as well plead guilty. I been in jail seven months . . ."

"Seven months!"

"Yessir. Couldn't get no bond. Might as well plead guilty now. No use a-layin' in jail when I ain't gittin' no creditin'."

"You shouldn't have been in jail that long. I'll probate you."

A stocky Negro youth limps forward. His left leg is badly twisted.

"My record states you broke into a post office after telling a policeman you were going to."

"Yassah."

"What in the world did you do that for?"

"I've heard the gov'ment has places where they can take care of you right. I wanted t' get sent up fo' a year to get my leg straightened out."

"How did you get your leg in that shape?"

"I got shot and it never was set."

"Would a year in jail do just as well as a year in a reformatory?"

"Nossuh, it wouldn't, but I guesses if you gives it to me it'll have to do the best it can."

"All right. I'll send you to Chillicothe. They can fix you there."

With a hitch at his trousers a handsome man of about thirty saunters before the judge. Nervousness, a sallow complexion, and shadows under his eyes mark him as a drug addict. He is charged with possessing marijuana. He maintains that he went fishing and, finding the weed growing on a bank, decided to try a little. He gets two years.

A thin woman whose bright rouge ineffectually conceals her paleness moves forward. Her chest is shallow. Her hair is in kinky curls. She is dressed in a cheap rayon dress. Her patent-leather shoes are run over at the heels. Her story:

"Judge, I admit selling whisky, but I've got seven children to support. My husband's in the pen. He's been there more'n a year. I've tried to get work and nobody would have me. I tried to support the kids and me on $1.50 a week relief money, but I just couldn't do it. We almost starved, Judge. I picked up a little extra one way and another, and then I started buying a little whisky and peddlin' it. I never made none."

"You say you have seven children. How old are you?"

"Twenty-eight."

"Twenty-eight!"

"Yessir. I was married when I was fourteen."

"You speak as though you've had some education."

"I started to high school."

"You've been in jail for some time. Where are the children?"

"They've scattered around."

"Where did you get the money to purchase the whisky with?"

"Well——"

"Did you use the relief money?"

"Nosir."

"Then where did you get it?"

"Well——"

"Never mind. Your record shows that your reputation is none too good, but I can't send you away from those young children. I'll give you a probated sentence. Try again to get a job, won't you?"

"Yessir."

A man of sixty and his eighteen-year-old son are the next defendants, charged with distilling.

"Do you two wish to enter guilty pleas?"

"Yessir," the old man answers. "But I've got sixteen children, Judge, an' . . ."

"All of you seem to have plenty of children, and you seem to be leading one of your boys in a bad path."

"I'm not leadin' him, Judge. He's a grown man of his own will. He's married and has three kids."

"What!"

"Yessir."

Judge Ford shakes his head. "I'll probate you," he tells the old man. "But I'll have to give this 'grown man' thirty days."

Ushered before the judge now is a burly, middle-aged Negro who tries to look jaunty in a striped silk shirt, a bright red bow tie, and a frazzled, hand-me-down blue serge suit. He is charged with using the mails to defraud.

"What's all this here on the record about perpetual motion?"

"Yassah, Yo' Honor, thas me!"

"That's you?"

"Yassah. I'se de inventor of perpetual motion."

"I see. That's very interesting. Just how did your perpetual motion bring you here?"

"Wal sah, Jedge, I been workin' on this he'e motor fo' a long time. I got de model all worked out and I'se sho it'll rebolutionize de airplane industry. But you know how 'tis, I couldn't get nobody to put up de do, re, mi. I trabel from town to town tryin' to get some of them financeers t' back me up, an' finally I jus' plain got tired o' trablin'. So I fo'med me a co-poration an' writ to people sellin' shares. I didn't do nuthin' dishonest, but the nex' thing I knowed, th' gov'ment had me, an' here I is."

"Uh huh. Of course you're smart enough to do what the most learned physicists have been unable to do, but still you didn't know you were using the mails contrary to the law?"

"Nosuh, Jedge, I didn't know I was breakin' no law!"

"Well, suppose you take a couple of years at Atlanta. It will give you time to perfect your invention."

"Try to help th' gov'ment and it lands you in jail," he mumbles as he is led away.

Shuffling forward is a man wearing overalls, a red-and-black-checked shirt, a blue serge coat, and a bandana. He pleads not guilty to distilling, tells the judge he is forty-five, has eight children, lives on a thirty-acre farm that is mortgaged for more than it's worth.

"You say you're not guilty?"

"Yessir."

"But the still was found on your farm not 200 yards from your house."

"Judge, I didn't know nothin' but say-sos 'bout that still bein' thar."

"I guess you didn't know about the malt corn found in your shed either?"

"Yessir, I knowed 'bout that thar corn in the shed, but hit warn't malt corn. Th' children put it a-soakin' thar so th' leetle chickens could di-gest it."

Laughter.

"All right. If you want to plead not guilty you'll have to stand trial. I'll set your case for tomorrow."

A former deputy sheriff, more recently a deputy constable, steps up as his name is called.

"It is a sad state of affairs when an officer of the law is charged with possessing illicit liquor."

"Yessir, Yer Honor, I've been done an injustice."

"But you were caught with the liquor."

"I was just a-haulin' them drunk boys who had th' whisky."

"What drunk boys? I don't see any names but yours listed in this case."

"They run."

"They were so drunk they had to be hauled, and still they ran away without the revenue men seeing them?"

"Yessir, I reckon they did."

"You're pleading not guilty then?"

"Yessir."

"I'll set your case for the day after tomorrow."

The judge swings his chair around as the marshal leads a fifteen-year-old lad before him.

"Son, you're no more than a child. You should be in school instead of running a moonshine still."

"Yessir. That's why I was a-runnin' hit, so's I could go to school."

"I don't believe I follow that reasoning."

"I was a-makin' it t' sell and buy some clothes and shoes t' go to school. Pap's got nine other boys and five girls t' git clothes fer."

"Well now, let me see, young man. This was in July when you were caught making whisky. Did you need shoes so badly at that time of the year that you had to violate the law to get them?"

"Nosir, Judge, but hit's agin th' law t' go naked."

The judge ponders a minute. "I don't want to send you to jail, and there's no use probating you. Several members of your family are mixed up in the moonshining business and you wouldn't have a chance of getting away from it. I'm going to send you to a Federal juvenile school where you will be taught a trade and given a chance to be a decent citizen. Does that suit you?"

"Yessir."

A raw-boned young fellow, his hair dangling in his eyes, stalks forward.

"I'm guilty of distilling, Yer Honor, but I'm askin' fer a break."

"You got thirty days in 1937 on a similar charge, didn't you?"

"Yes."

"Apparently it didn't do much good."

"Well, it slowed me up a bit."

"You certainly don't deserve any 'break.' I'll try again—year and a day."

A gray-haired man of medium build and regular, deeply lined features shuffles up to the bar and hesitantly offers the judge a folded piece of paper.

"What does the county attorney mean by writing that you haven't given 'much' trouble?"

"Does he say that?"

"It's in the letter you handed me."

"Wal—I didn't take time t' read hit fer a fack. I don't ricollect givin' NO trouble."

"You're pleading guilty to distilling?"

"Yessir."

"Well, I'll try you on thirty days since it's your first time."

Judge Ford settles back in his chair but comes forward to stare despite himself, for before him now is a man who shakes as though with palsy, a man whose face is gray and haggard.

"You don't look well. Is there something seriously wrong with you?"

"Wal, I take lak fits. Kain't do no work to 'mount to nothin'."

"How are you going to get along if I probate you?"

"I don't ritely know, Jedge, but I'll swar I hain't gonna make no more licker."

"If you're not sure you'd better take thirty days, for if I give you a three-year probation and you break the terms you'll have to go to the penitentiary for the whole three years."

"I'll swar and de-clare I won't make none, Yer Honor."

The defendant answering the call now is a youth of about twenty who looks half-witted. He is charged with distilling.

"I had you here in 1937, didn't I?"

"Nosir, hit musta been another feller."

"I believe he's right, Judge," the district attorney interjects. "There's another man by the same name who has a record. I don't believe we've had this boy before."

"All right. Thirty days."

Next on the list of accused is a chinless man with a bulbous nose. He is deaf. The judge tries shouting, then the clerk, then the marshal.

"You were probated in 1938 on a distilling charge?" the judge shouts and the marshal repeats.

He nods his head and mutters, "Yes."

"Year and a day."

"Eh?" He cups both hands behind his ears and leans over the clerk's table in front of the bench.

"I'll take him outside and tell him," the marshal offers.

A small, sandy-haired fellow whose weak, watery blue eyes blink behind thick-lensed spectacles paddles forward timidly.

"I'm guilty, Judge, but let me tell you why I done it."

"Go ahead."

"I don't know where I ever got th' crazy idear, Judge, but I jes' had to have some money from some place. I got five children and th' doc said my least 'un was a-goin' blind lessen I got glasses fer him. I been a-workin' at anything I could git fer fifty cents a day, but I jes' couldn't pay out on that and so when I had to have those glasses I jes' started makin'."

"Did you get the glasses?"

"Nosir. They cotched me with th' first batch—but, Judge, if you'll be merciful I'll stop, so help me heaven I'll stop. I been in jail forty-two days and while I been thar my woman up an' left, jes' left th' leetle fellers a-standin' on th' railroad an' I don't know who's a-takin' keer o' them. I wanna gather them up and make a home fer 'em."

"Probation granted."

A withered, tight-lipped little woman in a freshly starched gingham dress steps timorously before the judge. The court record says she is thirty, but she looks forty. The record states also that she has used the mails to defraud—by making false statements to a wholesale concern in order to become its agent, obtaining merchandise worth a total of $9, and selling the goods without making remuneration to the company.

"You don't look like the kind of woman who would steal."

"Nosir, Judge, I hain't."

"But what you did actually was stealing. You had no right to state in a letter to this company that you owned your home. That was a fraudulent misrepresentation. Moreover you had no right to sell goods you obtained and keep the money."

"I know, Judge, but I didn't mean to keep the money."

"You didn't mean to?"

"Nosir, I shore didn't. I got five young 'uns, an' I needed some way of makin' a leetle money. I didn't have nothin' and I had to say I owned th' house in order to get to sell their things. But I meant to sell honest, I swar I did. I sold them $9 worth o' things, but then my least 'un he tuk down with pneumoni-fever an' I had to use th' money to buy medicine an' I never could git that much agin t' send in."

"I have a great deal of sympathy for you, because I don't believe you are really dishonest. But you simply must find some other way of supporting your children without resorting to such tactics. If I probate you will you promise never to do a thing like this again?"

"Yessir, I shore will."

"All right. Probated for three years—call the next case."

A heavy-set, baldish man of forty-five hitches forward. A broken back prevents his standing erect.

"I got hurt three year ago when I was a-groundhoggin' coal. I owned a leetle lease o' land then, but hit soon was et up. My woman, she left me when I couldn't work none. Thar I was a-ailin' and with eight young 'uns. I tuk th' bankruptcy law, but then we had t' pull out of th' place where I'd lived all my life. After I got so's I could git around I tried to git work, but I couldn't find none. I rented a house fer me an' th' kids from a nigger feller, and I couldn't pay th' rent fer it even. So then I tried makin' a little whisky."

The judge sighs again, rubs his eyes with his finger tips.

"I don't know what to do with people like you. I can't probate everybody that comes before me. It isn't right that I should and it isn't fair to the officers. I know that many of you are going to be right back in the business again. But here you are, a cripple, obviously not able to do any manual labor and not equipped with an education that would make it possible for you to do anything else. And you have eight youngsters. All of you complicate the problem by your many children. If I probate you the chances are you'll be right back making whisky. If I send you to jail eight children will become public charges. What am I to do?"

The man shakes his head slowly, surprised that the question has been put to him.

"I don't know, Judge, but if you'll let me off this time I'll try not to make no more whisky. Hit don't pay nothin' nohow."

"All right. I'll put you on probation. But remember this, you'll be closely watched, and if you break the terms of your probation, off to the penitentiary you'll have to go. The probation officer will explain what you must do—next case."

The youth who answers has a red nose that contrasts sharply with his pale face. His haircut is of the bowl type. One red bandana protrudes from a hip pocket of his rivet-studded overall pants, and a second embellishes the top of a brown sweater. The soles and uppers of his shoes meet only in spots.

"Didn't I have you before me at Frankfort for making whisky?"

"No, hit musta been some other Tipton by th' same first name."

"Is there another?"

"Yessir."

"Are you related to him?"

"Don't ritely know, Judge. They's famblies o' Tiptons of th' same blood, an' then they's famblies o' Tiptons of diffrunt blood. I hain't shore whether mine gits to his'n er not."

"My question was, are you related to this other man?"

"Could be, Judge."

"Do you plead guilty or not guilty to this distilling charge?"

"I plead guilty, but I wisht you'd probate me so's I could git my diplomi from the eighth grade."

"You're eighteen?"

"Yessir."

"When are you going to get this diploma?"

"Rite now pretty soon I reckon. I been goin' reg'lar this term."

"How regular?"

"Wal, I hain't missed more'n five, six days in th' last two weeks."

"Thirty days."

Called now is the case of Rance and Jim Johnson, the two

whose arrests resulted from the sunrise raid. They see me, stare, then turn their attention to the judge.

They plead guilty, and Rance tells the story.

"Your story is like so many others—poor, big family, can't see any real harm in making whisky. This is your first time before me, isn't it?"

"Yessir."

"I'll probate you," he says to Rance, "so you can go on home and take care of your family. But you must give up making whisky or you'll spend a year in a penitentiary as sure as you're here today. Jim, though you have a wife and baby, I can't probate you. You're a young, able-bodied man. Thirty days, since it's your first offense, but the next time it will be much worse."

"There won't be any next time, Judge."

"I hope so."

A cross-eyed youth of twenty who looks feebleminded moves forward with his father. He is charged with breaking into a country-store post office.

"Is he mentally deficient?" The judge addresses the father.

"Well, he hain't much in th' head. Seems like his sickness kindly dulled his memory."

The judge, the father, a lawyer, and the district attorney hold a mumbled conference.

"Son, I'm going to give you a year and a day at Chillicothe in order that you may have proper care and treatment."

For the next man, charged with distilling, the judge reads a long list of previous offenses.

"Judge, I wasn't guilty the biggest most of the time."

"Year and a day."

A nice-looking young man whose cold gray eyes are the only signs of a criminal nature pleads guilty to using the mails to defraud. "But, Judge, I been in jail four months at Jackson and Moscow."

"Moscow, where?"

"Moscow, Idaho."

"What's Idaho got to do with this case?"

"They just kept me there for a while."

The district attorney explains that the man had skipped bond and had been caught at Moscow.

"Year and a day."

A jovial-looking old fellow in overalls, gum boots, and mackinaw marches forward.

"You were given thirty days and paid a $50 fine in 1935. Right?"

"Yessir."

"Now you are charged with possessing again?"

"Nosir. I wasn't havin' it. They got me for sellin' it."

"How in the world could they get you for selling it if you didn't have it?"

"That's what I want to know."

"I ought to give you a year, but I'll be generous this time. Sixty days."

To a cream-colored Negro woman Judge Ford says, "Lucy, your face looks familiar. Weren't you before me at Lexington several years ago?"

"Yassuh."

"Now in this case you took the liquor to a church in a basket and were selling it, weren't you?"

"Nosuh."

"Then what were you doing with it?"

"I didn't even know it was there."

"You didn't know it was there? Then what are you pleading guilty to?"

"I was caught with th' goods."

"Is this man" (referring to a black buck who is co-defendant) "your husband?"

"Nosuh, he . . ."

"I know. He boards with you."

"Yassuh."

"Did you know the liquor was in the basket?" He addresses the man.

"Nosuh. I was jus' carryin' it fo' Lucy."

"Thirty days each."

Before the judge now is a gray-haired man whose upper lip curls, baring yellow teeth. His vicious grin is not in keeping with his frail figure and his houndlike eyes.

Judge Ford looks at the record, then opens a heavy envelope lying on his desk and pours out the contents.

"Did you make these things?"

"Yessir."

"They are exceptionally crude, but they are counterfeit coins nonetheless. What did you do with them?"

"Judge, I was over to a place where I seen a machine with a handle on it. I seen fellers puttin' money in hit and wheels went around and sometimes they got a lot o' money out. I drapped in some nickels, though, and nuthin' come out, so I figured I'd make me some lead slugs to put in thar. I didn't aim t' cheat th' gover'ment. I jest wanted t' git even with that thar machine."

"These things could be used to operate legitimate machines, and your declaration of innocence regarding slot machines is not convincing. Year and a day."

Another father and son charged with distilling answer the next call. The father is sixty-five, the son twenty-one.

"A still was found in the loft of your barn. What have you to say for yourselves?"

"I didn't know hit war thar," the old man answers, "leastwise not till th' day afore th' law come. When I seed it I tol' th' boy he'd have t' git shet of hit, an' he said he 'lowed to do it first off."

"I can't believe a still was in your barn without your knowing it."

"Hit's a fack, Judge. Please don't send me t' jail. I got

thirteen children–three boys married, three girls married, and eight at home."

"That doesn't make thirteen."

The old man studies a minute.

"Nope, that hain't right. I guess they's jest seven at home."

The judge looks at the son, who has his arm in a sling and a patch over his left eye.

"Do you plead guilty to the charge?"

"Yeah." His answer is surly.

"How did you get hurt?"

"Car wreck."

"Your car?"

"Yeah."

"You be a little more polite, young man!"

"Yessir."

"I have no sympathy for you whatever. If you can buy a car, at whatever price, you can make enough to live on without moonshining. Thirty days for you, and it's going to be a year the next time you are before me. I will put your father on probation."

A heavy-set man of thirty-five, dressed somewhat better than most of the defendants, walks up to the clerk's desk before the bench.

"I plead guilty to the still, Judge."

"Thirty days."

As he is led to the door he stumbles and pulls away from the marshal.

"Come back here!" the judge orders. "Have you been drinking?"

"Nosir."

"Then what's the matter with you?"

"I jes' wanted to speak a word."

"Go ahead."

"I've got a mother eighty years old, Judge, an' I've got a little farm, a horse, a cow, and a thoroughbred bull which nobody can't handle but me. They ain't nobody t' take care of them if I'm in jail, and I don't know how they'll make out. Can't you give me probation?"

"You should have thought of those things before. You are a man of better than average intelligence and have the facilities with which to get along. There was no justifiable reason for your making whisky, and I'm not going to let you hide behind the skirts of your old mother now. Thirty days."

Four tatterdemalions answer the clerk's call. A grimy old fellow badly in need of a haircut and a shave, a hard, gold-toothed woman with a tight hair knot atop her head, and two rough looking boys of fourteen and seventeen compose the quartet.

"Well, Katie, we meet again. You are one of my most consistent guests. What's your tale this time?"

She scratches her ear with a hairpin, shifts a wad of snuff from one cheek to the other, and begins in a raucous voice, "Jedge, Yer Honor, I hopes t' fall flat o' my face an' die dead rite hyar if I'm guilty of doin' ary thing agin th' law."

"Of course. Of course. But weren't you operating that still the officers found?"

"No. Lord–I didn't even know it war thar! Hit's whisky-makin' country all right, but we live on a big lease o' land and 'shiners kin sneak in an' set up without me ever a-knowin' nuthin' about hit."

"Is this man your husband?"

"He's th' pappy o' my chil'ren."

"Are these two part of them?"

"Wal, this hyar one is," grabbing the sleeve of the younger, "but t'other one hain't. He's my son-in-law."

"He's rather young to be married, isn't he?"

Katie surveys him as though she hadn't thought of that before.

"Wal, he is kindly runty-like, but he seems t' satisfy my gal."

The marshal raps for order.

"All right. Do you wish to plead guilty or not guilty to the charge?"

"We hain't guilty, Jedge."

"Then be here for trial on the fifteenth."

A tall, middle-aged man in ragged and faded overalls strides forward. He pleads guilty to distilling, but before sentence is passed he hands up a letter, purportedly from his fiancée. It declares she will see that the man goes straight and asks for clemency. The judge considers the letter for a moment. "I'll take a chance. If a woman can't set you right nobody can."

The next man is a walking corpse in rags, a pariah even among the canaille. The skin is drawn tautly over the skeleton of his emaciated body. The top of his head is bald as a monk's, and the knotted hair around the bare spot strings below his ears. A bright spot of pink tops each of his sunken cheeks.

The judge stares. "You look critically ill, my man."

"Yessir, Judge. Lung consumption. I'm barely able to git about." His voice is husky.

"Your name was called earlier on the docket. Why weren't you here?"

"I walked fifteen mile, Judge. I couldn't git here no sooner."

"You walked fifteen miles!"

"Yessir. Th' sheriff said he couldn't send after me."

"Are you married?"

"Yessir."

"How many children?"

"Six leetle ones."

"How are you going to get along without making whisky if I turn you loose?"

"Wal, we been diggin' a little sassafras fer a livin'. Hit

shore don't pay much, but we'll do the best we kin with it." He coughs violently and a bloody froth flecks his hand.

The judge swallows hard. "I'll probate you—and I'll see that you get home without walking. Court's adjourned until one-thirty."

The marshal raps. "The court will recess until one-thirty o'clock this afternoon. Walk out quietly please."

XVI

Some Fun!

THE MOUNTAINEER's principal form of recreation is reflected in an annual addition to the family, but he has several other amusements that help while away the leisure hours.

Take singing. The average highlander sings worse than the average outlander, since he adds a nasal twang to a monotone. But he likes to sing, and so he sings.

Sometimes he sings to himself, though not in the bathtub, since there aren't any. Sometimes he and half a dozen neighbors get together and blend their voices with the notes of a fiddle, guitar, or banjo. He always sings at church meetings and public speakings, and annually he sates himself at one of the big singing conventions.

The "singin' gatherin's" are held during the summer at central points, and the hill folk come from miles around to participate and to listen.

To Pikeville each June they come from Kentucky, West Virginia, and Virginia to pour out their hearts in hymns and spirituals. Generally they meet in the park, and their voices echo from the hills. Last summer rain forced them into the courtroom.

Pikeville is no crossroads town, and the circuit courtroom is large—but not large enough for the hundreds that packed it that stuffy summer day. The master of ceremonies mopped his brow as he announced, "We dedicate this program to the praise of God, and give thanks we are living peacefully and able to hold such a gathering while those across the waters are slaughtering each other."

The Joe's Creek Four, three men and a woman, opened the program with "Stay on the Way." They patted their feet and worked up some pretty good rhythm. That's one thing the mountain people have right down in their souls. They can get more rhythm out of a stick and a fence post than Stokowski can out of his percussion section. But part singing just doesn't come naturally to the mountaineer as somehow it does to the Negro. In fact after one has listened for a few minutes to an amateur mountain quartet he is ready to believe part singing doesn't come at all. Most of the singers don't know a half-note from a question mark, so without a natural harmony the only variation between voices is in quality—and quantity. Volume is most important.

But lack of harmony doesn't worry the singers, nor for that matter members of the audience either. They sat there in wrapt attention for eight hours, sweating and fanning and coughing and nursing their babies.

The spokesman for the Lonesome Duo announced, "We want to sing for the unsaved among you. We aren't good singers, but we make up our own songs."

The leader of the Joyful Harmonizers sounded a note on a harmonica. The four emitted a groaning chord and let loose. In the middle of the first verse the woman member coughed, sputtered, and stopped. The other three followed suit. There was an embarrassed silence and then another chord. This time they were off for fourteen verses.

The Heavenly Spirits Singers let out a "mi, mi, mi," then attacked with a gusto that would have brought joy to the heart of a brass-band leader. A bald-pated man held up his britches with one hand and slapped his thigh with the other to the tune of "We'll Have a Long, Long Time Up There to Stay."

The Pick-up Quartet proved with painful monotone that its name was well chosen, but a woman across the aisle remarked, "They really can sing, can't they?"

A woman fainted over in the front corner of the room, causing a bustle there. But the carrying-out didn't disturb the Four Clouds of Joy as they proclaimed, "I Want to Settle Down in Heaven."

"This here's Smoky Joe, that there's little Emmy Lou, that there's Susie Jane, and this here's yours truly, Slim Jordan," announced the leader of the Thousandsticks Harmonizers. "Labor On," they implored, and Slim was taking the labor seriously. His shirt was wet clear down to the pants line.

All took their singing seriously for that matter. Few smiled, and occasionally one wore a "not of this world" expression.

A 250-pound woman with a face like a full moon reared back and sang in an ultra-high soprano, "I Would Have to Cross Jordan Alone."

"There wouldn't be room for anybody else," stage-whispered a young-blood to the giggling girl beside him.

His remark was met by cold stares from around him.

Three little girls and a boy, the Kiddies Quartet, squealed to accordion accompaniment, "We Love Him Still."

"Ain't they cute!"

The Home-baked Four sang "I'll Be Among the Numbered." A stocky little woman stood on tiptoes to reach the high notes, swinging her pocketbook vociferously to keep the tempo.

After each group had sung twice somebody made a speech apropos of nothing. Then everybody went home.

At some of the gatherings they sing the old ballads—not

so much of their own choice as of that of some outlander who insists they must "retain their ancient culture." The ballads, of course, are songs that tell a story in many verses having the same melody. Most of the stories are sad, though a few are ribald. The old ballads had no individual author. They evolved from singers as far back as sixteenth-century England and Scotland and were handed down from generation to generation. The newer ballads may have been composed by one or more persons and generally recount some event that strikes the imagination of the people, as "Floyd Collins in the Cave." New and old alike are on the monotonous side, and many have absolutely no beauty.

The truth is that there's been entirely too much bunk written about the ballads and too much emphasis placed on the old ballads simply because they're old. Writers like Jean Thomas and John Jacob Niles would have one believe that every-other mountaineer goes around singing quaint, beautiful sixteenth-century ballads as he plunks on a dulcimer.

Now in the first place thousands of hill dwellers know no old ballads and other thousands know the old ones but prefer the newer ones. In the second place 90 per cent of the ballads and 90 per cent of the ballad-singers stink. There are of course ballads that are pure poetry, lovely things with all their sadness. And when they are sung by someone with a voice they are enchanting. But the vast majority are neither poetry nor music, and the nasal wailing with which they are presented is not song.

Further, the only dulcimers left in the hills are gathering dust on the walls of the settlement schools. The mountain people found out long ago there wasn't any music in the damned things, and so they discarded them for fiddles, banjos, and guitars. But that didn't suit Thomas, Niles, and Company. The mountaineers had to be quaint, even if they had to make 'em quaint.

Such determination led to hoaxes like the one Jean Thomas

perpetrated with "Jilson Setters, the Singing Fiddler of Lost Hope Hollow." She took this "typical representative of the quaint mountain folk of Kentucky" to New York and to London and made quite a name for herself and him. But though he might have been Jilson Setters to the New Yorkers and the English he was James William Day (nicknamed "Blind Bill" Day) to the people in Kentucky who knew him. There may be a "Lost Hope Hollow"–they name them everything–but nobody in the Kentucky mountains ever heard of it. Observe this sickening piece of unadulterated boloney that came out of New York as a result of an unsuspecting reporter's interview with Miss Thomas:

"From Lost Hope Hollow, Ky., where they still celebrate Christmas on January 6, the date on which it was generally observed until some time in the fifteenth century, Jilson Setters, an aged mountain minstrel, came to New York today.

"In a black oilcloth 'poke' tied up with a string, Setters carried his fiddle under his arm as he stepped off the train. . . .

"The remainder of his baggage consisted of a patchwork quilt made of bits of homespun from the shirts and jeans of his father, grandfather and great-grandfather, and a homemade basket containing an extra shirt and pair of trousers, a corncob pipe with a bowl four inches deep and a gourd to serve as a drinking cup.

"He had no overcoat and departed from the Pennsylvania Station wearing a raccoon coat belonging to W. H. Egan, stationmaster, who has framed in his office autographed photographs of five presidents and the Prince of Wales.

"He was a little worried because he won't be in Lost Hope Hollow January 6 to play 'lonesome times' at the Christmas celebration. . . ."

The January 6 "Old Christmas" hasn't been observed in any part of the mountains since the days of John Fox, and most Kentuckians have forgotten there ever was such a custom. Even Bill's wife said, "I never heard anything about

Christmas being in January at all until I saw it in the papers."

But the most laughable part of the whole affair was that Bill Day had lived for years in Ashland and Catlettsburg, and of all the sections of the Kentucky mountains, that in which the two cities lie is the most modern. Ashland is an industrial city of more than 30,000 population, and Catlettsburg is almost a suburb. The Big Sandy Valley was opened up years before southeastern Kentucky, and thus if one is to find any "quaintness" at all he must get out of the Big Sandy country.

The people of Kentucky laugh at Miss Thomas' stuff, but people outside the state are willing to lap it up.

There was no particular harm of course in changing Bill Day's name to Jilson Setters if the latter sounded more poetic—or something. Names are changed every day in Hollywood. The harm came in pawning off Bill, well-coached in quaintness, as a representative of the Kentucky mountain people. Miss Thomas quoted "Jilson" as having made this pretty speech upon his return from England: "I everly had a favorance for the Englishers. You see my grandsir come from that country. And when it comes to song ballets and lively ditties they're a mighty knowin' race. What's more, they're a powerful friendly turn. Bless me, the elder cyarved me a fleek of ham-meat the size of my pam spread plum wide. And that young striplin' that stood afore the foir-board and sung that Riley ballet; eh, law, he were for a fact a doughty fellow." Quaint, eh? Right out of one of Miss Thomas' books.

The trouble with most of the ballad-pushers, as well as of the other "native culturists," is that they're seeking their own exaltation under a guise of working for the benefit of the mountain people. Niles hasn't caused any rebirth of dulcimer-playing in the hills (thank God!), but he has got himself on the radio. And one wonders as he watches the American Folk Song Festival whether it's all for the glory of

God, art, and mountain balladry or of Jean Thomas, Jean Thomas and Jean Thomas.

In somewhat the same category as the ballads are the chants intoned at Baptist foot-washings and funeralizings. People who have studied them say they were handed down from the days of Pope Gregory in the sixth century, just as the ballads were handed down from the days of Queen Elizabeth. Weird, primitive things, they sound as though they antedate the Christian era, and to hear one of them is fascinating. But one is enough! They are monotonous, unmusical, and nothing can make them otherwise.

Edith James of Prestonsburg organized the Floyd County Plain Song Chanters and presented them at various places. She even got them on the radio by springing that old "fostering-a-native-culture" plea. As oddities the chanters were all right. As artists, even of a primitive art, they were ridiculous. I have seen the mountain people, the people for whose benefit the culture was being nourished, walk away laughing when the chanters began to chant.

With both ballads and chants it all boils down to this: They are part of a primitive culture and must come naturally. As forced, hothouse growths, produced for sale by promoters, they are no good.

Many of the mountain people still sing ballads, but for the most part they are of a more modern type. They are still sad, telling of disaster and unrequited love and dying sweethearts, but songs like "I'm Thinking Tonight of My Blue-eyes," "Red River Valley" and "You Are My Sunshine" have been substituted for "Barbara Allen" and "The Turkish Lady."

In sharp contrast to the melancholy chants and ballads is the merry rhythm of the "break-downs" and the whimsical measures of the yodeling songs. One can heap scorn if he wishes on the corny hillbilly music, but it is the music of the hills today just as the old ballads and chants were the music of yesterday. It is the music they sing and whistle. It is the music they listen to when they turn on a radio. All efforts to force it out with the old ballads are useless. As much is gained in telling a young mountaineer he should sing "Lord Thomas and Fair Elender" instead of "They Cut Down the Old Pine Tree" as in telling a jitterbug he should hum "Prelude in C-Sharp Minor" instead of "In the Mood." And for that matter, plenty of mountain youths can swing with the best.

Square dances are less frequent than in former years, but they are by no means a thing of the past. Public square dances often are held in vacant storerooms or at roadhouses, and occasionally young folk and old alike gather at a neighbor's house for a private hoe-down.

Space being scarce, furniture is moved outside or into the other room. The fiddler places his instrument across his knees or against his shoulder, the banjoist or guitar player plunks a few warm-up notes, and they're off on "Sourwood Mountain," "Turkey in the Straw," "Cacklin' Hen," "Big-eared Mule," "Chicken in the Dough-Tray," or "Gamblin' Man." Here's where the old music actually still lives. One man calls the set and dances; the others just dance, clapping their hands, patting their feet, and exerting more energy than they would in a day of plowing—"Bird hop out and hoot-owl in; three arms around and hootin' again. Swing and circle four, ladies change and gents the same; right and left; the shoo-fly swing . . ."

Other folk dances, or singing games, like "Skating Away," "Jeanie Crack Corn," "Papaw Patch," and "Brown-eyed Mary" are taught at the settlement schools—as another one of those native cultures—but the people seldom if ever engage in them for their own amusement.

Play-parties or socials sometimes are held in conjunction with the square dances, sometimes by themselves. At these, childish games are played with childish abandon. Grown men and women—yes, old men and women—find fun in "Spin the Plate," "Going to Jerusalem," "Thimble," "Pleased or Displeased," "Cross Questions and Silly Answers," and "Bean Bag."

Fewer each year are the old-time combination workings and socials, such as house-raisings, fodder-pullings, husking-bees, bean-stringings, apple-peelings, quilting parties, and sorghum stir-offs. They are, however, still held occasionally, and since they once were such an important part of the social life of the community they should be described.

They are alike except in the type of work that precedes the frolic. Let's go to a stir-off.

It is fall, and the air is exhilarating. The sunlight is soft in the valleys, and a blue haze hangs over the hills. The woods are magnificent in their autumn trim. The green of the pines and cedars and laurels sets off the flaming red of the gum trees and the brilliant yellow of the maples.

To Jasper Stinnett's the neighbors come, and in Jasper's back lot all is in readiness. Old Sol, the mule, is hitched to the long arm of the sorghum mill, ready to begin his circular tramp. The fire is smoldering in its trough under the shallow, oblong cooking vat and smoke is curling from the stack at the lower end. Long shafts of cane are heaped about the mill.

The youngsters scamper about the lot playing tag and chasing Wolf, the friendly mongrel. Young Dewey rolls an old automobile tire under Sol's belly, and as the mule kicks up its heels Jasper warns, "Now you look-a hyar, Dewey. Roll that thar thing some'eres else. You're a-goin' to have that mule rippin' up th' whole blame mill."

"Aw, all right," Dewey replies petulantly. "Come on, Jason. Let's go over in the woods and make us a bark whip."

Bark whips and whistles of hickory or papaw are two principal playthings for youngsters in the land of make-things-yourself-or-do-without. But though the mountain child has almost no manufactured toys, and though he starts working at an earlier age than the average child, he is not to be pitied. He has the outdoors and his own resources.

The courting couples make a show of helping with the sorghum-making, but they're really there to watch the older folk work, to laugh and talk and wait for evening and the real fun. Bob peels a green stick of cane and hands it to Alliefair. "Sweet like you, honey," he proffers gallantly. She blushes and giggles as she sucks the sweet juice from the cane.

Jasper seats himself in an old kitchen chair beside the mill, picks up four or five stalks and sticks their ends into the grinder. "Gid ap, Sol!" As Sol begins his counterclockwise motion the crushed stalks come out under the tablelike structure on which the mill is mounted and the juice trickles into a wooden keg.

When the keg is full a couple of the boys carry it over to the cooking vat and place it upon a stool. A spigot at the keg's bottom is over the higher end of the slightly tilted vat. The vat is about eight feet long, a yard and a half wide, and six inches deep. It has a metal bottom, wooden sides, and wooden partitions at twelve-inch intervals.

Jasper's woman, Miranda, turns the spigot and the juice begins to flow from the keg into the first section of the vat. It sizzles a bit as it hits the hot metal bottom and finds its way slowly to the notch in the first partition. As it drifts through one partition and then another down the incline, it begins to boil and bubble and throw off a yellow steam.

"Grab that there dipper, Susan, and skim off that scum," Miranda instructs.

Susan picks up a shovel-like dipper and skims a heavy green substance from the liquid at the lower end.

"How's it lookin'?" Miranda asks later.

"Pretty nigh done."

"Here, let me have that dipper." She scoops up a dipper

full of the syrup and lets it drip back into the vat. Her trained eye tells her it has just the right "runiness."

"Hit's done all right. Pull out the bung."

Susan obeys, and the syrup at the lower end flows into a bucket, ready next morning for hot biscuits, ready–in days gone by–for nearly every sweetening purpose. "Long sweetnin' " it was called to differentiate it from white sugar, which was "short sweetnin'."

When Jasper has made up his cane he'll make up some for Mike and Lee and Henry. Not everyone has a sorghum mill.

At dusk Miranda announces results of the womenfolk's work of the afternoon with, "Supper's ready. Come and wash up!"

The men eat at the first table, smacking their lips over hog meat, beans, corn bread, biscuits, 'taters, pickled beets, and canned blackberries.

After the women and children have had their turn and the dishes have been washed and put away, the men move the chairs and two beds out of the living room, and the frolic is ready to begin.

Dan tunes his fiddle and strikes up "Sugar in the Gourd." Bob sings out, "Choose yer partners . . . Oh, eight hands up and go to th' left; half and back: corners turn; partners sashay . . ." Swiftly and smoothly they follow Bob's call of the intricate figures, sustaining the rhythm with clapping hands and gliding, shuffling feet.

The moon is riding high and the glow under the cooking vat is gone when the last good nights are called and the neighbors start for home.

More actual work is done at some of the other workings. When the folk gather in to help a neighbor "out of the weeds," every available hoe and hand is pressed into service, and by the time supper is called the corn stands up proudly among the rocks. At fodder-pullings young and old walk down the rows, stripping the leaves from the stalks. Leaves are shocked or heaped in the barn. Stalks are left to be plowed under when springtime comes. At husking-bees, apple-peelings, and bean-stringings, work precedes the fun.

Hunting and fishing were major pastimes in yesteryear, but hills and streams are nearly barren today. Yet the mountain youth or man likes nothing better than to set off with rifle or pole in a day's search for squirrels, rabbits, or perch.

Around the country stores horseshoe-pitching shares interest with whittling, tobacco-chewing, and discussions of politics and theology. Amazing is the mountaineer's ability to interpret Biblical passages to his own peculiar fancy. The most irreligious can quote long passages, and he'll swear and bet and offer to prove with fists, knife, or gun that his interpretations are the only correct ones.

Labor Day is observed in the mining camps and Fourth of July in all the towns, but Christmas is about the only holiday observed throughout the hills. Years ago the folk observed both "New Christmas," on December 25, and "Old Christmas," on January 6. The latter apparently was a holdover from centuries past when the calendar was changed and the country people of England and later of the colonies refused to accept the new Christmas date. To the early mountaineers Old Christmas was the real, the solemn Christmas, and they believed that at midnight on Old Christmas Eve the cattle kneeled and lowed as they did in the story of the birth of Christ. New Christmas was observed with a jug and a pistol—and to a certain extent it still is. A backhillsman who can't get drunk at Christmas and shoot his gun in the air a few times hasn't had any Christmas at all.

The importance of church meetings, revivals, speakings, funeralizings, and foot-washings to the social life of the mountain community has been discussed elsewhere. But with all these and the other forms of recreation there still is not an adequate social life. The people hunger for occasions that will bring them together. This fact accounts in large part for the mushroom growth of the roadhouses and for the tremendous drawing power of the carnival.

Carnivals are confined to the towns, but the country people get there. They make it a point to get there. They plan for days, maybe weeks, in advance.

Carnivals are of two types: The professional traveling show, and the show arranged by the American Legion or some such organization.

When the Legion at Hazard puts on a celebration the people come from Perry and Leslie and Breathitt and Letcher and Knott counties to have a good time without spending much money. Lots of them bring their lunches so that they don't have to spend any money at all.

Because there was almost no level land upon which to build a town, Hazard has only two streets running through the business section. Both are so narrow you can pretty nearly jump from one curb to the other. On carnival day they are jammed with people and automobiles and trucks. The sweating policemen have a hard time trying to keep the automobiles from running over the people and the people from climbing over the automobiles. The roped-off square in front of the courthouse is the only safe place—safe except that you get your feet stepped on and maybe get splashed by a none-too-carefully-aimed stream of tobacco juice.

All eyes are turned to the platform built out from the courthouse steps. The program is ready to begin, but somebody is making a speech. Nobody wants to hear a speech. Everybody wants entertainment today. The sun bakes down and the people sweat. But they came to see the show and they're going to see it. Some are lucky. They've found vantage points in the office windows across the street. The speech is over. Here comes a trio—guitar, banjo, and fiddle. Favorite of favorites! One of the three is a boy painted like a clown. He wears a bright yellow shirt, patched trousers, and a red bandana. He makes a face. The people laugh. The first piece is finished. Everybody claps hard. The trio bows and smiles. The clown grimaces. Everybody laughs some more. Four guitar players in cowboy garb take the stage. They sound good to the crowd too. A clog-dancing couple performs. That's great! Now the yodelers. Sound just like they do on the records.

Left my gal in the mountains,
Left her standin' in the rain.
Went down to the railroad,
Caught myself a midnight train.

Beat my way in Georgia.
Landed in a gambling town.
Got myself in trouble.
Shot the county sheriff down.

Yoo-de-li-de-lehi. Oh-lehi-dio-oh-lehi-dio . . .

A blackfaced comedian entertains. His jokes bring roars of laughter. Now it's time for the Old Fiddlers Contest. Most are too young for old fiddlers, but they fiddle, and the crowd likes it. Most of the hearers are pulling for Boone Cornett. He's the oldest. He announces he'll play "She Lost Her Shoe at the Ball." He's a good fiddler. He gets the most applause. He wins the $5. Now somebody else is making a speech. The crowd thins out. It's too hot to stand in the street and listen to speeches. There'll be more entertainment in the afternoon. And tonight–there'll be a huge, gigantic, colossal, stupendous, dazzling display of fireworks. The handbills say so. It will last twenty minutes.

Unlike the Legion carnival the traveling show costs money. Yes, everything you do costs money there. But the people go. They have fun. Their money comes hard, but it goes easy. They won't have enough for a sack of flour next week, but they'll have fun tonight. The carnival is in a field at the edge of town, toward Jackson and Hyden. The tents are arranged in a great ellipse around the Merry-go-Round and the Ferris Wheel. It costs a dime just to get in and look. But the dimes pour in. Everybody wants at least a look. The people on the whole are a crumby-looking lot—the carnival people and the visitors too. They are stoop-shouldered, pasty-faced. The young girls' clothes are cheap and tawdry. The women's clothes are cheap. They don't fit right. Some of the men wear overalls. Others wear pants and shirts. The pants hang down around their hips as if about ready to fall off. The shirts bag because the tails are not in far enough. Men and women walk around with their mouths open. "Hur-ry, hur-ry, hur-ry, folks! Step right up and take a chance. Only a dime, ten cents for a chance to win a valuable prize. You pay your money and you take your chance. A winner every time." A young show-off with his hat on the back of his head steps up and plops a dime on Red No. 13. Others follow his lead. The board is covered. The operator spins the big wheel. "And the winnah! No. 9. A BeUtiful baby-doll." The bumpkin ducks his head and takes his two-bit plaster kewpie. He hands it shyly but proudly to his girl.

"Step right over here, you big handsome boys. Spill the milk and win a cane. Here you—yes you with the big broad shoulders. Come over here and show your strength." The temptress is a hard-looking female with bright-red cheeks. The boy throws. He knocks off all the wooden milk bottles but one. "Mighty good. You're just warming up. Here, try again. You'll get 'em next time." She puts her arm around him. He throws some more. His companions try too. They win canes. Only cost them fifty to eighty cents apiece.

The thump of a drum and the blare of a cornet sound from the other side of the Merry-go-Round. A hootchie-kootchie dancer wiggles and squirms, throwing her hips enticingly. The people move toward the sideshow like metal shavings move toward a magnet. A kid of seven or eight walks over in the shadow of a tent and takes a leak against a tent pole.

Bloody Ground

Three girls passing by look at one another and snicker. A red-lipped girl in a tight-fitting dress saunters along in the crowd. She moves over in front of a tent and gives a boy the eye. He angles over. She says something and they laugh. They disappear into the night. Half an hour later the red-lipped girl in the tight-fitting dress is sauntering along in the crowd again.

XVII

Frontier Nurses

THE FLICKERING, globeless, oil lamp cast an eerie light on the rough board floors, the two iron beds, the rickety chairs and table. On the great open hearth a fire blazed, seeming to strive for warmth and cheer, but it was snowing outside, and the wind whistled down the chimney and through chinks in walls and floor. A ghostly quiet, an air of suspense, of fear, pervaded the lonesome one-room cabin at the head of Turkey Branch.

Cordelia sat hunched on a backless cane chair in front of the fireplace and stared at the smoke-blackened stones. Why should she be afraid? She had already borne five children under almost identical circumstances. She had been able to work outside this very day, chopping the wood that was burning now. And Aunt Phronie had come; Aunt Phronie, the old, old grannywoman with the weather-beaten face and piercing eyes; Aunt Phronie who had "cotched" Roby and Americee and Louizy and Beth and Little Tad, who had lived just a week. Chad had fetched her five miles through the howling night on his mule when it was evident Cordelia's time was near

But Cordelia was afraid. Perhaps it was because of the

pain she had refused for weeks to heed. Perhaps she realized that at twenty-five she was an "old" mother now. Perhaps it was because she felt so weak, so unfit for an ordeal like those of the past.

She looked at Chad, and he smiled wanly. Chad was frightened too, but then he was always frightened when birth time neared. The four little ones huddled under their too-thin quilts. They should have been asleep hours ago, but pairs of wide eyes peeked now and again from beneath the covers. Only Aunt Phronie seemed calm and unperturbed. For her it was just another night's work. She had ushered thousands of babies into the world in this country where doctors were unobtainable. Her ways were the ways of her grandmother, part voodoo, part folk medicine, all primitive. But she maintained she had lost only three mothers in her time, and they were all "goners" when she started. She took the blackened lard pail of steaming water from its hook above the fire and poured some in a cup. She was brewing verbena tea, her stand-by as a mild stimulant. She laid out the butcher knife, a piece of twine, two or three old newspapers, and some rags. She set within easy reach a cup of hog grease to smear upon her hands. She was ready.

Pain struck Cordelia and all but wrenched her from the chair. A moan escaped through her teeth. Tears ran down her cheeks. Aunt Phronie was ready with the herb tea, and Cordelia felt better when she had drunk it. Then pain filled her body again, and she knew she had never before been so ill. Her hands clenched and unclenched. She wanted to scream, yet felt she mustn't. She wanted to lie down, but Aunt Phronie always had insisted that she sit up. It was better that way, the midwife said. The other five children had been delivered as she sat upon this chair or on Chad's knees. But this time it could not be. Pain gripped her like a giant vise, and she rolled to the floor.

Quickly Chad sprang to her side, lifted her in his arms,

and placed her gently on the bed. She tried to smile but could not.

The old woman spoke, and her voice was rasping. "Quick," she ordered Chad, "drive three nails over th' door sill, fer th' witches er shorely in 'er." Chad complied dumbly. The rap of his hammer came to Cordelia like noises from afar off. Roby, the oldest, had stared like a frightened deer when his mother fell from the chair. Now he looked in wonderment as his father carried out the strange ritual.

Cordelia was seized again, and this time she screamed. Chad shuddered. Roby buried his head in the covers. The midwife pulled a sheet over Cordelia's tortured body, undressed her under the cover, then presently straightened up. "She's a-bleedin'. Go an' git yer ax fer t' stop hit."

Again Chad complied like one in a dream. He brought in the ax from the woodpile, handed it to the grannywoman, and she slid it under the bed, edge up, to stop the hemorrhage.

But the ravages of hookworm were not to be overcome by black magic. Cordelia's strength waned through the tragic night. Her eyes grew glassy and her breath came in short gasps as her lifeblood soaked the miserable shuck mattress. The old crone's lips muttered incantations and her greasy hands labored first in an effort to stanch the bleeding and then, when she knew there was no hope for the mother, to deliver the child. She beat and pounded and rubbed and pulled until Cordelia's poor body was blue.

The crucifixion was over with the dawn. Cordelia lay dead, her child still unborn. The four youngsters sobbed in their bed, comprehending only that something terrible had happened. Chad stared at the walls but saw nothing. Aunt Phronie wiped her hands on the corner of a cover. Old she was last night, but unbelievably ancient now. She dropped on the broken chair where Cordelia had sat, and when she looked at Chad her eyes were dull. "I done what I could," she muttered. He didn't hear.

Tragic as was Cordelia's death, the real tragedy lay in the fact that hers was not an isolated case. Thousands of mountain women have suffered and died as Cordelia did. Mrs. Mary Breckinridge recognized this when she made a survey of a section of the hill country in 1923. She recognized too that something could be done, and so she founded the Frontier Nursing Service.

Long before I visited the service I had read about it. Ernest Poole had written *Nurses on Horseback*, Caroline Gardner had published *Clever Country*, and numerous writers had composed magazine and newspaper articles. I had heard about it too from speakers, from doctors who had aided at clinics, and from other visitors. As a result I had a jumble of impressions: A nurse riding out in a blinding blizzard at midnight to deliver a baby in some cabin miles from the nursing center; a horse fording a swirling, muddy river; a glamorous debutante looking rustically attractive in overalls as she groomed a horse or performed other duties of a courier; clinics where the mountain people appeared with every ailment from chigger bites to scurvy; log-cabin nursing centers with great open fireplaces; mile upon mile of horseback trail; dying patients being brought on homemade litters to the stone hospital at Hyden; women who had lived so long to themselves they seemed a bit strange; English nurses who were somehow different from American women. Now I was going to see for myself.

Somehow I hadn't realized that the headquarters at Wendover were no longer far from a highway. Only a few years ago staff members had to ride horseback about twenty-three miles from Hazard, and even after the Hazard-Hyden highway was completed they had to ride five miles from Hyden. But now Wendover was only three-fourths of a mile from a highway jutting through the valleys toward Harlan.

I hadn't waited long beside the road when I saw the courier who was to meet me riding a dappled gray and leading a black across a ford in the Middle Fork. But she looked more like an Indian than a debutante. Slender and boyish, she was sunburned a reddish-brown. She wore no hat, and her overalls were rolled above her knees.

We jogged along a mud road up the river and a few minutes later turned in a gate that opened on Wendover. The main building, a rambling, two-story log structure, sat high upon the slope among the trees. It looked for all the world like a vacation lodge. Near it were the caretaker's home, the stables, the office building, an apple house, a blacksmith shop, and the quarters for clerical workers, secretaries, and couriers. Around the hill, a little piece past the stables, was the center's own drift mine and coal chute. Wendover looked comfortable, self-contained, and picturesque.

The main building included a big living room—attractive and equipped with the great fireplace I had expected—the dining room, kitchen, post office, clinic room, guest room, nurse's room, and Mrs. Breckinridge's quarters.

I stretched out in an easy chair and waited for Mrs. Breckinridge to come downstairs. I knew the service's founder and director by sight. I knew her background from what I had read. Her father was Clifton R. Breckinridge, who had served in the Confederate army when he was fifteen and later had become minister to Russia under Grover Cleveland. Her grandfather was John C. Breckinridge, one of Kentucky's foremost statesmen, Vice-President during Buchanan's administration, major general in the Confederate army, and secretary of war for the Confederacy. Her great-great-grandfather was John Breckinridge, attorney-general in Jefferson's Cabinet. Some twenty years after the death of her two young children and after her marriage had been dissolved she took back her family name but retained the matron's prefix.

During her childhood she spent twelve winters in Washington and two in St. Petersburg. Most of her summers she spent near New York with a great-aunt, a Kentuckian who had established a number of schools in the mountains. Mrs. Breckinridge's early schooling came at the hands of French and German governesses. Formal education was obtained at Lausanne, Switzerland, and the Low and Heywood School at Stamford, Connecticut. Then at St. Luke's Hospital, New York City, she became a registered nurse.

She organized nurses for overseas service during the first World War, and in January 1919 went to France for two years' service with the American Committee for Devastated France, organizing while there a public health service for the Department of Aisne which cared for thousands of French children.

It was during these two years in France that Mrs. Breckinridge made an exhaustive study of the training, the work, and the supervision of the French midwives and also made her first approach to England for a similar study in the British Isles.

After her sojourn in France and the completion of a public health course at Columbia University, Mrs. Breckinridge, in cooperation with the state Board of Health of Kentucky, made a survey, at her own expense, of several mountain counties to discover not only the health conditions there of mothers and babies but also the type and status of the mountain midwife. The findings of this survey were so enlightening as to the need for change that Mrs. Breckinridge immediately set sail for England to get the necessary midwifery training, not available in America, so that she could undertake her work, the present program of the Frontier Nursing Service.

At the completion of her training in England, Mrs. Breckinridge worked as a district midwife in the East End of London. Then she spent some time with the Queen's Nurses in England and Scotland to test their technique for application to a remote section in the United States and to study the scheme of organization of the Highlands and Islands Medical and Nursing Service.

I had just started thumbing through one of the service's bulletins when Mrs. Breckinridge came down the steps. She is a stocky, vital person who wears her gray hair in a boyish bob. Her features are handsome, her eyes keen and knowing. Her smile is warm, but somewhat condescending. She moves rapidly, talks rapidly and decisively. She smokes many cigarettes except when she is in uniform on duty. During my first talk with her I recognized a characteristic that later was described by a mountaineer who serves on the citizens' committee of one of the centers. "She is," he said, "the strong-headedest woman I ever seen in all my borned days." She is for a fact a one-way woman, and that way is her own. Her strong will so molds the members of the service that they come to think as she thinks. I do not mean that the staff members are lacking in intelligence or courage. They have both. I mean that Mrs. Breckinridge possesses that quality of leadership which makes her followers see her way. She runs her service as a colonel runs his regiment. She asks nothing that she herself cannot and will not do, but she is the commander, and duty is duty.

During our talk I learned many things about the service. Two years after the survey in 1923 Mrs. Breckinridge and two nurse-midwives opened in Hyden the first nursing center. Soon thereafter Wendover was built. The service covers approximately 700 square miles in Leslie, Perry, Owsley, and Clay counties. A twenty-bed stone hospital and a Midwifery Training School are located at Hyden. Wendover serves as administrative headquarters as well as a nursing center. There are six outpost stations, three along the Middle Fork and three on Red Bird River and its tributaries. The outlying centers differ in type of construction, but each has an eight-room house that includes a living room such as that at Wendover, dining room, bedrooms, porch, clinic rooms, waiting room—and a bath that more than likely is the only one in the section. Each also has a stable, cowshed, chicken house, and pasture land. Although all have running water, only at Hyden is there electricity. Since the service is operated on a decentralized basis, the stations are located from nine to twelve miles apart and the nurse-midwives carry on their work in districts of approximately seventy-eight square miles each. The centers have local committees composed of citizens in the districts who meet twice each year to discuss problems and hear the nurses' reports.

"We work through rather than for the people," Mrs. Breckinridge emphasized. "We make them feel that this is their service. They are proud people, and they must feel that they are helping themselves. Thus we charge what they can pay—five dollars, the amount generally charged by the old midwives, for prenatal, delivery, and postpartum care; a dollar a year for each family for complete nursing service; a dollar a day at the hospital for persons over sixteen years of age who are not midwifery patients. When the people can pay more than these fees they usually do. On the other hand when they can't pay in cash they pay in labor or produce."

The territory in which the service operates was chosen because it was one of the most isolated and poverty-stricken in all the Appalachian highlands. Mothers were having their numerous babies with no care other than that afforded by the untrained and often ignorant and superstitious granny-midwives. Doctors were unobtainable. Epidemics of typhoid, smallpox, and diphtheria were almost yearly occurrences. A large percentage of the people were infested with hookworm. Sanitation and hygiene were unknown.

To meet the problems presented by such a region the service carries three main phases—midwifery, general care of families, and prevention of disease, with especial emphasis on the first. Until recently the nurse-midwives were trained in

Great Britain because midwifery training was not available in the United States. But the second World War changed that situation. It caused eleven of the nurses to return to England to take up war duties, and it forced the service to adopt immediately a plan it had long considered but was not entirely ready for—the training of midwives in its own hospital and territory. Under the press of necessity the plan has worked well. The course, following requirements of the British Central Midwives Boards, lasts six months, and three nurses can be trained at a time. The pupil is "taught to care for the normal; to recognize the abnormal and give first-aid treatment when necessary. Class instruction by a graduate, registered nurse-midwife, lectures by the medical director, demonstration and practice on a manikin, actual prenatal and postpartum work in the homes and the Hyden clinics, and deliveries both in the homes and in the hospital are included in the course, as required by the English and Scotch Central Midwives Boards."

In addition to the director of the service, the medical director, and the district nurse-midwives, the staff includes an assistant director in charge of field work and nursing correspondence, an executive secretary and her assistant, a social service worker, a hospital superintendent who has one nurse-midwife and four non-midwife nurses under her, secretaries, bookkeepers, statisticians, and the couriers. The couriers are society or college girls, usually in their early twenties, who come from distant cities. They volunteer their services and pay their own expenses. They care for the horses, serve as guides and messengers, and do in general whatever is asked of them. They come because the duties sound like a combination of service and adventure. When their six weeks or two months are up most of them are ready to stay longer or to come again.

The cost of running the service each year is in the neighborhood of $98,000, about $53,000 of which goes for salaries.

Only the medical director receives more than $125 a month, and each staff member pays her own living expenses of about $40 a month. The money is obtained from contributors throughout the country, from endowments that are being built up, from an annual grant by the Alpha Omicron Pi national sorority for social service and from nursing-center, medical and hospital fees. The fees, however, account for only about 6 per cent of the income.

The Frontier Nursing Service has made a remarkable record. It has changed a high maternal death rate to one of the lowest in the world. It has given typhoid, diphtheria, and smallpox immunizations by the thousands until the diseases have been all but eliminated in the territory. It has fought hookworm until the people look more like the old mountain stock. It has saved lives through the proper care of accident cases. To centers and the hospital it has brought specialists in trachoma, pellagra, pediatrics, obstetrics, gynecology, and dentistry for clinics that have improved immeasurably the health of the people. It has preached sanitation until most of the families in the territory actually have screens in their doors and windows. It has kept records on each member of the thousands of families in the area so that case histories are always at hand. It has, in short, made rich in health a section extremely poor in wealth.

It was four o'clock when the director and I finished our talk, and the staff members had come in for tea. The daily tea custom was established partly because most of the nurses were English and partly because Mrs. Breckinridge is an Anglophile. Long before other Americans were advocating all-out aid for Britain Mrs. Breckinridge was calling for full cooperation with England and a union of democracies. The war was the principal topic of conversation at Wendover. No matter where discussion wandered, it always returned to the conflict. Even the mountain families in the area were more than ordinarily interested because of the nurses' concern. I found some resentment among the people in the summer of 1940 at Mrs. Breckinridge's contention that the United States should take a full and active part immediately, but usually the men said, "We fought once, and we'll fight again." And I remember a remark by a man whose son had been nursed through a serious illness by one of the English nurses. "If I get a chance," he said, "I'll fight in this war. I owe England a son."

Between tea and dinnertime I wandered about the settlement, asking questions and looking. After dinner most of the staff members gathered in the big living room, but there was a stiff politeness that didn't make for camaraderie. Each member of the staff seemed occupied with her own thoughts.

Next day I rode a district with an English nurse, Sybil Holmes, who was making a farewell trip before returning to her battle-scarred homeland. She told me there had been epidemics of scarlet fever, measles, and influenza during the winter; that at times when she was called on maternity cases it was so cold in the cabins the water froze in her sterilizing pan. But now it was summer, and the families in her district were nearly free of complaints.

At each stop Sybil talked jovially with mothers, fathers, and children, offering advice on everything from care of the potato vines to care of a tubercular. At one home she would examine an expectant mother; at another she would prescribe an ointment for the children's infected gnat-bites. Time after time she told mothers, "The children are looking sort of puny. Better have them wormed again." Always she instructed, "Come to the clinic this week so we can give you a checkup."

The log homes, the board homes, the frame homes we visited were much the same as those in other sections of the mountains except that on the whole they were neater and their inhabitants cleaner and healthier. A few houses were screenless and as dirty, bare and unkempt as any in the hills, but they were exceptions. They reflected the character of their occupants, men and women who were shiftless and slovenly despite all efforts to change them. By and large one could tell immediately where the nurses' districts ended, for even the crops looked better in the service's area.

At one house Sybil took a pink-and-white nine-month-old baby in her arms and told me she had delivered it in a truck. Later, as our horses jogged along by the speckled green water of the Middle Fork, she explained: "The baby was the mother's first and the family kept insisting that I call a doctor or take her to the hospital. I knew she was going to get along all right, but the parents and the aunts and the uncles kept worrying until they had the girl hysterical. I knew I had to get her away from there, and so I told them I'd take her to Hyden. They got a little pick-up truck and we made a bed in the back end. I knew when we started we'd never get there, but I had everything I needed in my saddle-pockets, and a delivery out in the open was far better than a delivery with all those people standing around. We weren't more than ten minutes away from the house when I rapped on the cab for the driver to stop. The baby came right there, and everything went off fine. We held up the mail and a few other travelers for a little while, but I don't think they minded waiting when they heard what was taking place. After the baby was delivered we just turned around and went back home."

Toward the end of our ride we stopped at a house where a gold-toothed woman with a face like tanned leather was excitedly waving a snake on the end of a long stick. Without even the usual "hi-de-do" she started telling us about the snake. "Hit's a copperhead," she declared. "I seen it while I was out a-huntin' sang. I've been a-sangin' all day—that's why I've got these here overhauls on. You'll have to 'scuse me fer 'em. Sang—I guess you-all call hit ginseng—hit's mighty scarce anymore. I been a-diggin' since sunup an' got only 'bout half a pound. I was just a-fixin' t' come on home when

I spied this feller here. He was all quiled up ready t' strike with that nasty little ole head o' his'n when I flung a rock at him. But rocks don't do no good. I shoulda knowed that. You kin pile rocks at 'em all day, an' they just bounce right off. A big club of a stick is the onliest thing that'll faze 'em. . . . Come on up on th' porch an' set down a spell." She talked unceasingly while Sybil took a look at the children. She told me about her flowers, about her garden, about her dogs, about her husband. She showed me the potato hole under the house where potatoes were buried under boards and dirt to keep during the winter. She told me the bugs had just about taken her potato vines until she found a way to combat them–she had tethered her hens in various sections of the patch, and they and their broods had found the bugs appetizing.

As we rode back to Wendover, Sybil remarked that she would miss the friendly people of the hills when she returned to England. I asked her if she didn't find the life of a frontier nurse abnormal. She considered a moment before replying. "Yes, it is abnormal and at times terribly lonely, but it all depends on the individual as to how it affects her. Some of the girls say that a year or so is long enough, that a person grows strange if she stays longer. But for my part I could stay for years. You know we get long vacations, and Mrs. Breckinridge asks that we spend them in an atmosphere as different from this as possible. I feel like a bird out of a cage when I get to a city during my vacation, but in a few weeks I'm more than ready to come back."

Early next morning women, children, and a few men began to gather at Wendover for the clinic. Clean, fairly well-dressed, and healthy-looking, they made up, I was told, quite a different picture from that of the clinics in earlier years.

First in the clinic room were five children of one family. The nurse weighed and measured them, made notations on their permanent record cards. She looked for signs of ringworm they had had and at places on their hands from which warts had been removed. She examined their teeth and tonsils and apparently was satisfied. She told the smallest of the five she must finish taking her typhoid shots.

An old lady came in. She talked almost as much as the woman who'd killed the snake. "I seen a baby swallow a No. 8 nail t'other day. His mother finally retched it out, but by the time she did th' blood was a-spurtin'. . . . My boy Ruby's as stout as a bear-dog to what he use t' be. . . . I've lost nigh onto ten pound a-workin' in th' corn, but I'm feelin' right peart. . . . They's really nuthin' th' matter with me. . . ."

A pretty young woman, leading one child and carrying another, shyly took a seat in the corner. She lived away up Hurricane Creek, but she was nicely dressed in a flowered rayon dress, brown oxfords, and silk stockings. The nurse repeated the weighing, measuring and checking process, advised the mother to keep her children wormed. "Worms," she said in an aside, "are our worst enemies. We've got to fight them constantly or they wreck the health of our people."

The next woman and her three children furnished a contrast to the Hurricane Creek family. She was worn and tired-looking, and her faded gingham house coat and run-over shoes added to her sad appearance. The children were shabby in gingham and overalls, but they looked healthy enough.

And so the clinic went throughout the day, with records being brought to date, minor complaints cared for, and more serious ailments noted for further treatment.

On the day after the clinic Mrs. Breckinridge and I sat down in the living room for another talk. After we had discussed various phases of the service's work I asked her a question. It was one that had been asked of her many times before and, because I had read what she had to say on the subject, I already knew her answer. Even so, I wanted to hear her. The question: "Since overpopulation seems to be the core of the problem, why not spend the $95,000 to $100,000 a year on teaching the people birth control instead of in helping them to have more and healthier babies?"

Her reply was this:

"Birth control is not a panacea for the ills of this or any other region. Do not misunderstand me. I am not opposed to birth control. At our regular weekly clinics for women at the Hyden Hospital our medical director gives birth control information and it is given with special care and with repeat visits for checkups in every case. I do not think any woman who wants it should be refused this information, and I have always been against legislation prohibiting or restricting dissemination of birth control information. I do think, however, that the procedure should always be taught by a physician, as is done here, and should be suited to the individual case, as is done in all gynecological work, and should not be handled by people ignorant in gynecology. Properly carried out it is a source of benefit to a number of women who wish to space their families and who should be given the opportunity to do so. On the other hand, where it is physically dangerous for a woman to have any more children (such as in certain advanced forms of kidney and heart disease) it is far safer and better for her to consent to sterilization, and that procedure we prefer for such cases.

"I don't think, however, that birth control is a panacea, because I don't believe in universal panaceas. They are like that kind of patent medicine that claims it can cure most of the ills to which human flesh is heir. Furthermore a policy of persuading normal and superior individuals to have fewer children, coupled with the incessant child-bearing (which birth control can't stop) of the sub-normal group, is a dangerous policy in a democracy.

"Psychologists tell us that in most population groups there are approximately ten per cent superior people with superior mentality and ten per cent people with low-grade mentality, and that the great mass of us lie in the 80 per cent between. You can readily see that if we foster a policy of limiting the upper level while the lower level breeds unchecked we are adding greatly to the dangers of a democracy. District nurses know that women who have no methodicity and apparently cannot boil a baby's infected drinking water steadily every day for a week are not able consistently to apply a birth control technique. Therefore it isn't a procedure open to the lower mental range of people anywhere. To such people I personally would apply my 'red hat theory.' I am against compulsion on such a subject as sterilization, but I think most district nurses could persuade feebleminded girls they personally know to consent to sterilization if they offered them a red hat. In extreme cases, throw in a red dress as well. I should like legislation to permit this.

"We have really not learned very much scientifically about population since the days of Malthus, but anyone with even a little knowledge of biology and history finds much food for thought in a direction not indicated by Malthus. Lower forms of life, such as fish, have vast quantities of offspring. Higher forms of life, such as bear, have few offspring. When we get to human beings, we find that the trend of history seems to limit the size of families (always with exceptions) almost in inverse ratio to their mental ability and the degree to which it has been cultivated and used. With the postponement of the age of marriage, so that most people of good mentality no longer marry in their teens, and with the more advanced education afforded women, the modern tendency is for small families in the upper ranges, irrespective of what anyone does about it.

"Such a subject, however, is far too complex, and we are too ignorant of nature's laws for anyone to say that this aspect covers the question. Studies that have been made of various economic levels would indicate that when one raises the economic level of a group of people, then automatically the birth rate goes down. On the other hand, luxury seems to have an inhibiting effect on fertility even with animals. Definitely city life tends to infertility and rural life to fertility. Cities hardly reproduce themselves and depend on their population growth mainly from the influx of people from rural areas. Rural areas more than reproduce themselves.

"On so highly complex a subject as population trends we need a great deal more research before we can be in a position to establish even approximate laws. In any case, I am convinced that in raising the economic level of any people one is assisting nature to produce fewer and better citizens."

When Mrs. Breckinridge had explained her position she didn't ask whether I agreed or disagreed. I had asked a question, and she had answered it. That's all there was to it.

That afternoon I ended my stay at Wendover, and as I rode back to the highway, impressions of the Frontier Nursing Service turned over in my mind to reach this summation: Stripped of the romantic aura thrown about it by writers and speakers the organization is one that has an exalted opinion of itself, but which, paradoxically perhaps, has good reason for that opinion. Its ideals are high, its purposes definite. It is sincere and efficient. It is doing its job and doing it better than well.

And then I thought about Mrs. Breckinridge's reply to my question. I could only shake my head. She had said the birth rate could be lowered only by raising the economic level. I had always felt, and still felt, that the economic level could be raised only by lowering the birth rate. Here was a steel-rimmed circle.

XVIII

Plagues, All Colors

THE CLAY COUNTY health officer stopped one day at a two-room shack so loosened from its foundation that it seemed to rest upon the air. When he left he felt a bit ill. In the shack he had found the head of the family of twelve lying on a pile of rags, a fly-covered tin can for a sputum cup at his elbow. He would die first. The mother still dragged herself about the cabin, but her eyes were hollow and her chest sunken. Two of the ten children coughed repeatedly. The other eight were pale and anemic. They too would have the white plague.

The doctor had seen such sights before in his territory, but their frequency didn't lessen their effect. The hopelessness of the situation made him despair. These people had no money. They didn't even have food, clothing, or adequate shelter, and there was no place to send them. Kentucky has one state-operated tuberculosis sanatorium—with 110 beds for 120 counties. It was horrible to have to stand by and watch a family die, slowly, one by one.

Most of the mountain doctors feel overwhelmed by the magnitude of their tasks. In the thirty-four hill counties are

401 doctors for 900,000 people. Thousands of these people live in almost inaccessible places. They do not have proper diet. They do not have proper sanitation. They have pellagra, trachoma, rickets, scurvy, tuberculosis, pneumonia, diarrhea, heart disease, diphtheria, smallpox, typhoid, scarlet fever, cancer, syphilis, gonorrhea, stomach ulcers, influenza, complications from hookworms, whooping cough, measles, chronic bronchitis, asthma, and "risin's" of every known kind. They produce children in such profusion that the birth rate is the highest in the nation. From 45 to 85 per cent of the births, depending upon the county, still are attended by granny-midwives.

Yet health officers and other mountain physicians can take heart from the fact that conditions are infinitely better than they used to be. Communicable diseases are not so uncontrolled as in former years, and one of the doctors' greatest enemies, superstition, does not have so strong a hold.

Unscientific treatment of ailments, formerly encountered constantly and still found all too frequently, can be divided into two groups—plain voodoo and home remedies. As examples of the first, consider these:

To cure the phthisic stand the patient up beside a door sill, bore a hole even with his head, and plug the hole with a sassafras stick. When he has grown taller than the plugged hole his consumption will have been cured.

To cure a baby's thrash let a person who has never seen his own father blow down the baby's throat.

To remove a corn rub a snail over it between 7 and 11 A.M. each day for three days.

To prevent headache place a paper under your chair while you're having a haircut; then bury paper and hair under a rock.

To cure a bad cold kiss a horse on the nose.

To cure rheumatism cut a lock of the ailing one's hair and place it in the forks of a beech tree, or cut a double slit in the skin of his arm and pull a horse's hair through the slit.

To heal a cut quickly place a peach leaf over it.

To ward off influenza place a bit of sulphur in your shoes.

To prevent or cure sores refrain from bathing during dog days

To remove a sty from the eye rub it with a gold ring.

To kill little snakes under your skin (varicose veins) special incantations are required.

To stop the nosebleed tie a red string around your finger or drop a key down the back of your neck.

To prevent scarlet fever, whooping cough, measles, chicken pox, and mumps stick five pins in a piece of flannel and place under the child's bed.

To prevent lockjaw from a nail wound grease the nail with bacon fat and carry it in your pocket until the wound heals, or inhale the smoke from burning flannel rags.

To keep a child from being afflicted constantly with bad colds ween it only when "th' sign is 'tween th' shoulders and the knee."

To stop night sweats place a pail of water under the bed.

A child who has the "bold hives" will get well, but a child who has the "stretchin' hives" is doomed to an early death.

To remove warts there are many methods. Among them: (1) place three drops of blood on a grain of corn and feed the corn to a black hen; (2) rub a bone over the wart nine times, throw the bone over the left shoulder, and don't look back; (3) tie into a piece of cloth nine pieces of gravel found in a corner where the rain falls from the roof, drop the cloth and stones at the forks of a road, and the warts will be transmitted to the person who picks up the parcel; (4) steal a dishrag from a neighbor, rub it over the warts, then hide the dishrag.

Home remedies generally are more effective, though they

may be more dangerous. Repugnant as is the idea, cow manure spread on sunburn does tend to heal the burn, because the manure contains tannic acid. Clay placed on a wound sometimes stimulates tissue growth. Doctors have employed the idea in using sand on an ulcer. Many of the herb teas contain medicinal qualities, and most of them are useful if for no other reason than that they produce heat in the body. Beet leaves and fat meat unquestionably bring a boil to a head. Foolish-sounding onion, flaxseed, turpentine, and lard poultices are useful for the heat they radiate to congested chests. Here are several other "cures" I picked up from old mountaineers and doctors, some of them quoted verbatim:

To purify the blood make a potion of yellow poplar bark, sarsaparilla, wild cherry tree bark, dogwood, whisky, and water. Take a tablespoonful three times a day.

To quench the "burning thirst" occasioned by fever take a teaspoonful of glycerine and lemon juice.

To overcome nausea pour a small stream of water on the back of the neck.

For sprains, "take the root of the black locust tree and wash well, then scrape off the skin and pound it until it is well mashed; pour on enough strong vinegar to make it thick as mush, and apply with bandages." Poultices of vinegar and clay or vinegar and brown paper also are good for sprains.

To heal old sores use red oak bark tea or lye.

For colds, "make a very strong ooze of wild cherry bark, boil down, then add one pint of white sugar and boil to one pint of syrup. Take three times a day."

For scrofulous sores, "take five or six roots of lamb's tongue, cut it up, and stew it slowly with old bacon; strain and rub on the sores well. Use with it a tonic made of a handful of the roots of wild violets and a quart of whisky. For the first few doses take one-half teaspoonful three times a day. Then increase the dose to one teaspoonful."

To treat dysentery, "mix a heaping tablespoonful of salts, a level teaspoonful of laudanum, and a level teaspoonful of cream of tartar with twelve teaspoonfuls of water. Take a teaspoonful every two hours."

To cure tetter let a mixture of yellow dock root and strong vinegar stand for twenty-four hours, then apply it to the hands.

To relieve pain from a bunion fill half a lemon with salt and place it in a cup of vinegar. After the lemon has soaked well tie it on the bunion during the night, then put it back to soak some more next day.

For use in almost any ailment make a salve of one pound of red lead, one quart of linseed oil, and one quart of sweet oil; boil "over a slow fire, stirring constantly to keep lead from settling, until it is as stiff as jam."

To make a salve for chapped hands and face mix a teacupful of freshly churned butter and half a pound of beeswax and boil until dissolved; strain and place in a mould.

To prepare a poultice for a pneumonia sufferer, "take one gill of old whisky, a piece of old butter the size of a walnut, a piece of beeswax the size of a partridge egg, and one teaspoonful of black pepper and stew until the whisky evaporates; spread on a cloth and sprinkle black pepper thickly over it."

For poison oak and poison ivy apply a paste of gunpowder and milk.

To "break out" a measles patient give him "nannie tea," made from sheep droppings and boiling water.

For the "yaller janders" mix live lice in small pellets of bread dough and swallow.

To stanch bleeding place burnt flour on the wound.

To cure a running sore place a well-chewed cud of tobacco on it and bind tightly with a cloth.

For worms drink half a pint of tea made from tobacco stems and boiling water.

To remove a sty use an eyewash of fresh, undiluted urine.

For "withered hand" (paralysis) drink a tea made of boiling water and crushed earthworms.

To cure the mumps bind "hawg dung" on the jaws.

For a sore throat bind a dirty sock around the neck.

To bring a "risin' " to a head apply soot to it.

To cure the shingles drink half a glass of the blood of a black cat.

For inflamed eyes: "Take white sugar, pound it, and sift it through a piece of muslin; hardboil an egg, cut in halves lengthwise, and remove the yolk; place the whites in boiling water. Dust some of the sugar on the eyeballs, then take the hot cups made from the egg white and place them over the eyes."

For "pneumony fever" make a salve from sassafras, goose grease, turpentine, and lard and apply to the chest.

To ease a baby's teething rub its gums with the brains of a rabbit.

For smallpox bathe in the blood of newly killed chickens.

Probably only the mountaineer's remarkable ability to endure pain keep some of these "cures" from killing him outright. Horace Kephart tells an amusing story that pictures the mountaineer's barbarous minor surgery and his fortitude under severe pain. He recounts a conversation with an old highlander on the subject of "tooth-jumpin'," a kill-or-cure process that was not uncommon two or three decades ago:

" 'You take a cut nail, not one o' those round wire nails,' the old fellow explained, 'and place its squar p'int agin the ridge of the tooth, jest under the edge of the gum. Then jump th' tooth out with a hammer. A man who knows how can jump a tooth without it hurtin' half as bad as pullin'. But old Uncle Neddy Cyarter went to jump one of his own teeth out, one time, and missed the nail and mashed his nose with the hammer. He had the weak trembles.'

" 'I have heard of tooth-jumping,' said I, 'and reported it to dentists back home, but they laughed at me.'

" 'Well, they needn't laugh; for it's so. Some men git to be as experienced at it as tooth-dentists are at pullin'. They cut around the gum and then put the nail at jest sich an angle, slantin' downward for an upper tooth, or upwards for a lower one, and hit one lick.'

" 'Will the tooth come at the first lick?'

" 'Ginerally. If it didn't, you might as well stick your head in a swarm of bees and ferget who you are.'

" 'Are back teeth extracted in that way?'

" 'Yes sir; any kind of a tooth. I've burnt my holler teeth out with a red-hot wire.'

" 'Good God!'

" 'Hit's so. The wire'd sizzle like fryin'.'

" 'Kill the nerve?'

" 'No; but it's sear th' mar [marrow] so it wouldn't be sensitive.'

" 'Didn't hurt, eh?'

" 'Hurt like hell for a moment. I held the wire one time for Jim Bob Jimwright, who couldn't reach th' spot for hisself. I told him to hold his tongue back; but when I touched the holler he jumped and wropped his tongue agin the wire. The words that man used ain't fitten to tell.' "

James Watt Raine, of Berea College, tells a story along the same order. In his, the rough treatment is meted to a baby:

" 'Come right in, Miz Lombard. You ketch'd me this time shore. I'm mightily tore up, and everything untidy, but I'll find ye a chair.

" 'I been up the holler, sittin' up all night with Sally Ann's baby. Hit's jest a week old.

" 'Yes, mighty puny. Atter I'd studied on it consid'able I 'lowed hits head were sprung, so I bound its head with a cloth I tore up.

" 'Then I thought maybe hit were liver-growed. You

don't know what that is? Well, you take the child by the right hand and left heel and make 'em touch behind. Then I tuk the left hand and right heel and they wouldn't touch. So I jest pulled. The child cried mightily, but I knowed hit had to be done.

" 'Then hit looked hivey to me, so I given it teas all night. Shore enough, agin mornin' thar was the hives out plumb thick.

" 'Hit's a mighty sick child yit, but with its head bound up, its liver let loose and it hives out, hit stands a good chance to git well.' "

Barbarous, too, is the obstetric practice of those grannies who have not been trained in midwifery schools conducted by the county health officers. Even those so trained are scornful of weakness and are forever lamenting that "women is shore weaker than they use t' be." Those who have not been trained employ their own ungentle methods, using only such materials as are available at their patients' cabins.

Many of the midwives—and it must be remembered that they still deliver more than half the babies in the hills—began on horses and cows, and there are those among them who continue to mix what might be called veterinary and medical practice. Others started because "somebody had to cotch the baby" and they happened to be available. Still others learned midwifery from their mothers and grandmothers.

One of the last group is Mrs. Sylvania (Granny) Duff, of Hyden. Seventy-odd now, she told me, "I've cotched 700 or 800 babies since I was twenty-six. My mother and my husband's mother was midwomen, and I learned from them." Until recent years she answered calls with nothing but her hands to work with. "All I needed," she explained, "was a pair of scissors or a butcher knife, some water, a few newspapers, a bar of soap, and some rags.

"Lots of times," she reminisced, "when I had to ride a

long ways on a mule th' baby would be borned when I got there, and more'n once I've found th' mother up and a-cookin' breakfast. They always worked right up to their time, and seemed like it never hurt them none. My own mother had a baby in a sugar-cane patch, and she warn't none th' worst fer it. She was workin' out there when she felt th' first pangs. She started for th' house, but she never made it. When th' baby was borned she jest wropped it up in her apron and walked on to the house, and hit ever' bit of half a mile."

Granny Duff never used any sort of stimulant, sedative, or anaesthetic, "and didn't need one. Nature took better care of them than medicine would. Course it seems like women today jest can't stand what they used t' could. They're gettin' plumb lazy and soft, that's what they air!"

Her fees were about the same as those of the other midwives—two to ten dollars, depending upon the ability to pay and "th' hardness or th' goodness of the times."

She maintains she never lost a baby "or a mother what was a-livin' when I got there." It could be true, but most of the old midwives make a point of forgetting the horrible deaths they've witnessed.

During the last few years she has carried on her practice under the general supervision of the Leslie County health officer, for despite the fact that the Frontier Nursing Service operates over a large part of Leslie, 45 per cent of the births still are attended by granny-midwives, many of whom now, however, have some equipment and primary training. Each of the midwives who can be persuaded to come to the health officer's office is supplied with a kit that contains soap, a hand towel, a nail brush and file, two pairs of scissors, tape for tying the umbilical cord, a cap and mask, two bundles of clean cloths, two aprons, silver nitrate, a book of birth certificates, a small basin for boiling ties and scissors, four sterile eye wipes, cord dressings, safety pins, and a flannel band. Each reads, or has read and had explained to her, a *Primer for Midwives in Kentucky*, published by the state Health Department. This booklet gives in question-and-answer form simple and specific directions on cleanliness, delivery of the child and care of mother and baby, and methods for emergencies. Although all do not attend the midwifery schools, and many of those who do attend will not follow instructions, the plan unquestionably has reduced the suffering of mothers and lowered the maternal death rate.

Concerning the midwives the health officer who serves Leslie and Clay counties said: "The plan works fine if you can get the grannies to learn just the necessities and no more. If they don't learn elementary hygiene and care of mothers the results are terrible. On the other hand the results are not much better if the women get to thinking they know a lot. Then they will try to handle difficult cases themselves, use crude instruments, or give drugs instead of calling a doctor."

The diet of the mountaineers is enough to kill them even after they've survived the rough handling of the midwives, the "stretchin' hives," the strength-sucking hookworm, and all the gamut of diseases. Of course it varies somewhat with the seasons and economic circumstances, but corn bread and pork are to the highlanders what rice is to the Chinese. Green vegetables and fruit are all too rare, and even when vegetables are served they're so greasy as to be well-nigh indigestible. Everything is fried, and not well fried at that. For some reason the highlanders put great store by grease. I heard a story once about a mountaineer who went down to Mt. Sterling to visit a relative who had prospered in the comparatively level land. Upon his return his report was this: "You know, Maw, I don't think Tom and them is so well off as we thought they was. They got a nice house and a lot o' nice stock, but they didn't have hardly no grease on the table a-tall." The mountaineers aren't immune to the ills of their diet even though they've developed a tolerance.

Those "risin's" they're always talking about are largely due to the grease they consume, and I have an idea a good many shootings stem indirectly from rebellious bellies.

Insanitation is another menace. Until the WPA came along with its privy projects—and they have helped only in limited areas—there either weren't any toilets or they were so filthy their presence was no gain. Screens still are luxuries, and flies are as numerous inside as out. Families at the "head of th' holler" dump all their filth into the little stream that helps to feed the wells and springs of their neighbors a little way down. Only wholesale immunizations have cut down the tremendous incidence of typhoid. Few highlanders bother to wear shoes in the summertime, and hookworms infest the soil about the outhouses and stables. The worms lower vitality, stunt physical and mental development, and make the body a fertile field for numerous afflictions. When one member of a family contracts a disease the chances are that every member will have it, for the sick and the well sleep together, use the same towels, eat out of the same utensils, even wash their teeth with the same toothbrushes. It's taken for granted that any disease which gets a start will ravage the whole family. " 'Pears like hit jest takes a family that-a way."

In attempting to obtain a general picture of health conditions in the mountains several factors must be considered. In the first place counties vary widely in their facilities. One, like Boyd, may have a sufficient number of doctors to care for the population, whereas another, like Breathitt, may have one practising physician for 10,000 people. Further, several of the counties, as Harlan and Magoffin, have no health department, and thus statistics are unavailable. Even the figures kept by health officers, moreover, do not always give a complete picture, for countless cases of disease and thousands of deaths are never reported. The Breathitt health officer estimates that 56 per cent of the people who die in the county never have the services of a physician.

After taking these factors into consideration there are several generalities that can be applied to the region. Tuberculosis is much more prevalent than in the state as a whole. Hookworm is an unyielding enemy. Trachoma, pellagra, scurvy, and rickets are still present. Rheumatism is a common ailment. Teeth are unusually bad. Dr. Philip F. Barbour, consultant on child diseases for the state Department of Health, said recently, "Perhaps nowhere else in the nation are there so many children with such poor teeth." In recent years venereal disease rates have risen alarmingly. The number of crippled children is enormous, and most are without care. A shortage of hospital facilities as well as of physicians exists.

A look at a few of the counties one at a time through the medium of the health departments will bring the picture into sharper focus.

In Breathitt the death rate from tuberculosis has increased during the last ten years, whereas the state rate has decreased. "One is faced with the distressing economic problems of the county in dealing with tubercular patients," says the health officer's report for 1940. "The families are extremely poor; it is the breadwinners who usually contract tuberculosis; they must work in order to live; if they work they cannot live; consequently they become worse, spread the disease to others, and die." Syphilis and gonorrhea are pressing health problems. Incidence of both has increased during the last decade. Typhoid and diphtheria have been controlled by immunizations despite the fact that it is estimated 80 per cent of the wells in the county are contaminated. There has been no smallpox since 1938, when one case was reported. Trachoma is largely confined to one isolated section. As to dysentery, "In the rural sections with poor water, little refrigeration, and no protection from flies, the rate must be high, but it simply is not reported." Midwives in

Breathitt, "almost all of whom are ignorant and untrained," perform 85 per cent of the deliveries. Little advancement has been made in preschool hygiene because of the inaccessibility of the children's homes, but progress has been recorded in school hygiene. "Any curative medicine that is practised is done at the expense of needed preventative practice. . . . The situation in Breathitt County presents a problem that is almost overwhelming. To be able to see the vast amount of good that could be done and, at the same time, to realize that human endurance will permit so little is most depressing. But at the same time in reviewing the accomplishments of the health department for the year 1940 one finds that almost unbelievable gains have been made. . . . Truly we have made great progress, but much more remains to be done. We are beset on every hand with problems that cannot be met until the educational and economic level of the people is raised. . . . The innate ability is there, but it is stifled by poor environment, poorly fed bodies, superstitions, and the lack of proper facilities for training."

The birth rate in Leslie and Clay counties, only slightly higher than that in others of the region, is 41 per 1,000 population as compared to 21.5 for the state. In Clay, 80 per cent of the births are attended by granny-midwives; in Leslie, 45 per cent by native midwives and 49 per cent by frontier nurses. Five years ago the number of persons who had smallpox was larger than the number immunized. Recently thousands of school children in the two counties have been vaccinated, "but this service needs to be extended to reach infants and preschool children." Diphtheria and typhoid have been brought under control, but "we cannot expect to get rid of typhoid fever or of hookworm disease until privies of the sanitary type are in general use." Trachoma, dysentery, tuberculosis, and venereal disease incidences are high. Pellagra is becoming increasingly rare, but rickets and scurvy are still too common.

Perry County has thirty-eight physicians as contrasted with six in Clay, three in Breathitt, and two in Leslie, counting the health officers in each. Venereal disease rates are going up—the health officer blames the "jenny-barns" more than any other factor—and the tuberculosis incidence is extremely high, "especially among the mining population." Typhoid, diphtheria, and smallpox rates have been lowered, but trachoma, pellagra, and the common communicable diseases are prevalent.

"In a county like Knott," said the health officer, "where there are only one or two physicians doing private practice, we have so many cases that have no medical care that diseases are unrecognized until everyone in the community has been exposed." Trachoma was rampant even as late as 1939 but since then has been brought under control. Tuberculosis, with an increasing incidence, is "the most serious and distressing problem in Knott County." Diphtheria and smallpox have been almost eliminated, and typhoid incidence has been greatly reduced, "not through sanitation but through immunization."

In Floyd County, where the birth rate is 30 per 1,000 and one-third of the births are attended by midwives, "typhoid fever, the scourge of the hill country in the past, was more prevalent during the past year than for a number of years. . . . There was not a single case of smallpox . . . and that is quite a change from early days of the health department when smallpox appeared to be endemic. . . . Only twelve cases of scarlet fever were reported during the past year. . . . Rabies is so prevalent in this county and other sections of eastern Kentucky that I am of the opinion that the wild animals have become infected. . . . With regard to diphtheria this county was very fortunate as compared with some of our neighboring counties, which had quite large epidemics early in the year. . . . The month of July was the beginning of the biggest epidemic of infantile paralysis ever to visit this county and probably ever to occur in a single county in the state. Sixty-seven cases were reported. . . . Tuberculosis is very prevalent in Floyd County, causing a large number of deaths each year. . . . The control of venereal diseases is one of the most serious problems of this health department."

The Pike County health officer declares, "It is estimated that 55 to 60 per cent of Pike County residents have or have had a venereal disease. . . . In 684 reported cases of communicable disease, the fatality percentage was 5.7. This high fatality rate is in no manner a reflection on the physicians who treated the cases. As a matter of fact some cases never had a physician until they were moribund or death had occurred."

XIX

Hell in the Hills—I

THERE IS NO PEACE in the Harlan-Bell coal field. There is only an occasional calm, as when a live volcano smolders.

On March 22, 1941, William Turnblazer, hard-bitten district president of the United Mine Workers of America, stood before a throng of miners at Pineville and declared, "There has been more peace and prosperity in the Harlan field during the last two years than ever before." The "more" qualified his statement. During the year and eight months he referred to as the "last two years" Harlan's strike average had been more than one a month. And even as he spoke southern operators and the U.M.W. were disagreeing in New York over a new wage contract.

When the March 31 expiration date of the old contract arrived two statements were made. Taken together they meant just one thing: trouble. "In view of the almost certain fact that no agreement will be reached in New York between miners and operators by midnight tonight," said George S. Ward, secretary of the Harlan Coal Operators Association, "a majority of the operators in Harlan County feel that a large number of their employees will want to continue work and at the same wage scale and under the same hours and working conditions as prevailed under the expiring contract." Asserted Robert Hodge, district U.M.W. secretary-treasurer, "Mines that attempt to open after expiration of the contract will be picketed."

And so next day the headlines screamed that guns had barked again in Harlan. Mine Guard Earl Jones, the stories said, was fatally wounded at the Mary Helen Coal Company, six miles from the town of Harlan, and Bill Gibbs, a miner, was arrested. A couple of hours later Frank Joyner, a union picket, was shot in the leg at the Harlan-Central Coal Corporation. During the afternoon some 250 wandering pickets exchanged shots with men in a mine tipple at the R. C. Tway Coal Company, "then motored to a mine at Crummies, where heads were bashed in on both sides."

That was only the beginning. On the following day, April 2, pickets roamed the coal field, union miners held a rally at the Mary Helen mine, and a machine gun rattled at the Crummies Creek commissary. Four died at Crummies Creek, and five carried slugs away. Spokesman Hodge declared that union miners went to a company store "for a soft drink" and that as they entered the door they were "fired on by a machine gun and pistols." Company Manager L. P. Johnson retorted that the shooting occurred "only after a large group of union pickets, armed with forty-fives, entered the store, abused the store manager, Noble Smith, and attempted to force several nonunion men to sign union checkoff slips."

At Frankfort the Governor denounced the whole thing as a "disgrace that must stop," but he didn't follow the usual procedure of sending troops–the state militia was in the army. Maybe he wouldn't have sent troops even had he had them. At any rate it must be said to Keen Johnson's credit that he helped to negotiate a truce between the union and the operators instead of trying to strong-arm the union.

It was a grim "peace" that prevailed in the Harlan field on

April 3, but under the agreement the operators closed the mines and the union abandoned its picket lines.

The truce was marred during the next eleven days only by a cutting scrape between a mine boss and a union miner, but on April 15 hell broke loose over on the Kentucky-Tennessee border. Apparently this is what happened: The Fork Ridge Coal Company, located in Claiborne County, Tennessee, just over the Bell County line, had continued to operate. Union miners from Harlan and Bell, possibly 250 strong and determined to close down the Fork Ridge, drove to the vicinity of the mine before daylight. On a road not far from the tipple they met three or four carloads of company men, including the Fork Ridge president and vice-president. An argument took place, and then the shooting began—shooting in which rifles, shotguns, pistols, and sub-machine guns were used at close range.

When the battle was over there was no positive answer to the old question of "Who shot first?" but there was a new answer to the old question of "Who died?" This time two "generals," Company President C. W. Rhodes and Vice-President E. W. Silvers, had met the death usually reserved for hirelings. A Tennessee deputy sheriff, Bob Robinson, and a Bell County miner, Sam Evans, died too, and at least twenty-five others were wounded. Bell County Attorney Walter B. Smith, of whom we shall hear more later, proclaimed that the gunplay was "one of the most cold-blooded mass murders that has ever been committed in the history of this county." Warrants were sworn for nineteen men, among them District President William Turnblazer, Union Auditor A. T. Pace, and Union Organizer J. W. Ridings, who at one time was Bell County sheriff. Turnblazer was not indicted. The other eighteen, all union men, were.

The last week in April came, and the Southern operators, having bolted the New York conference, seemed further than ever from an agreement with the union. For once at least they appeared to have good reason for not signing. The union was demanding elimination of a forty-cent wage differential through pay increases of $1 a day in the North and $1.40 in the South. The Southerners couldn't hold still for that. They couldn't, that is, until the Federal government, through its mediation board, said they must.

Meanwhile thousands of mine families in eastern Kentucky were hungry. Surplus commodities by the carload were ordered into the hills, but continued restlessness was shown on April 28 when maintenance men at the High Splint Coal Company were fired upon from ambush.

Then on the very day of the volley Southern operators announced to the President they were ready to open their mines. They would pay an additional $1 a day, the same as the Northerners, and would negotiate further over the forty-cent differential while the mines were operating.

Union mines reopened under the temporary agreement, but the numerous "independent" or nonunion mines did not. In early May Governor Johnson called a conference of nonunion operators and representatives of the U.M.W. It availed nothing.

On the day the conference ended, Walter B. Smith exclaimed for benefit of the press, "Roving bands of pickets are shooting at and terrorizing miners who want to return to work!" Hodge retorted there was "nothing to it."

When at last, on July 5, 1941, representative Southern operators and the U.M.W. signed a two-year contract Harlan operators still were recalcitrant, and there will be other shootings, other deaths before this book can be published. There is no peace in Harlan and Bell.

It was back in 1750 that Christopher Gist, one-time guide for George Washington, first noted that nature had given eastern Kentucky bituminous coal. Nature not only put coal in Kentucky's hills; it put it where it could be easily taken out. Most of the seams run horizontally through the ridges, and the streams have cut the old Appalachian Plateau until the coal seams are above drainage, ready to the drift miner. He had merely to cut a few trees, scrape away the sandy loam, and begin to pick. He dug back fifty or a hundred feet without timbering, and when the roof began to show signs of collapse he opened a new drift mouth. He left coal that never can be mined. But what of it? Coal, like timber, was inexhaustible.

Fifty years after Gist noticed the coal outcroppings farmers who saw a possibility of adding to their incomes began to dig more than they needed from coal banks along the waterways and to send it downstream on barges. By 1840 a river traffic had been established, but even then production gave no indication of what was to come.

In the latter part of the nineteenth century railroads branched along the streams barges had followed in the Big Sandy country, changing it from peaceful mountain wilderness to bustling, ugly mining camp.

It was not until 1911, however, that Harlan's industrial-day history began. In that year a railroad jutted into the county, and Ford, Insull, and Mellon sent in their capital to exploit its great resources. Here was the first development by the big money, and the change was revolutionary. Roads left the creekbeds and wound along the hillsides. Power lines stretched over the ridges and down the valleys. Mountaineers, heeding the call of the big money, left their log cabins and moved into board shacks around the tipples. Negroes and honest-to-God foreigners, not just "furriners from the Bluegrass," descended upon Harlan. The big money made more money.

In 1915 the first World War sent prices soaring. The market was wide open. Every man who had a nickel bought stock in a mining company or organized a company of his own. Banks were ready, willing, and able to lend money on coal land. Every man who didn't have a nickel grabbed a pick and went to work in a mine, for the inflated wages were like a Siren's singing.

Coal boomed in the Harlan and other Appalachian fields from 1915 through 1918, dropped sharply in 1919, and then, with a shortage in Europe and a heavy demand in America, boomed again in 1920. Prices skyrocketed to $20 a ton. Operators made fabulous profits despite ridiculously bungling management. A few miners made $60 a day, many made $500 a month. Everybody was dizzy, but especially giddy were those poor benighted people who hadn't made $500 before during their entire lives. They went on buying sprees Saturday afternoon and got squalling drunk Saturday night. They bought silk shirts for $10 apiece and threw them away when they got dirty. They bought electric washing machines and set them in their front rooms as exhibits of prosperity. They bought automobiles for so much down and gave not a thought to future payments. They scorned savings accounts, for money spent today could be replaced tomorrow. Coal was king, and all fattened who served him.

Then in the next year European mines began to function normally, meeting the European demand. American manufacturing plants caught up with their orders, and many of them, determined not to be caught short again, opened mines of their own. Others improved fuel utilization or found substitutes in oil, gas, or hydroelectric power. Prices slumped. King Coal was sick. But his subjects, positive he would recover, kept gathering in his kingdom, and it was not until 1923 that the number of mines and miners in Kentucky reached an all-time high. Then, with the market shrunk and mine capacity at its peak, the real pinch began. Fly-by-night operators salvaged what they could and got out, leaving their employees to shuffle for themselves. Operators who had big investments cut down expenses by whacking wages. A miner who made $60 a day in 1920 did well to make $60 a month in 1924. If he wouldn't work for that there were plenty who would. Thousands of miners from throughout Appalachia migrated to Detroit and Akron and Cleveland. They were lucky. Those who stayed through 1929 had no place to go. Twice during the 20's the backward swing of the pendulum was temporarily halted. In 1926 strikes in England caused an abnormal demand for bituminous coal, but the demand was soon gone. And the good year of 1929 was followed by the depressed 30's. Business has improved considerably in the last two years, but the current war will no more cure the ills of the coal industry than a hypodermic will cure a man with rheumatism.

From 1920 to 1929 the Southern operators were further harassed by a series of legal controversies known as the Lake Cargo Coal Rate Cases. Prior to 1909 the Pennsylvania operators enjoyed a monopoly of the Northwest coal market. Between 1909 and 1920 the Southern fields opened and poured coal into the Northwest, but they didn't worry the Northern operators too much: the market was ample. After 1920, however, when the market shrank and a price war was on, the Pennsylvania operators began to press in earnest an expedient they had launched as early as 1912, a demand for a wider freight rate differential on coal shipped to lake ports for distribution over the market of the Northwest. Kentucky and West Virginia operators paid $1.91 a ton on coal shipped to the lake ports; Pennsylvania operators paid $1.66. The Northern interests maintained that the rates weren't proportionate to the respective hauls; the Southern interests contended that the differential was too much, asserting they could not absorb even that additional twenty-five cents and meet the competition of the Northern fields. Case after case was fought bitterly, and in 1927 the Northern interests finally succeeded in widening the differential to forty-five cents by obtaining a lower rate from railroads that hauled their coal. But lines serving the Southern fields depended largely upon them for existence; and so down came the Southern rail rate, and back went the differential to the same twenty-five cents. Realizing at last the futility of the prolonged controversy the Northern and Southern railroads made an agreement January 1, 1929, under which the differential was fixed at thirty-five cents. Rail rates have varied since that time, but the difference has remained.

There were 169 miners in Harlan in 1911; about 10,000 in Kentucky. By 1923 there were 10,000 miners in Harlan alone; 620,000 in the state. Though many miners left the state after 1923 to seek other employment, the number actually increased in Harlan until after 1930. Some 15,000 are still there today, many more than are really needed.

In 1920, 700,000 American miners produced nearly 569 million tons of bituminous coal. That was 34 million tons more than in 1929, when the largest tonnage since 1920 was mined. It was 116 million tons more than in 1940, when the coal industry was responding to the impetus of war. Yet potential capacity today is many times the 569 millions of 1920.

Price failed the coal industry. When price was high it attracted capital and labor to the fields; but when price dropped, production didn't slow down accordingly. For this there were four main reasons. Mines deteriorate rapidly when not in use, and so operators of big holdings kept them producing at a loss. Machinery was installed in many mines, increasing their output. The coal market is less flexible than many other markets. Prior to 1929 miners still remembered the great days of 1920 and were reluctant to leave to seek other jobs; after 1929 there were no other jobs.

During the 20's many operators sold out at tremendous losses, but the majority of them held on—by cutting prices to find a place in an ever-shrinking market, by slashing wages, and by increasing operating efficiency. Here was a survival in which the strongest—and the hardest—survived.

In 1920 union mines produced nearly 70 per cent of the bituminous coal in America, but as the industry sickened, union agreements were repudiated, and by 1930 union mines produced only 20 per cent. In 1924 the U.M.W. obtained an agreement in Pennsylvania, Illinois, Ohio, and Indiana under which miners received a basic wage of $7.50 for an eight-hour day, but operators in Kentucky and other Southern fields would have none of it and by cutting their prices forced the Northern fields to abandon it as quickly as possible.

Finding their wages cut to a bare subsistence level the miners felt their battle was with the flinty-hearted operators who tightened the purse strings. Finding their industry yielding diminishing profits or none at all the operators felt their battle was with the mulish miners who had the effrontery to resist. Actually both were in the same boat because price and free competition had not adjusted mine supply to demand, but neither seemed to realize this basic truth, and both grew more obdurate as the Great Depression added to the woes of their ailing industry.

In the spring of 1931 agents of the U.M.W. went into the Harlan field. If they'd known what was in store they probably would rather have tried organizing the Tibetans against the Lamas, for if ever men were born to hate the very sound of the word union they were the Harlan operators. Among them were men who swore they'd close their mines and let nature reclaim them before they'd submit to the outrage of a union contract. Such a stand they were willing to defend to the death—of the last subsidized deputy sheriff.

Rebellious at unemployment, starvation wages, and the highhanded rule of the operators and their gun thugs the miners were ready to try anything. But as soon as they joined the union they were blacklisted, cut off at the company commissaries, and evicted from their slovenly shelters.

Thus was the Harlan stage set on May 5, 1931, when three automobile loads of deputies and other company men drove down the road from Black Mountain to Evarts. They were armed and ready for trouble. Along the roadside near Evarts sauntered more than a score of disgruntled miners. They too were armed and ready.

God knows who fired the first shot—the testimony of more than 100 witnesses at long and bitter trials never fully determined that—but when the shooting ceased, two deputies, a commissary clerk, and a miner lay dead, and nearly every participant had been hit. Among those who limped away from the Battle of Evarts were miners mortally wounded. That much is known. But who they were may never be known. They were buried secretly lest their families suffer the revenge that was sure to come.

The next day troops rode into Harlan, and Governor Flem Sampson proclaimed, "Communists—Reds—from outside the state, men who do not belong in Kentucky, are at the root of these disorders."

The Red herring had been produced.

Continuing, the Governor stated: "Recently a number of Harlan miners have been let out of employment, and some have been evicted from their houses. Numerous of these seem to have assembled at Evarts, which is eight or ten miles from Harlan. Stores have been broken into by numbers of men and robbed of wholesale quantities of provisions. Both the workers and the mine operators have appealed to me for troops to protect them. In one case the workers claimed that officers had invaded their groups and shot two. The operators insisted that the men provoked the trouble. It is very difficult to get at the truth. The citizens there, most of them, are as blameless as you or I. But they are living under a reign of terror brought on by interlopers and those who wish to take advantage of discontent to bring on a bad situation."

The National Guard commandant looked the situation over and reported a few days later that he had found "no trace of communist workers." That must have made the Governor swallow, but he had sounded that battle cry, and the operators had no intention of letting it die.

In the following weeks the independent mining camp of Evarts became the rallying ground of the unemployed. In a month the population of that little town on the banks of the Clover Fork of the Cumberland grew from 1,800 to 5,000. As the disinherited crowded in, Evarts took on the appearance of a movie version of a boom town in gold rush days—except that there was poverty instead of riches. Tarpaulin tents were pitched in back yards and along the roads. Huts were built from sign boards, tin cans, and paper boxes. Evicted families piled their meager belongings wherever they could find room and slept where they happened to be. Armed men in overalls and checked shirts lolled about the camp. A Tennessee hardware salesman reported that his firm had sold more pistols and high-powered rifles in four weeks than during the entire preceding year.

Things were too hot for the United Mine Workers. Their organizers moved out, and the National Miners Union took up the fight. Now the Red-baiters really had something to howl about. The N.M.U. definitely had Communist backing.

Six months after the Battle of Evarts the "Committee on Defense of Political Prisoners" arrived to investigate the "reign of terror" in Harlan and adjoining Bell County. Headed by Theodore Dreiser, it included John Dos Passos, Lester Cohen, Celia Kuhn, Samuel Ornitz, and Bruce Crawford. The miners didn't know Dreiser and company from Mohammed's handmaidens, but they sounded important and they gave promise of assistance from the great outside world. The operators didn't know much about them either, but they feared they were "radicals." Their fears were confirmed when Dreiser declared he was "personally in favor of organized labor" and that although he wasn't a member of the Communist party he agreed with many of the party's principles.

The committee made a tour of inspection and held a few sessions during which it heard of threats, beatings, shootings, evictions, and starvation. It found conditions even worse than it had expected but was able to do nothing to correct them. At first it met only amused defiance at the hands of the operator sympathizers. A group of Pineville wiseacres formed "The Society for the Protection of Defenseless Children from Wholesale Slaughter by Gangsters on the Sidewalks of New York." But as the investigation progressed and Dreiser's indignation was poured forth in acrimonious articles the defiance of the operators and their supporters turned to belligerence. They framed Dreiser on a morals charge, asserting that a young woman had gone into his hotel room one evening and was still there the next morning. He left the state before the warrant was served, but the assertions caused him to make a public statement that it was physically impossible for him to have committed the acts charged. On the heels of his departure, too, came an indictment for criminal syndicalism. The investigation served only to confirm Dreiser's opinion of Kentucky mountaineers and to focus the spotlight once more on Harlan.

By the first of January 1932 National Miners Union organizers, feeling they had sufficient strength, called a general strike in the Harlan-Bell field despite the fact that the coal business was in such condition that many of the operators were glad of an excuse to close their mines. A week after it began, 1,500 striking miners marched in the streets of Pineville while deputies armed with machine guns stood ready to fire should an attempt be made to free six women and three men arrested for "strike activities." These "activities" were the making of speeches in a land where free speech is supposed to be an inviolable right, but the nine were not the first to feel the weight of Kentucky's criminal-syndicalism law as applied by a self-appointed protector of "the American way of life against the encroachments of communism." The protector was Walter B. Smith, young and educated but reactionary and intolerant county attorney of Bell.

Union organizers called a mass meeting for January 16 at Harlan town. Forthwith Sheriff J. H. Blair and Mayor L. O. Smith, die-hard opponents of unionism, swore such a meeting wouldn't be held, come hell or high water. Declared Blair in a country where freedom of assembly is supposed to be another inviolable right, "If the National Miners Union holds a meeting in Harlan County, any place, these Communists will have to whip the sheriff's office first." American Legion posts at Harlan and Pineville, always ready to battle Communism in all forms, existent and nonexistent, supported the stand of the mayor and sheriff. The meeting was not held. Jubilantly the sheriff of Harlan proclaimed, "The Red revolt in Harlan county has been crushed!"

Ruby Laffoon, Democrat, had taken over the governorship from the Republican Sampson soon after the unhappy visit of Dreiser's group. Old, lumbering, kindly Ruby was even less able to cope with the situation in Harlan than was Sampson. When miners went to him at Frankfort to tell him conditions were unbearable he gave "mouthful after mouthful of sympathy but promised nothing"–and did nothing.

The miners made eleven requests of Ruby. They asked for $10 a week for unemployed, striking, and blacklisted miners and $3 a week for each dependent, the money to be obtained by a state appropriation and distributed by a miners' relief committee. They asked for unemployment insurance equal to the average wage; for the immediate release of all imprisoned miners and strike leaders. They asked that no striking or blacklisted miners be evicted. They asked for withdrawal of armed forces from the coal fields; for abolition of all existing injunctions (many operators had obtained injunctions both through state and Federal courts); for the unrestricted right of miners to organize, picket mines, and hold meetings. They asked that there be no discrimination against Negro miners;

that Jim Crow laws be abolished. They asked that no foreign-born workers or organizers be deported. They sought repeal of the criminal syndicalism law—the law that was invoked every time an organizer opened his mouth or passed out a handbill. They asked for free luncheons, clothing, and medical care for unemployed miners' children.

They might as well have asked Ruby for heaven in a goldfish bowl.

Fuel was heaped on the strike fire by the trials of one after another of the forty-four indicted after the Battle of Evarts. In January at Mt. Sterling, through change of venue, seventy-seven-year-old illiterate William H. Hightower, president of the Evarts local, sat with his twenty-seven-year-old wife to hear that he plotted the shooting that brought death to three company men. (Apparently the miner didn't count.) By admission of the prosecution Hightower was at Harlan when the guns were popping, but the state contended he had previously called a meeting of miners and had told them to "come to Evarts with your rifles and shotguns and bring a good head. We'll win out if we have to wade in blood up to our necks. We won't have those Black Mountain gun thugs to contend with much longer."

As an added fillip a freedom-of-the-press issue sprang from this trial, which already involved so many "freedom" issues. The circuit judge, Henry R. Prewitt, barred from the courtroom a reporter from the Knoxville *News-Sentinel* who, he charged, made "remarks derogatory to the court." According to the special prosecutor to whom the reporter made the remarks so distasteful to the judge here's what happened:

One of the attorneys called a Negro "Mister" while making a cross-examination. Warned the court, "You can't 'Mister' niggers in my courtroom." Commented the reporter, "What chance has a man for a fair trial in a case of this kind?"

But the real reason for Judge Prewitt's wrath was the comment of the Knoxville paper after William B. Jones, union secretary, was sentenced to life imprisonment for the Evarts killing. The newspaper said in part, "There is no fair-minded man who has followed the Jones trial who can help wondering in his own mind whether the Harlan County leader was convicted and sentenced to life imprisonment for murder or for being a labor leader." The judge admitted that the paper's statements prompted his action when he referred to "scurrilous and unjust attacks" in the Knoxville paper and barred not only the one but all representatives of the publication.

Despite efforts of its counsel, the late Newton D. Baker, former Secretary of War, the *News-Sentinel* failed in an effort to have the court of appeals reverse the judge's order. The jury of eleven farmers and a barber found that Hightower had counseled the death of the Harlan deputies, and they fixed his penalty at life in the penitentiary. Another man and a newspaper had met Kentucky justice.

(In the spring of 1941, after nearly a decade of never-ceasing effort on the part of the union and its sympathizers, the last of the Battle of Evarts miners were freed. While Keen Johnson was out of the state Lieutenant Governor Rodes K. Myers pardoned Al Benson. Three weeks later he signed paroles for Jones, Jim Reynolds, and Chester Poore. Hightower, Elzie Phillips, and William Hudson had been released through executive clemency in 1935.)

Despite the abortive effort of January 16, 1932, the National Miners Union tried again to hold a mass meeting. Word went out that Allan Taub, New York attorney and representative of the N.M.U., would speak at Pineville on Sunday, January 24. But before the mists had cleared from the hills that Sunday morning sheriff's deputies, city police, and 100 special officers armed with rifles and shotguns blockaded roads leading into the town and stopped all cars and trucks carrying miners. They told Taub to get out. He did. But two weeks later he tried again.

This time he came with Waldo Frank and three truckloads

of supplies for the miners. Walter B. Smith, that shining young defender of Americanism, and his entourage met them at the courthouse with warrants charging "disorderly conduct."

On the same February 10, 1932, Harold Hickerson, playwright, and Doris Parks, strike leader and secretary of a relief committee, were arrested when they attempted to address a group of miners. Until Walter B. could make up his mind what count to place against them they were held in jail without charge.

Also on that day city police raided N.M.U. headquarters and arrested nineteen men. Officers said the culprits had been calling police headquarters and demanding release of persons previously incarcerated, and "we got tired of it."

Less than twelve hours after Smith's welcoming committee greeted Taub and Frank at the courthouse a "vigilance committee" escorted the two to the state line at Cumberland Gap, commanded them to get out and stay out. To make the ouster impressive the defenders of democracy bludgeoned Taub and Frank over the head, then spread the jeering word that the two had wounded each other in a fight. Two days later the lawyer and the writer, their pates bound in gauze, asked, as Dreiser had asked, for a Congressional investigation.

One day in March the circuit judge at Pineville dismissed a criminal syndicalism charge against a miner when the defendant avowed he didn't know what Communism was and thus felt he didn't support it. "I'll dismiss a like charge against anyone who will make a similar avowal," the judge announced. There was a dearth of knowledge about Communism in the hills for the next few days, but when Doris Parks was haled before the bar of justice she would make no such statement. She admitted–yes, unholy of unholies–she admitted she was a Communist. What was more, and a thousand times worse, she declared her only religion was the "religion of the workers." That settled it. Communists were among the strike leaders and Communists did not believe in God. Her testimony was spread at large over the mine fields. Communists were among the strike leaders and Communists did not believe in God. That theme in a land of literal believers broke the strike when machine guns and horsewhips and starvation and Walter B. Smith and his criminal syndicalism charges had failed.

It was anticlimax, that flood of pesky college students that poured into Harlan's troubled waters around Easter time of 1932, but it also was another dark page of Harlan-Bell history. The first group got in—and got more quickly out. Succeeding delegations were met by Walter B. and his border patrol and, despite protestations to the Governor, were denied entrance. The more they came and the louder they decried violations of their rights the more bellicose the good citizens of Bell and Harlan grew. The inevitable happened. The vigilantes tied members of an Arkansas student delegation to trees, whipped the daylights out of them, and threw them bodily from Harlan's sacred soil.

It was not until three years later, near the end of his reign, that Ruby finally admitted what Dreiser and others had screamed to the world in 1931 and 1932. Reported he, as though announcing a great discovery: "There exists a virtual reign of terror, financed in general by a group of coal mine operators in collusion with certain public officials; the victims of this reign of terror are the coal miners and their families. . . . We found a monsterlike reign of oppression whose tenacles reached into the very foundation of the social structure and even into the Church of God. . . . There is no doubt that Theodore Middleton, sheriff of Harlan County, is in league with the operators. The proof shows that the homes of union miners and organizers were dynamited and fired into, that the United States flag was defiled in the presence of and with the consent of peace officers who were sworn to uphold the principles for which it stands. . . . It appears that the principal cause of existing conditions . . . is the desire of the mine operators to amass for themselves fortunes through the oppression of their laborers, which they do through the sheriff's office."

XX

Hell in the Hills—II

FIVE YEARS after the hell of 1932, the Federal government finally got around to doing something about Harlan. That afflicted county's troubles had never ceased, but they had lessened somewhat in 1933 when the miners and the operators got together on a contract under the NRA. While it was in effect the union gained strength, but after it expired in 1935 the old fight against the union was renewed in full. So rank was the stench emanating from Harlan by 1937, when the U.M.W. again made a concerted effort to organize, that the Senate Civil Liberties Committee, headed by "Young Bob" La Follette, undertook to investigate. As a direct result of this probe and the work of the G-men, a special grand jury sitting at Frankfort on September 27, 1937, indicted twenty-two Harlan coal companies, twenty-four operators or company officials, and twenty-three company-paid "peace officers." The United States charged that men and companies had conspired to violate the Wagner Labor Relations Act. Further, since this hitherto untested law of 1935 had no teeth, the government rang in a statute adopted in 1870 to protect Southern Negroes from oppression during Reconstruction. It prohibits two or more persons from conspiring to "injure, oppress, threaten or intimidate any citizen in the free exercise or enjoyment of any right or privilege secured to him by the Constitution or laws of the United States," and provides a fine up to $5,000 and imprisonment up to ten years.

The government charged "conspiracy," showing that it would not concern itself primarily with individual acts of violence and oppression but would try a principle—the right of working men to join or organize labor unions of their own choosing and to bargain collectively through agents of their own choosing. On this principle the Wagner act was built, and in this trial the act was to be given its first real test.

Into the little, mineless hill town of London on May 15, 1938, poured defendants and their witnesses and attorneys, government officials and their witnesses and attorneys, prospective jurymen, curiosity-seekers, hot-dog vendors, pottery salesmen (dispersing Ohio-made merchandise), mountain minstrels, reporters, and newsreel cameramen. The "Trial of the Century" was ready to begin.

For five days counsel hammered at one after another of 150 men before a jury of eight farmers, two country storekeepers, a bookkeeper, and a carpenter finally was agreed upon. That jury was to sit for ten weeks while 192 government witnesses told of arson, spying, shooting, kidnaping, dynamiting, gassing, and murder by the operators' hired thugs, and 377 defense witnesses either denied all or declared the union itself committed the offenses.

Opening for the prosecution, handsome, young Brien McMahon minced no words. He called names and linked them with harsh deeds. He declared the government would prove the Harlan County Coal Operators Association was held together by a "common hatred of unions"; that it contributed as much as $2,000 a month to Ben Unthank, ruddy-faced chief field deputy whose benign appearance belied his reputation as "head road-killer," and that Unthank used this money to fight the operators' war of terrorization.

Hell in the Hills–II

What a different picture Chief of Defense Counsel Charles I. Dawson painted! All was sweetness and light in Harlan until 1931, "when a bunch of outside organizers came into Harlan County and undertook to compel the men, by all sorts of intimidation, to join the union." He asserted the Harlan operators had been tolerant of unionism until the Battle of Evarts, and that "that dastardly outrage" was the cause of all the trouble. His version of the battle was this: "The sheriff sent a posse of deputies, good citizens of Harlan County, to guard a miner who wanted to go to work in a picketed mine. As they were escorting him up the road they were fired upon from ambush, and when the smoke had cleared away three sons of Harlan County lay dead. The murdered men belonged to honored and widely connected families, and that dastardly outrage inflamed the whole country." (That poor damned miner mowed down by the deputies' bullets still didn't count.)

The sides had chosen their positions, and the big guns were brought into play. For a month and a day the prosecution shelled the defense ramparts. The first G-man on the stand testified that George Ward, high-salaried secretary of the operators' association, had admitted he had destroyed records of the association in anticipation of the investigation, that Unthank was "general field man" for the association, and that Unthank hired men whom the operators "didn't know and didn't care to know."

After testimony of the G-men came that of a surprise witness, E. J. Asbury, straight-talking superintendent of the Black Mountain Coal Corporation and former member of the operators' inner circle. He had been a defendant until the week before he took the stand, but the charges against him and his company had been dismissed a few days after a $500,000 fire of mysterious origin razed the company's tipple, conveyor, and headhouse. Asbury leaned forward in his chair and told the jury the association had assessed his company $600 to $750 a month for the "war chest," that no financial statements were prepared after the La Follette investigation, that Sheriff Theodore Middleton and Chief Field Deputy Ben Unthank attended operators' meetings and took part in discussions about suppressing the union.

Clinton C. Ball, former Harlan jailer, testified he had jailed 14,000 persons during his four-year term and that he came to the parting of the ways with Sheriff Middleton when he (Ball) started refusing to lock up men who had committed no offense. He told of the sheriff's "whisper room," a room that was to be darkly mentioned many times during the trial. Opening from the sheriff's office it was a one-windowed room where conferences of deepest secrecy were held, where "an arsenal of guns was kept in a safe."

On May 27 the Louisville *Courier-Journal* reported:

> Another sorry pageant of beatings and threatenings, of sulphurous swear-words, of dirty linen soiled in the coal field strife between union men and operators moved across the record in Federal Court here today as government counsel tugged at the lasso with which it is trying to tie up more than a score of Harlan county coal operators and the law forces of former Sheriff Theodore R. Middleton in a common conspiracy.
>
> Today the record fairly bulged with stories of discrimination by certain of the defendant companies against United Mine Workers members. It cried out with tales of deeds of violence by law forces. It kept the defense objecting feverishly, and, in cross-questioning, attempting to show that many of the stories were sheer fabrications, that others were distorted shamelessly and that the alleged discriminations either did not occur at all or were amply provoked.

One of the deeds of violence was the kidnaping and ousting from the county of a local union vice-president on September 25, 1935. Another was the breaking up of a meeting called at Evarts on July 7, 1935, to celebrate passage by Congress of the Wagner act. At that meeting, according to the testimony, deputies who stalked through the crowd, waving their guns, threatening and cursing, knocked the speaker—a frail, oldish man who was hard of hearing—from the pile of ties he had chosen as a platform. Still others were the tear-gas bombing of union organizers' headquarters at Harlan and the dynamiting of organizers' cars, both on the night of January 23, 1937; three ambush firings on union organizers; the night attack on the home of organizer Marshall Musick that resulted in the death of his nineteen-year-old son, Bennett, on February 9, 1937; and the slaying of Lloyd Clouse, union sympathizer and part-time organizer, at Verda on the night of April 24, 1937.

The trial was not without its sidelights, humorous and serious, mostly the latter. Former Deputy Sheriff John P. Hickey was a big, red-faced, blatant threatener of miners who was referred to time and again as the toughest of them all. For day after day he had listened intently as witnesses told of his actions with his "two big guns" and his caustic tongue, but one day he didn't answer the roll call. When the trial judge, H. Church Ford, asked where he was a defense lawyer explained that Hickey was "a little under the weather today." Next day Hickey sneaked in sheepishly and took his usual seat. A titter ran over the packed courtroom and the judge had difficulty in restraining a laugh. John Hickey had two of the most beautiful black eyes you ever looked at.

One of the defense lawyers told after the trial of a bit of amusing strategy. He instructed a witness, "Now when you get on that stand I want you to remember this if you forget everything else including your own name. One of those jurors is a Sizemore and I know that clan sticks together. I'm going to ask you why you're down on the union, and you look right at that jury and say . . ."

The witness took the stand.

Q. "Now tell the jury why you dislike the union."

A. "Wal, it's like this. About five years ago er sech a matter one of them union fellers shot up one o' my best friends—a man name o' Sizemore—an' I ain't had no love fer 'em since."

The Sizemore on the jury rolled his eyes first toward the man on his left and then toward the man on his right. The lawyer beamed. His strategy had worked.

On the serious side were: the fatal shooting of a government witness, Lester Smithers, former president of a U.M.W. local in front of a saloon at Gulston, near Harlan; the kidnaping of John Isom, another government witness; the "self-defense" shooting by Lee Fleenor, a defendant and former deputy, of a man once convicted of killing Fleenor's father; the fatal shooting of another deputy-defendant, Frank White, allegedly by a government witness; the admission by a defense witness that he had been paid $50 to "lie-swear" and the subsequent disbarment of a defense lawyer; an unsuccessful attempt by the defense to have two G-men held in contempt of court for alleged "interference with defense efforts."

But perhaps the most serious of all the sidelights from the standpoint of the trial itself was an event that took place on July 22 as the case neared its end. Many persons believe to this day that the occurrence had a profound effect on the jury, perhaps cost the government its chance of winning convictions; although others believe the minds of the jurors already were made up. The jurymen were lolling on the grass in front of the jury house one afternoon when a group of men walked along the sidewalk across the street. The group included Merle Middleton, former deputy who was on trial, and three Clay County men (one of them a son of one of the jurors) who had come into town with Defense Attorney A. D. Hall. They walked past the house twice with their arms around one another, showing by their actions how friendly they were.

When, next day, Judge Ford heard what had taken place he was furious. His secretary, Miss Genevieve Newman, said it was the first time in her long association with him she had ever seen him really angry. His face blazed and he pounded the desk as he delivered a tongue-lashing to the participants. Probably he would have jailed the men had he not made it a practice never to sentence defendants when he was out of sorts. That same day the jury house was roped off and no one was permitted to walk in front of it, but it is possible the jury had been reached.

When the defense rolled out its big guns it followed on a broader scale the tactics it had used in cross-examining prosecuting witnesses. It endeavored to prove that stories of acts of violence and intimidation were out-and-out lies, that they were greatly exaggerated or that the acts were amply justified. The prosecution, by way of example, had introduced testimony to the effect that two deputies had questioned a miner about his union affiliations and later had come to his home, drawn their pistols, beat him and his stepson, and cursed his wife. The defense version was that the miner was drunk and had created a disturbance at a poolroom, that he had had to be taken home, and that when he got there he beat up his wife and his stepson. The defendant deputies declared they didn't go to Evarts on July 7, 1935, to break up the celebration. They said they went there to keep order and that some of the celebrants got rough. They said they didn't shoot into the home of organizer Musick and kill his son. They said union organizers did it to bring the wrath of the miners on the deputies. They declared that night riders had threatened to "shoot the damn hell" out of miners who wanted to work during a strike, and that they (the deputies) had to get tough once in a while "to preserve law and order."

The *Christian Science Monitor* put it this way:

> After five weeks of being told by government witnesses that the Harlan County Coal Operators Association existed solely to keep unions out of Harlan and that its members and agents were liberal in their use of bullets, tear gas and dynamite to achieve this end, the jurymen now are informed by defense witnesses that, quite the contrary, the association existed for much

the same reasons a Rotary or Kiwanis club or a Chamber of Commerce exists in other lesser known communities.

According to defense witnesses . . . Harlan coal operators are a group of civic-minded business leaders who vote money for community Christmas trees, medals for bright Harlan school children and dictionaries to encourage "spelling bees" when they are not busy fighting freight rate discrimination, lobbying in Frankfort against bills to outlaw their deputy sheriff system of law and order maintenance, or planning to operate their mines with greater safety.

So there was the case. The jury, after ten hours of deliberation during four sessions, reported it was hopelessly deadlocked at seven to five for acquittal.

The government had failed in its mighty effort to convict the Harlan operators and their front men, but it had by no means failed to bring a degree of light to Harlan. Three years after the trial Judge Ford said: "I think the outcome was the best thing that could have happened. If the government had won and men had been sentenced to the penitentiary, bitterness would have been kept alive just as it was through convictions after the Battle of Evarts in 1931. If the defense had won there is no telling what would have happened in Harlan County. As it was those men were punished plenty. The trial cost the government $250,000, and it must have cost the defendants as much. Moreover they were shown the government meant business and they were kept on the uneasy seat not only during the time of the trial but for more than a year afterwards while the matter of a retrial hung over their heads."

But the trouble wasn't over at the conclusion of the trial, nor, for that matter, is it now.

In 1935, after not one but two Kentucky primaries, the commonwealth's electorate had chosen young A. B. "Happy" Chandler to the governorship. He was another "friend of labor" destined later to be called foe. On May 13, 1939,

Chandler followed the example of his predecessors at Frankfort and ordered troops to Harlan.

The recalcitrant Harlan County Coal Operators Association had by no means been whipped into line by the big show at London in 1938. It still had the same bosses, and they refused to sign an agreement reached after weeks of bickering at New York among representatives of the United Mine Workers and the Appalachian operators. Harlan miners had been on strike since the first of April, both sides were determined to fight it out, and things were getting rough. Faced with the fact that Harlan operators refused to ratify the New York agreement John L. Lewis touched off the fireworks by declaring: "Whoever thinks the mine workers are going to be starved back into the mines on a nonunion basis of operation is a fool. Those mines must be kept closed." Chandler immediately took up the gauntlet. "No one can tell our people to work or not to work and no one can come into this state and cause trouble." (Shades of 1932!)

So once more the kids of the National Guard, some of them not out of grade school, the majority of high school age, donned their uniforms and became men, men whose solemn duty it was "to preserve law and order in Harlan County and its environs."

Two days after the boys with the bayonets took over, one nonunion miner was killed in an argument with another, a man was shot in the legs as he walked along a main street in the town of Harlan, and one of the kids felt called upon to crack the skull of a union miner with the butt of his pistol. The guardsman said the miner tried to run him down with an automobile. The miner said the guardsman hit him because he insisted on crossing a bridge en route home.

The Harlan U.M.W. president echoed Lewis' cry, proclaiming to his striking miners, "Stick to your rights. They can't dig coal with bayonets and tin soldiers. . . ." Automobile loads of scabbing miners ran gantlets of stones flung by angry pickets. Throngs of sullen miners milled threateningly around the patrols, hooting and hurling epithets. The guardsmen were ordered to "shoot to kill if necessary." Chandler and Lewis engaged in a name-calling contest. Two hundred miners' wives descended upon the county judge and demanded that the troops be recalled—and were, of course, refused. Snipers fired at scabs and their soldier escorts. Every National Guardsman in the state was ordered to stand ready to move in.

For day after day, like flashes of lightning in a lowering sky, the exchanges continued until on July 12 the storm broke at a mine on Catron's Creek, five miles southwest of Harlan. A picket tried to yank a scabbing miner from an automobile. An officer of the militia interfered. When the smoke cleared away a picket was dead, an officer was critically wounded, two other strikers were carrying lead, and three other miners and a guardsman were injured.

The troopers started a roundup and by nightfall had 250 in tow, including oft-arrested George Titler, the U.M.W. officer who was in the thick of every struggle. Meanwhile another outburst of fire from the guns of the trigger-nervous boys wounded a miner and his mother on the streets of Harlan. That night prisoners overflowed the jail. The guardsmen roped off the courthouse square and set up machine guns.

These developments gave Chandler and Lewis a chance to get in a few more licks. The CIO leader charged that the Governor was "violating his oath of office and prostituting the power of his state." The Governor retorted, "Lewis has found one state where the people are not ready to be bulldozed. This is a new situation to him."

Three days after the battle on Catron's Creek two men met at a roadhouse and shot it out. The man who lived was the one who had sworn to warrants for 223 of the 250 arrested on July 12. The picket had failed to get his man.

Two other men died the same day, but their deaths wound

up the shooting for the time being, because on July 19, after a five-day conference at Knoxville, Harlan operators and union representatives set signatures to an agreement.

But it still was a draw. The union gave way on its demand for a union shop; the operators waived the clause imposing fines against the union for "illegal strikes."

Perhaps it should be explained that a union-shop agreement provides that all new employees must join the union within a stipulated period but does not require membership of non-union employees already on the job. The closed shop requires membership of all employees. To Harlan operators there is no difference. The union is the union, a thing to be feared, despised, and bitterly fought.

"To promote industrial peace" charges were dismissed in the fall of 1939 against 400 arrested during the troops' invasion. A few days later the Federal court conduced to that fragile amity by dismissing the antilabor conspiracy charges, and thus wrote finis to the government's expensive but not unsuccessful effort to point the right way in Harlan. The Kentucky General Assembly had done its good deed in 1938 by outlawing an old and vicious practice, company employment of gun thugs who wore the badge of the law as sheriff's deputies. Oh, mine guards still are employed, but at least they aren't deputies sheriff.

Those efforts relieved but, as shown by the outbursts in 1941, they did not cure. So long as there is stupid, pigheaded intolerance on the side of operators and miners alike there will be no lasting peace in Harlan.

During all the years of Harlan's hell the neighboring Hazard and Big Sandy-Elkhorn fields have had their troubles, but they have never known the strife and bloodshed that have scourged Harlan and Bell. The reason seems apparent. Operators in the Hazard and Big Sandy-Elkhorn fields—which include the counties of Perry, Letcher, Pike, Floyd, Knott, and Johnson—have taken a common-sense view of labor trends, have been tolerant of the union (for all they may not like it), and have fought out their problems over a conference table instead of a rifle barrel. Much more difficult to explain is why in attitude they differ from their brothers in Harlan. Men of Hazard and men of Harlan look alike; they talk alike; they dress alike. In the main they are the same type of men. But the Hazard employers just weren't born with the damnable perversity that nature crammed into the carcasses of the leaders of Harlan's operators.

The Hazard and Big Sandy fields have had their strikes, but generally they have been settled bloodlessly. The two-year Appalachian agreement under which the miners worked through March 31, 1941, for example, was signed after a short and shotless strike, whereas in Harlan the agreement, minus the union shop clause, was not signed until after weeks of bloody warfare. In the same manner the April 1941 shut-down was carried out peacefully in the Hazard and Big Sandy fields.

But conditions are bad enough in all eastern Kentucky fields—the pickup due to the war notwithstanding. An average Kentucky miner with a job (and there are still plenty who do not have jobs) earns maybe $1,000 a year. And even that figure does not represent true income. Many a miner, in Hazard as in Harlan, is lucky to have enough left for a bag of Bull Durham when the commissaries and that fiend "deduction" get through with him. His check may be, and usually is, debited for rent (for a company-owned house); burial fund (so the company won't have to bury him); insurance (so the company won't have his family on its hands); scrip (issued by the company); cash advance (allowed occasionally by the company); coal, explosives, smithing, lights, doctor, and hospital (all sold or controlled by the miners' owner, the company).

In justice it must be said that not all operators force their employees to buy their food at company stores at prices higher than the market, but in truth it must be said that a great many of them do. Uncounted miners have lost their jobs because they traded at the A.&P., and few and far between are the company stores that sell at A.&P. prices. Commissary operation and the scrip system have lent themselves to some of the most malignant practices in a noxious industrial order.

Scrip is nothing more or less than token money designed as a credit medium. In principle the scrip system is all right; in operation it is a racket. Miners' work is irregular, and semimonthly paydays are a long way apart. Few miners have bank accounts, and most of them need credit. Scrip seemed to offer a suitable credit medium. So far so good, but let's see how it works.

A miner is worth, say, $10. In other words he has worked a sufficient number of hours to have $10 coming to him. But he can't draw that pay until the regular payday. He can, however, walk up to the mine office and say, "Cut me $10 worth of scrip." The clerk punches a machine that looks something like a cash register and out come coupons about the size of bank checks. He makes a notation on the payroll sheet debiting Henry Poore, No. 540, $10. Then he writes Henry's name on the coupons, files one for the record, and hands the other to Henry.

The scrip thus issued has these advantages:

To the company: (1) The original scrip must be endorsed by the miner to whom it is issued, and for the most part it can be cashed only at the company commissary. Thus the company is sure to get part, and sometimes a very large part, of its wage money back through the sale of merchandise on which it realizes a profit. (Many a mining company, with the aid of scrip and high prices, has realized a greater profit from the commissary than from the mine.) (2) The company never issues more scrip than a miner is "worth," and so it extends a credit on which it can't possibly lose. (3) Scrip is issued only in even dollars. Thus bookkeeping at the mine office is simplified. (4) Scrip is handled just like cash at the commissary. No sales tickets and subsequent posting and billing are necessary.

To the miner: (1) He is extended a credit he cannot get elsewhere and so can buy necessities to tide him over until payday. (2) He can buy as much at the company store with $10 in scrip as with $10 in cash (overlooking the matter of higher prices).

After Henry has obtained his paper coupons he takes them to the commissary, endorses them, buys $3 worth of groceries and a pair of overalls, and gets $6 back in metal scrip. It says "non-transferable," but nobody pays any attention to that. In fact the Kentucky court of appeals held recently that custom had made scrip a medium of exchange. So Henry can sell his brass money or spend it elsewhere—at a discount. Maybe his wife and baby are sick or maybe he just feels a mighty thirst. Whatever the reason, he is willing to take the discount. It is indeed an odd quirk of human nature that makes a man willing, sometimes even anxious, to sell a hard-earned dollar for seventy-five cents, but Henry and many thousands like him will do it.

All in all Kentucky coal miners are a pretty Godforsaken class of people. The whole story, economically, can be summed up in the statement that tens of thousands of people are trying to eke an existence from an industry that might provide a decent living for a third or maybe a half their number. But that summary doesn't tell the story of their bleak, hideously ugly surroundings, of the squalid shacks they are wont to call homes, of the monotonous life of the mining camp, of the drudgery of families that increase as regularly as the seasons, of irregular work or total unemployment, of insufficient food or out-and-out starvation, of sickness, of the danger of fatal or disabling accidents, of the early age at which they will be finished as miners, of increasing crime and delinquency, of loss of hope for themselves and their children.

When the major coal seams were opened, most were off passable roads, removed from centers of population, and neither the mountaineers nor the outsiders who swarmed to the mines had money with which to build homes. Thus it was logical, though regrettable, that company-owned communities should be developed at the mine sites, where for the most part they still remain, although a number of companies now supply decent living quarters and a few have built model communities.

Improvements in roads and transportation facilities abolished the need for houses at the pit's mouth, yet in the majority of camps they still stand on the slag pike, with cinders and mud for yards, a pall of smoke for sky. The barrenness, the stark and forbidding ugliness of the camp are such as to discourage any thought of beautification. Many of the houses are almost past description—one can't put smell on paper. Unpainted board and batten houses of three rooms they are, roofs warped, porches staggering, steps sagging. Old newspapers cover the walls inside. Two or three rumpled beds take up most of the space. Three, maybe four cane-bottomed chairs squat forlornly in front of the sputtering grate fire. Gone, amid such surroundings, is the mountaineer's old love for his home.

If a miner starts work at eighteen, and if he is able to keep a steady job, the chances are one in three that he will die in an accident before he is fifty. The odds that he will lose an eye, both eyes, a leg, or an arm are many times greater. Do you see that fellow sitting over there in that dilapidated rocker on the porch? His back was broken in a slate fall. He's just thirty-seven, but he'll never enter a mine again. For $200 he signed away all claim against the company.

In mining camps, magazines and books are so rare as to be practically nonexistent. There are no golf links, no tennis courts, no country club dances, no bowling alleys, no hobby groups, no luncheon clubs, no swimming pools. In mining camps there is monotony, deadening, deteriorating monotony. Even when a miner is employed he has from two to five days of leisure time, time in which he has nothing to do but spit tobacco juice, chew the rag, get drunk, and shoot craps—or somebody else. When he is unemployed he has plenty of time to do a little thieving, a little moonshining.

But if a miner's life is dreary and monotonous his wife's is thrice so. On her falls the drudgery of bearing and rearing the many children, of trying to eke enough from her husband's meager wages to keep food in their bellies, of trying, despairingly, to keep them and the rickety house in some semblance of cleanliness. Nowhere in all the world is birth control needed more, but in mining camps it has made least progress.

Look at that sad-eyed, misshapen woman as she raises up from the cookstove, wipes her hands on her soiled gingham dress, and pushes her stringy hair back from her eyes. How old do you think she is? Forty? She's barely thirty, and once she was pretty by anybody's standards. Those six dirty-faced, raggedy children playing mountain goat over there on the gob pile are hers. What chance have they got? Schools are available, yes. But about the time they start, the miner-father will find it necessary to move on to another camp. The boys will grow up to be miners. They've got about as much chance of being anything else as a Russian peasant has of becoming a land baron. The girls will blossom at fourteen or fifteen and fade at twenty to twenty-five. Between those years they will marry miners—or become prostitutes. One life is about as hard as the other.

XXI

The Answer?

IT IS THE FASHION, in narrations such as this one, to follow diagnosis with prescription, the assumption being, seemingly, that once a man knows what's wrong he will know how to set it right. So common is the habit, indeed, that readers have come to expect of reporters a last-chapter accession to the seat of omniscience from which all problems are resolved into simplicity.

In disappointing that expectation, I can plead only that I'd prefer to let nature take its course than to bleed a sufferer from anemia, as doctors in their wisdom have been known to do. If a man thinks he has an answer I suppose the thing for him to do is to present it, though the presentation always seems to me a bit presumptuous and more than a bit futile. In the first place his opinion is apt to be worth no more than the next man's, and in the second who will heed him even if he's right?

I can sum up the problem of the mountains in mighty few words: There are too many people on too few acres, and mighty rough acres at that. But I am wholly unable to sum up, or even string out, the answer. The more I ponder the situation the more impossible seems a solution. Consider:

In the thirty-four hill counties of eastern Kentucky are tens of thousands of ill-clad, poorly educated, disease-ridden people striving to dig an existence from rocky, eroded soil or from the grimy coal pits. There was a time when the hills were covered with trees, when game and fish were plentiful and people were not, when the mountaineers lived a full, free, self-sufficient life. But that time has gone, not to return. As the population has increased, so has share-cropping. Farms have been divided and subdivided, trees have been cut away, and the topsoil has washed to river deltas. The little hillside farms can be made to produce more through the methods of the county agents, but they cannot be made to produce enough.

Mines and industrialism have come to the hills, but they have only complicated the problem. Industrialism superimposed upon a primitive economy has brought chaos. Moreover for every man who has a job there are ten who need one. Under the impetus of war new mines are being opened and old ones are stepping up production. A few more men will find jobs despite increased mechanization, but it is outside capital that will realize the profits—just as it has always been—and when the war is over the outside capital will move out again, and coal will hit a slump worse than it did after the great days of the first World War.

Originally the mountain people were of the best stock in the nation, but inbreeding during the long years of isolation plus migration of the more intelligent and energetic has impoverished the strain. And sociologists tell us that Appalachia is the nursery of future America. Ah America!

Kephart's hope of a salvation lay in the education of mountain leaders. During the twenty-five years since he expressed that hope educational standards have been raised and illiteracy has been reduced—though by no means, of course, to the extent they should be—yet poverty has grown, and the problems of the mountains are farther from solution than they were a quarter of a century ago.

The mountain counties are deeply in debt and can't get out. They are unable to provide adequately for the usual governmental offices, much less for hospitals, clinics, sanatoriums, and eleemosynary institutions. Some have given up their greatest asset, their health departments. To this sad state of affairs can be added the fact that the people are tolerant of political stupidity and corruption.

The attitude of the mountaineers doesn't conduce to changes for the better, even if such changes were possible. Always proud, the people have been victimized by profit-seekers—in business and "quaint" journalism—until they resent anything said about them or offered for them. Their attitude is either one of belligerency—"the mountains against the world"—or of lethargy—"what's the use?"

And always to be met at every turn is the major factor of an ever-increasing population. The problem would be difficult enough if there were just too many people, but when that too many people keeps increasing, it is insolvable. The percentage of population increase for Kentucky from 1930 to 1940 was 8.8. Among the mountain counties the increase ran as high as 56.1 per cent.

As an answer to the mountain problem one person suggests that thousands of people be moved out and that the hills be restored to the forests for which they are suited. Fine. But most of the mountain people are unmovable—and if you could move them, where would you put them? Others suggest birth control, the raising of educational standards, concentration on handicraft and home industries, intensive cultivation of the best lands and reforestation of the others, changes in the types of farm crops grown, redistribution of population through effective guidance, more assistance from the state and Federal governments, more roads, more manufacturies. Each of these probably would lessen but none would solve the problem.

What would?

I don't know.

Afterword

Harry M. Caudill

Since 1941, John Day has lived an interesting and successful life. As a Washington and then foreign correspondent for the *Courier-Journal,* vice president for news of Columbia Broadcasting System, and a foreign representative for Time-Life Broadcasting, he brought Americans the news from many quarters of the globe. For fifteen years now he has published a weekly newspaper in the Devonshire town of Exmouth. But his best work is *Bloody Ground.*

This book about the dilemma of eastern Kentucky in the great depression, written when Day was a young reporter for the Lexington *Leader,* left the presses just as a stupendous war burst upon the nation. With the attention and energies of the people focused on war to the virtual exclusion of all other interests, an American classic went largely unnoticed and unappreciated.

Will Henry Varney, probably the first writer to pick his way along the winding rock-strewn bridle paths of the Kentucky hills, traversed the Cumberland Plateau in 1869 and imposed a label that has endured. The hills, creeks, and valleys and their shy but often violent inhabitants puzzled him and he called them "a strange land and peculiar people." Many others passed through the hills in the next seventy years, as indeed they still do. The strange land and peculiar people have never ceased to fascinate, puzzle, bewilder, and sometimes infuriate their beholders.

John Day was in this tradition, but he wrote no brief magazine article heavy with superficial observations and hasty judgments. His pages graphically portray the nightmare that came into being when an archaic, deeply conservative society, born of the prolonged Appalachian frontier experience and preserved in the roadless hills for a full century, was struck by a whirlwind of industrialization. In little more than a decade this social backwater was penetrated by railroads, strewn with new towns, and turned from subsistence farming to mining. All this was accomplished in the heady atmosphere of the World War I boom, which abruptly ended in a resounding postwar crash. By 1940 the farms were depleted or covered with "camps," legal title to the region's mineral wealth reposed in absentee corporations, and ancient ties to the land had been shattered by the headlong rush to coal towns and scrip windows. A reliance on corporate paternalism had been shattered in turn by widespread corporate bankruptcies, and a demoralized, tattered, and hungry people were being sustained by federal relief. Day's brief final chapter sums up a dilemma that the intervening thirty-nine years have in no wise resolved. *Bloody Ground* ranks with Malcolm Ross's *Machine Age in the Hills,* and the two books should be read together by students of Appalachia. These two perceptive works leave one substantially wiser and much sadder.

The book avoids no important aspect of mountain life. Here is frank and honest discussion of the persistent scourge of illiteracy and ignorance, the fanatical and narrow "hard-shell" religion, the bloody feuds and the biases and hatreds that nurtured them, the entertaining but utterly unconstructive political practices, the grotesqueries of courts when one social class sits in judgment on another, the insuperable problems of superstition and poor health, and the brutal labor wars that killed many and resolved nothing. Here, in all their starkness, are the Appalachian coalfields of forty years ago.

But time does not stand still. Undreamed of whirlwinds of change swept through the hills after John Day went on to other things. The Second World War generated another boom and the battered miners gained strength and dignity through unionism. A million mountaineers left for more promising regions, spreading Appalachian mores and values far and wide. The old-time religion gave rise to a new wave of "born again Christianity," and the folk music of the hills blared across the land as the Nashville Sound, altered, but still distinctly Appalachian. Hill people saw some of their departing kinsmen move into the judiciary, the Congress, and important corporate positions in many states. Dolly Parton and Loretta Lynn became symbols of the triumphant spirit of a battered but unbeaten people. On hundreds of weekends cars of every age and quality carried pilgrims from the northern industrial cities back to the lost and lamented hills. "I wanna go home!"–wailed across the land from countless radio stations–became a lamentation for a new nation of Ishmaels who could never return to the old familar places they loved.

The late 1940s brought new coal depression, idleness, and welfare dependency. A new term entered the psychiatric journals–"the eastern Kentucky syndrome." Its victims were exhausted people who gave up and sank into a chronic state of dependency and passivity. The welfare rolls ballooned, many counties became little more than "welfare reservations," and the once mighty United Mine Workers of America shrank. Strip mining devastated hillsides, filled reservoirs and streams with mud, and turned once-beautiful vistas into sullen ugliness. New booms sowed millionaires across the plateau when Arab oil princes decided in 1973 that the world's free ride was over and that henceforth consumers must pay for the oil they blithely burn. Men died in spectacular mine explosions and stealthy, quickly forgotten roof-falls. Thousands of men wheezed and coughed their ways to the graveyards, their lungs choked with tiny particles of coal, sand, and slate.

New roads were built to bring tourists and "industrial diversification." Instead they gave rise to new coal mines and countless coal trucks. Federal funds built lakes and reservoirs for the enjoyment of those much anticipated tourists, but strip-mine spoil layered their bottoms with oozy mud and turned their sparkling water yellow. Floods occurred in a grim cycle as the hills fought back against mindless greed and exploitation.

Government struggled to impose order on this jumble, succeeded a little, failed often. A philosophical journalist who watched and wrote about it for four decades mused, "Perhaps eastern Kentucky is too much for democracy to cope with!"

Yet there has been much progress. The schools have improved enormously, and some children acquire learning. Roads, cars, schools, and television have ended the old cloying isolation and insularity. The welfare-fed multitudes are better fed than were the highest paid miners of 1941. After allowance is made for the monstrous "promiscuous pilling" of Medicaid, health standards have risen. Too much soda pop has displaced hunger as the scourge of school children.

There is no peace in the hills but there is less war. Courts are stronger but not necessarily more respected. An able state police force embodies a threat of retribution that did not exist forty years ago.

Like a giant who heaves himself upward out of a mire of sucking quicksand the Appalachian mineral fields struggle blindly and gropingly toward a better future in this Year Seven of the Energy Crisis. How will a perceptive reporter describe this land and people when another forty years have slipped away?